In
Memory of
William Hausmann

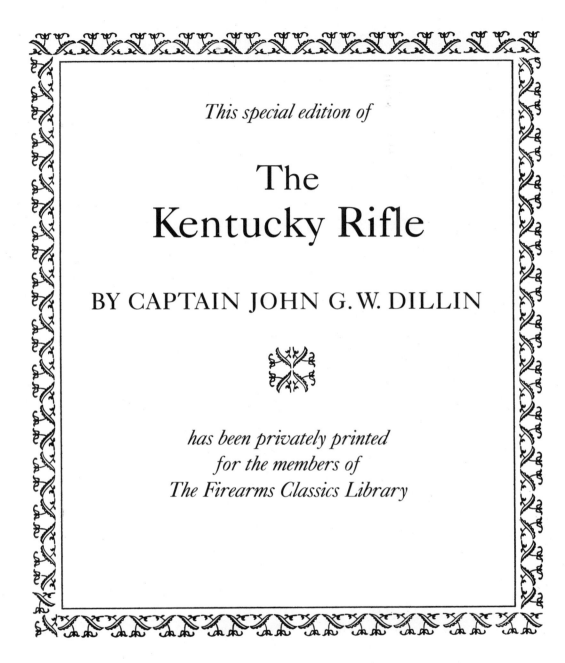

This special edition of

The
Kentucky Rifle

BY CAPTAIN JOHN G.W. DILLIN

*has been privately printed
for the members of
The Firearms Classics Library*

THE FIREARMS CLASSICS LIBRARY

PUBLISHED BY

PALLADIUM PRESS

Special Contents Copyright © 1998
PALLADIUM PRESS
Post Office Box 530065
Birmingham, Alabama 35253
Printed in the United States of America

Editor's Note

CAPTAIN JOHN G. W. DILLIN'S
THE KENTUCKY RIFLE

by Dr. Jim Casada

In the subtitle of *The Kentucky Rifle*, the book's author, Captain John Grace Wolfe Dillin, describes the gun as "a purely American type of firearm." This is unquestionably true, although students of firearms history trace influences on the rifle's crafting to the heavy, cumbersome, and short-barreled Jaeger rifles brought to America by early colonists from Germany, Holland, and Switzerland. But there can be no denying that the Kentucky rifle is, as George C. Nonte, Jr., puts it in his *Firearms Encyclopedia* (1973), "one of the purest forms of 18th Century Americana."

In appearance and performance, the gun far surpassed the Jaeger. On the frontier, a firearm that was easy to handle, economical to operate, and, most important, accurate at long ranges was a necessity. The rifle that ultimately emerged — truly an "American rifle," for although it was made primarily in Pennsylvania (its given name notwithstanding), it was made in Kentucky, North Carolina, Virginia, and Maryland as well — was a delightful blend of beauty and function. With a stock of curly "fiddleback" maple, polished until it almost glowed, and with a long, distinctive octagonal barrel and a slender design featuring a gentle drop terminating in a curving buttplate that nestled in the shooter's shoulder, the rifle was a visual delight. Individual examples of the guns featured an incredible array of decorative and artistic touches. Hinged metal covers of highly polished brass were commonplace in the compartment in the stock, which held patches and sometimes gun-cleaning accessories such as a worm. Fine carving or hand engraving was frequently employed, and the more striking guns are distinguished by additional attributes such as silver, brass, or pewter inlay along the stock. The rifles were never mass produced, and as Harold L. Peterson writes in his *Pageant of the Gun* (1967): "This was the American rifle, a gun that was more than a superior weapon. It transcended its place in history and became a part of the American legend."

At least a portion of that legend was created during the American Revolution. British redcoats and the Hessian mercenaries with whom they took the field had never seen anything quite like the Kentucky rifle. At the battle of Kings Mountain, in the hands of the expert woodsmen known as the "Over-Mountain Men," the rifle proved a devastating weapon of war. It was, simply, the sole instrument of victory at this watershed battle, for this was the only arm carried by the colonists involved. A generation later, the rifle loomed large in the battle of New Orleans during the War of 1812, where the British sustained an astounding 2,600 casualties, compared with a mere 13 for the American forces.

In these conflicts, as in hundreds of frontier skirmishes, the Kentucky rifle played a key role. Possibly even more significant was the constant use of the rifle for putting meat on the table. No pioneer family wished to be without one of the guns. As the rifle evolved, its caliber reduced, and in the gun's golden age (from the time of the Revolution until around 1830, when the percussion cap became widely accepted) it was the rifle of choice for anyone who could afford it. Daniel Boone, Simon Kinton, and Davy Crockett made the rifle almost an extension of the body, and sharpshooting and use of the rifle became synonymous. The Kentucky rifle was in every sense a gun for the times. The description offered by (editor) David E. Petzal in *Encyclopedia of Sporting Firearms* (1991) nicely captures the essence of its physical qualities: "The typical Kentucky rifle was a flintlock, had a barrel of 44 inches, was about .45 caliber, had a blade front sight of silver, a non-adjustable rear notch sight, a maple stock with a patch box, and a weight of 8 to 9 pounds."

This storied rifle was an integral part of American military history and everyday life on the frontier. No lad was considered worth his salt until he could "bark" a squirrel (shoot beneath the bushy tail so that the squirrel was killed by the shock of flying bark; this left the meat undamaged and enabled the marksman to retrieve his lead bullet for recasting) and judge "Kentucky windage." Likewise, the Kentucky rifle represents American enterprise, ingenuity, and craftsmanship at their best. These were the characteristics Dillin had in mind when he wrote his magnum opus.

While Dillin did not, to my knowledge, have any other notable literary achievements to his credit, his expertise on the Kentucky rifle is undeniable. He had the good sense to avail himself of a skilled editor, Kendrick Scofield, to ensure that his book read reasonably well. At times, such as when he describes the subject of the work as being "light in weight; graceful in line; economical in consumption of powder and lead; fatally precise; [and] distinctly American," Dillin writes wonderfully well. His book was the product of a decade of devoted research and a lifetime of love for the rifle. As the list of individuals thanked in his acknowledgments attests, he left few stones unturned in the preparations for the work's writing, and some measure of the respect in which he was held in the firearms community is provided by the fact that he was able to induce noted authority Captain William de V. Foulke to write a foreword for *The Kentucky Rifle*.

Unfortunately, we know little of Dillin the man, although the presence of a title before his name suggests he had a military career. Apparently Pennsylvania, the home of the Kentucky rifle, was also his home. The illustrations adorning his book indicate he enjoyed ready access to major collections of firearms across the country, and internal evidence from the work is suggestive of a voluminous correspondence on the subject of his interest. While we might wish to know much more of the man, in the present book he left a lasting literary legacy to the gun that for him transcended the level of focus of avocational interest to lay hold of a corner of his soul. For that, students of firearms history and those who enjoy reading about the American past should be eternally grateful.

Dillin's labor of love has proved an enduring one, and, despite being reprinted a number of times, the book remains a collector's item. The original edition, published in 1924 by the National Rifle Association and reprinted here, is a joy to behold, chock full as it is of fine illustrations, beginning with the singularly expressive photo of venerable rifle maker John Shell that graces the work as its frontispiece. Similarly, the attractive royal blue binding of the first edition, with its gold-embossed front and spine (some copies have a plain spine), immediately appeals through its tasteful simplicity. Interestingly, Richard A. Hand, in *A Bookman's Guide to Hunting, Shooting, Angling and Related Subjects* (1991), states that the first edition of the book is bound in black cloth. Possibly this is a variant binding; I have never seen one in this form. Nor have I been privileged to handle the extremely scarce deluxe edition, which was bound in red Fabrikoid with a rifle in gilt on the back.

On the odd occasions when copies of the first edition of *The Kentucky Rifle* are offered for sale by dealers of out-of-print books, the asking price is usually in the $200 to $250 range. In all likelihood, a copy of the deluxe edition in fine shape would fetch somewhere around $750.

A second edition was issued by George N. Hyatt in 1944. Two years later, the New York publishing firm of Ludlum and Beebe came out with a third edition, this one featuring different pagination (136 pages) and in a narrow quarto size with a slipcase. This is truly a new edition, inasmuch as new material is included, in the form of a chapter on the Kentucky pistol, with six plates illustrating these handgun "sisters" to the Kentucky rifle. Trimmer Printers came out with a printing of the work in 1954. This quarto-sized volume was clothbound, boxed, and 154 pages in length. These later editions or reprints are in less demand than the original, but even they bring substantial prices in the used-book trade.

From the time of the first appearance of *The Kentucky Rifle,* critics have hailed it as a volume of seminal importance. John C. Phillips, in his reference work *A Bibliography of American Sporting Books, 1582–1925* (1930), lists the book but offers no comment with the entry. On the other hand, in Ray Riling's *Guns and Shooting: A Bibliography* (1982), Dillin's book is described as "a standard reference work on the subject, not surpassed to date." Although almost half a century has passed since Riling offered that opinion, his judgment still holds. Two later works, Henry J. Kauffman's *The Pennsylvania-Kentucky Rifle* (1960) and Joe Kindig, Jr.'s *Thoughts on the Kentucky Rifle in Its Golden Age* (1960), should really be seen as supplementing, rather than supplanting, Dillin's study.

Meticulously researched, lavishly illustrated, and written as a labor of love by a man for whom Kentucky rifles were an abiding passion, Dillin's *The Kentucky Rifle* is a model of its genre and a landmark in the literature of American firearms history. Modern enthusiasts look back in longing on the superb craftsmanship that went into the finest of the Kentucky rifles, and it is small wonder that interest continues strong in making and shooting replicas of these remarkable guns. The book, like the gun, belongs to the ages. As such, *The Kentucky Rifle* is richly deserving of the place it now assumes in The Firearms Classics Library.

Jim Casada

ROCK HILL, SOUTH CAROLINA

John G W Dillin

The Author

THE KENTUCKY RIFLE

JOHN SHELL, RIFLEMAKER

Early in July, 1922, John Shell died at his home in Leslie County, Kentucky, where he had lived for more than a century. Shell claimed that he was born in Tennessee in 1788, and seems to have offered very strong arguments in support of his assertion. He paid taxes in 1809, and was too old for service in the Mexican War. He also distinctly remembered seeing Daniel Boone. He was the son of Samuel Shell, also a riflemaker. The Shells came from Holland about 200 years ago and settled in Pennsylvania.

Medical men who were attracted to Shell by reason of his advanced age were unanimous in declaring that he had undoubtedly passed the century mark by a good many years. When more than a hundred years old, he married for the second time. He retained his faculties to the very last, and suggested plans for his funeral a few days before his death. He has many descendants.

JOHN SHELL, RIFLEMAKER

Over his picture is the reproduction of a rifle made by him.

JOHN SHELL, RIFLEMAKER

Early in July, 1922, John Shell died at his home in Leslie County, Kentucky, where he had lived for more than a century. Shell claimed that he was born in Tennessee in 1788, and seems to have offered very strong arguments in support of his assertion. He paid taxes in 1809, and was too old for service in the Mexican War. He also distinctly remembered seeing Daniel Boone. He was the son of Samuel Shell, also a riflemaker. The Shells came from Holland about 200 years ago and settled in Pennsylvania.

Medical men who were attracted to Shell by reason of his advanced age were unanimous in declaring that he had undoubtedly passed the century mark by a good many years. When more than a hundred years old, he married for the second time. He retained his faculties to the very last, and suggested plans for his funeral a few days before his death. He has many descendants.

JOHN SHELL, RIFLEMAKER

Over his picture is the reproduction of a rifle made by him.

The Kentucky Rifle

A study of the origin and development of a purely American type of firearm, together with accurate historical data concerning early Colonial gunsmiths, and profusely illustrated with photographic reproduction of their finest work.

BY

Captain JOHN G. W. DILLIN

NATIONAL RIFLE ASSOCIATION OF AMERICA
WASHINGTON, D. C.
1924

❧ Dedication ❧

ROM *a flat bar of soft iron, hand forged into a gun barrel; laboriously bored and rifled with crude tools; fitted with a stock hewn from a maple tree in the neighboring forest, and supplied with a lock hammered to shape on the anvil, an unknown smith, in a shop long since silent, fashioned a rifle which changed the whole course of world history, made possible the settlement of a continent, and ultimately freed our country of foreign domination.*

Light in weight; graceful in line; economical in consumption of powder and lead; fatally precise; distinctly American, it sprang into immediate popularity, and for a hundred years was a model often slightly varied but never radically changed.

Legends regarding this rifle which have never been confirmed have drifted out of the dusty past; inaccuracies have passed for facts. Few writers have given more than a passing word to a weapon which deserves a lasting place in history, and it is a pleasure to present herewith the data collected during the past ten years and to dedicate this work to the KENTUCKY RIFLE.

JOHN G. W. DILLIN.

Media, Pennsylvania,
September 1st, 1924.

Acknowledgment

The task of collecting and collating the facts contributing to the development of that distinctly American weapon, the Kentucky Rifle, would have failed of its purpose had it not been for the assistance rendered by many persons interested in Americana.

It is therefore with deep appreciation that the author acknowledges his indebtedness to the following among the many who aided either by information or by photographs the production of this book: Horace Kephart, North Carolina; Judge Charles I. Landis, Pennsylvania; Walter M. Cline, Tennessee; Dr. Thomas B. Snyder, Pennsylvania; John Laidacker, Pennsylvania; Dr. A. G. Clyne and Mrs. Lucy Bosworth Clyne, of Arkansas; Captain Wm. de V. Foulke, West Virginia; Dr. O. W. Fergusson, Illinois; Colonel George E. Kemp, Pennsylvania; Charles Henry and sisters, Pennsylvania; William Lockwood, Pennsylvania; Milton Warren, Tennessee; Colonel Henry W. Shoemaker, Pennsylvania; S. S. Sherwood, Connecticut; Meredith Wolf, Tennessee; Major Townsend Whelen, U. S. A.; Constance Lindsay Skinner, Pennsylvania; T. T. Moore, Oregon; H. M. Boone, Pennsylvania; Hazel A. Spraker, New York; J. G. Schnerring, Pennsylvania; John and Samuel Huston, Pennsylvania; Charles Tryon, Pennsylvania; L. K. Siner, Pennsylvania; Clarence St. John, Michigan; Stephen Van Rensselaer, New York; Charles Strong, Pennsylvania; Witt Bowden, Pennsylvania; Col. Fred Olds, North Carolina; Humphrey Porterfield, Pennsylvania; Edward Marshall Purcell, Pennsylvania, and David Price, Ontario.

And in addition, these organizations: The Pennsylvania Historical Society, The Pennsylvania German Society and the Remington Arms Company.

Contents

CONTENTS—Continued

Very Early
Rifles
of
Central Europe
and
Old Swiss
Cross Bow

1   2   3   4

(Plate 1)

Foreword

By Capt. Wm. de V. Foulke

Honored by Captain Dillin's request to write the introduction to his interesting and valuable book, a tabloid history of the evolution of firearms has been chosen as most appropriate, believing it would enable readers who were not familiar with its subject to better understand and appreciate its contents. The history of our American Rifle is very scant; what has been written before, with few exceptions, has been largely fiction. In this book we have a mass of historical facts collected with care by a skilled rifleman and big game hunter whose reputation is nation-wide.

The Birth of Gunpowder

Sixteenth-century France was the pioneer in the slow improvement of gunpowder, discovered 2500 years before and rediscovered from time to time by such men as Bacon and the monk Schwartz. Early eighteenth-century France produced from these developments the practical explosive which made the straight-shooting Kentucky Rifle possible. This was a very hard-pressed powder of fine grain, with clean-burning qualities.

Meanwhile from the smooth-bore tube fired with a burning stick or linstock, through the match-lock, wheel-lock and snap-haunce eras, with various forms of rifling and shapes of bullets, there had emerged the flint-lock proper, in which a round ball was fired through a slow pitched rifling.

This powder, exported from France to America in large quantities, was found to be excellently adapted to the rifle of the period and gave the early American gunsmiths a practical combination of powder and weapon upon which they later built not only the Kentucky Rifle, but the long and varied line of breech-loading single shots and repeaters, for paper-wrapped loads or metallic cartridges, which appeared between that time and 1879, the advent date of Carl Ditmar's curious and erratic Nitro-Cellulose Smokeless powder.

FOREWORD

Low-pressure smokeless powders were now soon adopted. These nitro powders were an advance only so far as absence of smoke and greater cleanliness went; they were irregular in pressures, and most of them ruinously corrosive to the low carbon steels then used in rifle barrels.

Black powder now was improved by addition of picric acid and other ingredients, and in such types as "King's Semi-Smokeless" and "Lesmok" is far more accurate up to mid-ranges than any of the "Low-pressure Smokeless" brands now on the market.

The Colloid Hi-pressure Nitro compounds were the next step forward. These are practically smokeless, flameless, progressive in combustion, quite uniform in pressures and fairly friendly to the barrel steels.

Nitro powders were not serious rivals of Black powders until after 1904. They now seem more accurate than the old Black, but more than half of the credit for this must be given to the perfection of the "Jacketed Bullet" used with them.

Birth of Firearms

Discovery of gunpowder stimulated invention of engines for its utilization.

The first form of gun was a single, crude, short, smoothbore tube closed at the rear end where a touch hole was located to fire the powder by the application of a burning stick, or by a linstock.

Smoothbore tubes were used without other modification than an occasional "belling" of the muzzle until about the end of the fifteenth century. Because of the dirtiness of the early powders it was not practicable to use a tight fitting ball.

In Germany, the fatherland of rifling, efforts were being made to overcome this. The cutting of grooves—at first straight—lessened the time and labor of loading, formed a receptacle for a part of the powder dirt, increased the accuracy and, as well, the number of shots possible to be fired without cleaning.

At last Gaspard Zoller, a gunsmith in Nuremberg, Germany, having possibly by accident cut grooves in a barrel which departed from a straight line and noting an increase in the accuracy obtained, thereafter cut grooves in his barrels inclined around the axis of the bores, or the first real rifling.

Many are the experiments made since then with rifling. These cover number, form, depth, width and pitch of grooves, those forms best known being the oval of Lancaster; the two-grooved of Purdy, Jacobs and others; the Hexagon; the Hexagon with rounded angles of Whitworth; Hexagon with a "Land" in the angles, of Henry, Schalk, and others; Square, and square sides with rounded bottom; the Ratchet, the Segmental, and many combinations of the groove systems named.

Pitch of grooving was thrashed out very early. There are extant Arquebuses of early periods with many different rifling pitches, some of even twist, with increased twist, with increased twist reversed, with twist slow at breech increasing to middle of the barrel, thence decreasing to the muzzle. Every freak idea which could issue from the minds of men unacquainted with the laws governing the subject has been tried. Even now we are not yet able to certainly formulate mathematically the perfect pitch for a given projectile, but must cut and try.

For modern bullets with lengths of three or more diameters, the rifling pitches have increased much; one with a full turn in six and one-half inches is the shortest tried to date.

Groove width has increased, groove depth has decreased, and the "lands," or the projecting metal between the grooves which grip the ball to rotate it, are very narrow, all directly opposite to the early rifling system which had broad lands and narrow, deep grooves.

Double-barreled arms followed as the second type, then multiple barrels. To discard the weight and bulk of multiple barrels and yet retain several shots at command the revolving system was produced.

Revolving firearms are of early date, as specimens of revolving flint-locks testify.

To overcome the inherent disadvantages of the revolving system the breech-loader was invented.

In hand arms this came about the middle of the snap-haunce era, but these are antedated by a breech-loading carronade of Spanish make which was fished up in the Caribbean Sea.

The hand-operated repeater followed the breech-loader, the automatic self-loader came next and is the last word in firearms to date.

Ignition Systems

During the black powder era, many notable advances in ignition, which has ever been one of the most important factors in accuracy, were made, starting with the flint-lock.

First came the pill-lock, forerunner of the percussion cap.

Second, the tape-lock, an advanced form of pill-lock in which the pellets of fulminate were attached to a tape of paper or fabric and were successively fed to the firing position by action of the lock.

Third, the cap-lock, which used the fulminate enclosed in a cup or cap of metal fitting a nipple or tube connecting with the charge.

FOREWORD

Fourth, the paper or cloth cartridge which contained the powder, ball and a plaque of fulminate fixed either at base of ball as in the German Zindnadel jewels, or at the base of the cartridge, as in the *chassepot* of France.

Fifth, the rim fire system in which the hollow rim of the metal cartridge case is primed with fulminate, which is fired by the nose of the hammer or a firing pin driven by the hammer.

Sixth, the center fire cartridge with flash hole in the base through which the flame from tape primer or a percussion cap passed to the powder.

Seventh, the center fire system in which the primer became an integral part of the cartridge. The first primers were without an anvil, which was formed by a teat swedged up in the primer pocket, as in the Berdan system.

Then followed the inside primer as used in our early .45 cal. Springfield. Lastly, the center fire primer complete with anvil, the form in use today.

The Projectile

The first missile for the hand gun was a stone or stones, a chunk or chunks of metal, or a crude ball of metal hammered to supposed roundness.

Improvement came when moulds were invented which produced a ball more uniform in size and form.

The desire for a heavier and more destructive ball to be used in the same gun led to the Ovoid Slug. From the Slug evolved the Picket Ball; the base of this was its major diameter; the base might be one of several types, flat, rounded, etc. The point was Conical, Conoidal or Ogival. Its length seldom exceeded one and one-half diameters.

It was but a step from the Picket to a longer ball with a cylindrical bearing, those first made for use with patches having a single cannelure to accommodate the folds of the patch.

To do away with the time, bother and possible inaccuracy of the patch as then employed, a long ball with one or several cannelures filled with grease or beeswax came into use. The forms of these balls were many; the points and bases were changed again and again in the age-old search for accuracy.

Up to and during this period most of the long rifle balls were made groove diameter, or even larger, exceptions being the *Carabine à Tige* of France and the Bersaglieri rifle of Italy.

The expansion system, in which the ball was bore diameter, and upset by the blow of the powder gases, is to the credit of Colonel Minié of France. The Minié system used a ball with a deep cavity in the base; it had an ogival point.

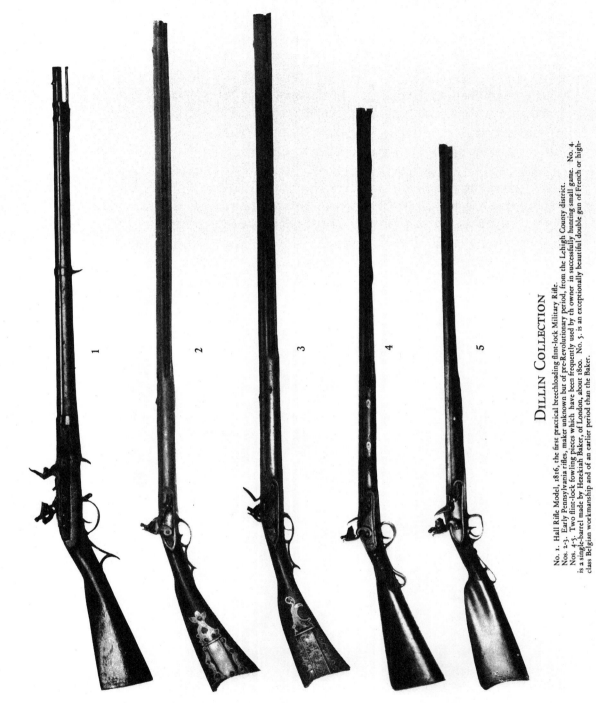

DILLIN COLLECTION

No. 1. Hall Rifle Model, 1816, the first practical breechloading flint-lock Military Rifle.
Nos. 2-3. Early Pennsylvania rifles, maker unknown but of pre-Revolutionary period, from the Lehigh County district. No. 4.
Nos. 4-5. Two flint-lock fowling pieces which have been frequently used by th owner in successfully hunting small game. No. 4.
is a single-barrel made by Hezekiah Baker, of London, about 1800. No. 5. is an exceptionally beautiful double gun of French or high-
class Belgian workmanship and of an earlier period than the Baker.

(Plate 2)

"MULE EAR" KENTUCKYS

Two splendid specimens of the Pennsylvania side-hammer or "Mule Ear" rifles. No. 1 shows the sett trigger model, right and left. No. 2 is a single trigger arm. No. 3 is a "boot" or flint-lock rifle breech-cover made of calf leather, an extremely rare exhibit from the Lehigh district.

"Mule Ear" rifles were made during 1850-1860, were usually highly decorated and were consequently expensive weapons.

(Plate 3)

Italy made the next stride in progress by using in its Bersaglieri rifle a long cannelured ball with a flat base, and of bore diameter. This system gave extreme long range and great accuracy.

Although the Minié and Bersaglieri balls were contemporaries, England, all Europe and the United States adopted the Minié system for their military rifles, refusing the Bersaglieri as too radical.

Our Ordnance Board was urged by skilled civilian riflemen (of whom my uncle was the leader) to adopt the bore diameter Italian ball, but "cits" were not then hearkened to as now, so Uncle Sam refused to do so.

As the long ball was accurate, of long range and gave good penetration, its length was further increased to secure more of a good thing.

Up to this time lead had been universally used for bullets, but it failed to give results when a ball was two and one-half calibers or over long. This caused adoption of lead alloys, with harder metals, tin being commonly used.

These extra long balls often upset too much in spite of the alloys used, and this led to the use of the fixed paper patch, and with this combination of an extra long smooth ball patched with paper, great accuracy was secured, but these were not practical for military use or for hunting.

The adoption of Smokeless powders giving great pressures and burning with heat too high to be stood by lead or lead alloy balls, forced adoption of the composite metal jacketed and solid bronze balls in use today.

Sighting Systems

The first gun had no sights, a front sight followed, a groove at the breech next was added, and this was followed by a rear sight at or near the breech.

The first rear sights in common use were of the open sort and set close to the barrel.

A rifleman finding himself annoyed by the heat waves rising from his barrel, and noting their absence when firing from a shaded spot, was led to make "shaders" covering at first the whole barrel. These did away with not only the glimmer from the barrel, but as well that distortion of aim caused by the sun's reflection from that part of the rounded front sight which was in line with its rays, causing him to shoot low if sun were at zenith, high if sun were behind, and to left if on his right, and vice versa.

Shaders led to use of fixed tubes of varying lengths and diameters, and these to the "peep" sight and the hooded front sights of various patterns.

A Telescope, with cross hairs, or an aperture ring, or a needle point, arranged in focus of the eye piece, is the latest and most accurate means of aiming in use today.

v

FOREWORD

For these "Scopes" micrometer mountings are used, and these are so finely graduated that the location of shots can be determined at will to within the limits of a rifle's accuracy.

Increase of the ranges at which rifles were used brought wind divergence of the ball forcibly to attention, and the "Wind Gauge" came into being. These were for a while a part of the front sight.

Frank J. Rabbeth made the first rear wind gauge sight seen at Creedmoor, about 1880. Modern target sights now have micrometer vertical and lateral traverses.

Loading Methods

The first guns were loaded by pouring a guessed-at charge of powder down the bore, a wad followed which was well rammed with the ramrod, then the slug or slugs, followed by another wad and more ramming.

This primitive procedure continued until close upon the era of rifling. In the early grooved barrels the ball was groove diameter or larger. It was pounded into the bore and down on the powder by strokes of a mallet on the ramrod.

These large balls were used bare and usually with no wadding over the powder. Of course the barrel leaded and the balls flew erratically, but they went harder and farther with much less powder than in the old way.

Here in America balls were cast smaller than the bore and were enveloped in a "patch" of leather or cloth to prevent lead contact with the barrel.

This patch enabled the American to load faster, and to fire longer without cleaning, and to outshoot all others of that time; it was the distinguishing difference between the American Rifle and those of Europe.

With advent of the long balls came the necessity of a "starter." This was a device fitted to a cylinder turned on muzzle of barrel concentric with the bore. The ram or follower was cherried out at its tip to fit the point of the ball, and the ball after being set fair at center of the patch on the muzzle was driven by a stroke of the hand on the ram into the bore and with its axis fairly true with axis of the bore.

Continued use of the rods in loading and cleaning soon funneled the muzzle and destroyed accuracy, and to correct this the "false muzzle" was invented.

This was a piece of the barrel which was bored for dowel pins, then cut off. The dowel pins were then fitted and the muzzle piece strapped in position, when the barrel and false muzzle were reamed and rifled as one.

The starter was fitted carefully to the false muzzle. The false muzzle was kept in place while loading and wiping, but was removed before firing.

It was possible to funnel and otherwise adapt the false muzzle to insure perfect entry of the ball into the bore with untorn, unwrinkled patch, while the end of the barrel proper could be left square and knife sharp for perfect delivery of the ball.

American Precision Rifles, the last word in the solution of the muzzle loading rifle, were all made on this plan. The powder charges used in them were sifted and carefully weighed; the patches were chosen from fine linen by using a magnifier; the balls were scraped to uniform weight and swedged to uniform size, shape and density; the barrel was scrupulously cleaned for each shot, and every stage of the loading process performed with the most careful exactitude.

These old rifles are today probably the most accurate on earth, but do not buck the wind so well as the swifter modern charges can.

The earliest breech loading American rifle was the "Hall." This was loaded by tipping up the pivoted breech block and pouring the powder into it from the torn cartridge paper; the round ball was then put on the powder and the breech closed; priming followed, for this was a Flint Lock arm.

The Sharps and other arms using a paper or cloth cartridge, all single shot arms, came next.

The Maynard with its metal cartridge case and tape primer ignition was next; then followed the rim fire single shot rifles, these succeeded by the Center fire, all of these being loaded by insertion of the cartridge by hand.

The first repeater was the revolving system, this followed by the hand-operated repeater, the cartridges for which were loaded into a magazine by hand and fed into the barrel by hand functioning of the mechanism.

The automatics are charged by clips, charges, magazines or belts and operated either by gases of discharge or momentum of recoil, and are the last form of fire arm to date.

As the American Rifles owed their superiority in large measure to the "Patch," let us follow the development from its origin. The first patches were just a square piece of wash leather, kid leather, buckskin or cloth, and about large enough and about thick enough, these were used greased.

The "Picket" demanded a thin patch of exact size, so for it patches were cut with a punch from fine linen, and in fact punch cut patches were used with all the long balls in the patch era of the muzzle loader.

Americans found out that a round ball loaded off center of a patch shot wild, and they insured the centering of the ball in the patch as follows: The buckskin or patching cloth was in a large piece; this was laid upon the muzzle of the rifle, the ball laid upon it over the bore, the ball was then pressed into the bore by pressure of the knife haft, and the left hand gathering the cloth between fingers and thumb pulled upward while a circular sweep of the knife blade (which lay against muzzle meanwhile) cut the patch off even at all points and insured a good delivery of the ball.

The increasing length of bullets with a corresponding increase in bearing surface on the bore had now reached a point where the linen patch would no longer answer, and the fixed paper patch, which was used with a smooth long ball of less than bore diameter, supplanted the linen. The paper patch in all its forms conduced to greater range and accuracy because a ball of greater length could be used and also one of practically bore diameter.

It was unfortunately not fit for either hunting or war because it had to be kept dry and unrumpled, and to secure its best work the rifle had to be cleaned each shot. When "no-cleaning" matches were inaugurated, the paper patch passed into practical disuse.

To meet these no-cleaning conditions, Mr. Braithwaite of the Ulster Rifle Club told me he had Kynock make him bullets for his .45 calibre long range rifle with a covering or "jacket" of copper, and that these had a square shoulder at front of bearing surface to act as a dirt scraper. And here we have the forerunner of the metallic jacketed bullets of today.

From the beginning human minds have ever tried to improve missile weapons, and in evidence will state that China discovered the principle of the lever-operated repeater, adapting it to a Bow Gun, circa 400 B.C. In the early part of the sixteenth century in Italy, Cellini, that soldier of fortune and world-famous goldsmith, states in his Autobiography:

"I found I could range farther and more true with my Arquebuse when I loaded it with powder of different grains, and these in series." He also states: "I loaded a long Culverin in like manner and with it killed a distinguished commander of the enemy at such a distance that the enemy had believed themselves safe." The Romans used peep sights on cross bows, as did the Chinese. The hair trigger is also a very old invention.

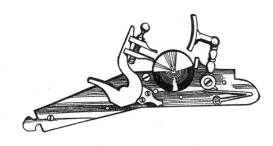

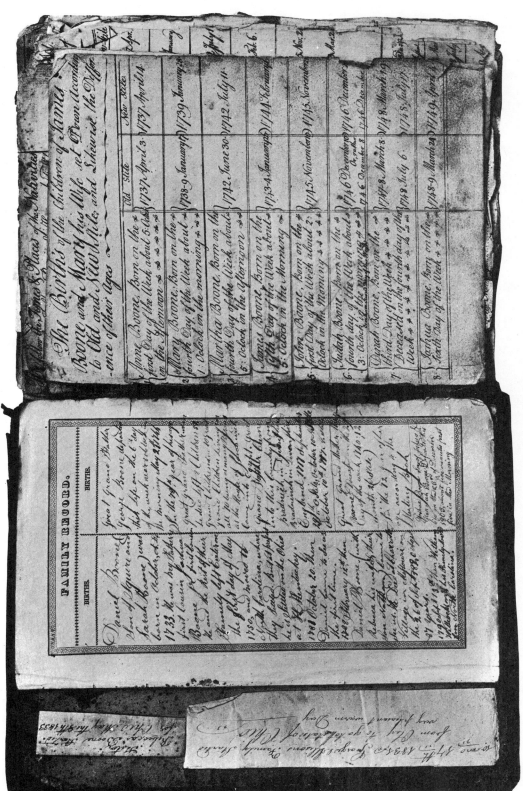

THE BOONE FAMILY BIBLE

This Bible, the property of the author, was obtained from the family of Joshua Boone, of Oley Valley, Berks Co., Pa., an uncle of Daniel Boone.

(Plate 4)

Fayette County August the 18th 1784

Sir I have miss'd several opper
tunitys of wrighting to you however it is never to
Late to do good your Land is all Survayd But that
of Martin flemans and that is to much Expos'd to
Danger to Survay at this time and I shall be
obliged to hire a man to go and show me Linns
improvement as I Do not no his from the Rest
and there is 4 or 5 on that Crick I winer Ket—
your horse till a bout 2 Wickes a go But Drovece
Carey to Sell him if posible but he Could not
then I took him to our Cort and Set the prise
of 250 pounds on him but I Coud Not get
a single Bid for him tho Every Man Liked the
horse But money is not to be had at any Rate
So I took him home and Swapt him for a—
Mare and Colt for my own use in Case I can
Sell hir to a good advontage and shall advance
5 pounds for you I Can a Sure you if I had
Cash I Could by 20 horsis in a week of pepel
who want to Lift there plots out of the ofis
the Ceasueys 2 plots for setolment and preemtion
and survays one all in the Regestors ofis your
Land obtend by tresury worrents the plots is not
yet returnd But will in afew Days I am
Sir your Most obedent
Daniel Boone

Letter written by Daniel Boone, upon his return from "The Dark and Bloody Ground," in 1784. This letter, written from Fayette City, refers to land surveys made by Boone.

(Plate 5)

The Name "Kentucky"

CHAPTER ONE

HE name "Kentucky," as applied to the American flint-lock hunting rifle, dates back to a time not long after that intrepid explorer, Daniel Boone, had returned from his memorable adventures in the wilderness to the west of the Cumberland Mountains and the region which is now included in the boundaries of the States of Kentucky and Tennessee. On his return in the year 1770, stories of his adventures and discoveries soon became the chief topic of conversation among the settlers along the entire Atlantic Coast. At that time the whole new region to the west of the Cumberlands was invariably referred to as Kentucky, and as the name of Daniel Boone was ever associated with the rifle, it is safe to say that the term "Kentucky," as applied to this weapon, came into use very soon after his return to North Carolina.

Boone had reported a region of marvelous natural wealth, a land of "milk and honey," so to speak, but at the same time he told the colonists, who at once began the consideration of conquest and settlement, that any attempt at invasion of this forbidden region was a perilous undertaking.

He was a practical man and no doubt fully informed his people of the important part the rifle must play in their undertaking. He found these sturdy people ready converts. They had been raised in an environment of adventure and privation and had heard the twang of the bow-string and the whirr of the Indian arrow.

Indian massacres were fresh in memory and dim echoes of the dreaded war-whoop still lingered over the eastern slopes of the Cumberlands. But, danger or no danger, a settlement to the west of the mountains was decreed, and after a period of general restlessness, actual preparations for the emigration pervaded not only the settlements in North Carolina, but all of the colonies. It is no stretch of the imagination to picture the Pennsylvania rifle makers working overtime to fill the ever-increasing orders for the long hunting rifles—the Kentucky rifles—of which these smiths had practically a monopoly, for these rifles played the most important part in this new drama of civilization.

Scouting parties were sent out to determine the course of a practicable trail over which the emigrants must pass and there is little doubt but that the mighty Daniel showed the way. Later came the axemen and bridge builders to clear the road and erect the crude bridges. Always a few rods away to the front, to the rear and on both flanks were the riflemen, selected for their skill, for their duty was to defend the road builders in case of an Indian surprise and furnish a supply of food from the game which roamed the forest.

History tells us that very soon after Boone's return in 1770, emigration was in full swing, and it is only reasonable to assume that every man carried a rifle who could get one. Some, doubtless, were armed with a smooth-bore, but from necessity, not choice. The Kentucky rifle with its great superiority over all other weapons was the regulation arm of the emigrant and his very existence depended upon his ability to use it.

Bogart, the historian, in referring to this phase of the drama, says of Boone and his companions: "No doubt they felt fearless, as their rifles gave them a power which the Indian dreaded," and it was ever so throughout the entire struggle for supremacy by the early frontier settlers. Their advance was contested at every advantageous point by the red warriors, and they must be outgeneraled and outshot or the cause was lost with a penalty of horrible torture and death.

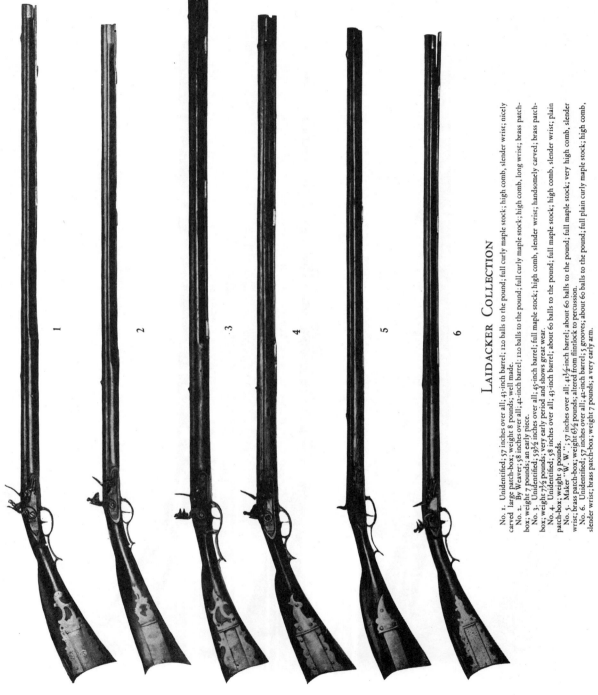

LAIDACKER COLLECTION

No. 1. Unidentified; 57 inches over all; 43-inch barrel; 120 balls to the pound; full curly maple stock; high comb, slender wrist; nicely carved large patch-box; weight 8 pounds; well made.

No. 2. By Weaver; 58 inches over all; 42-inch barrel; 120 balls to the pound; full curly maple stock; high comb, long wrist; brass patch-box; weight 7 pounds; an early piece.

No. 3. Unidentified; 59½ inches over all; 45-inch barrel; full maple stock; high comb, slender wrist; handsomely carved; brass patch-box; weight 7½ pounds; very early period and shows great wear.

No. 4. Unidentified; 58 inches over all; 43-inch barrel; about 60 balls to the pound; full maple stock; high comb, slender wrist; plain patch-box; weight 9 pounds.

No. 5. Maker "W. W."; 57 inches over all; 41½-inch barrel; about 60 balls to the pound; full maple stock; very high comb, slender wrist; brass patch-box; weight 6½ pounds; altered from flintlock to percussion.

No. 6. Unidentified; 57 inches over all; 42-inch barrel; 5 grooves; about 60 balls to the pound; full plain curly maple stock; high comb, slender wrist; brass patch-box; weight 7 pounds; a very early arm.

(Plate 6)

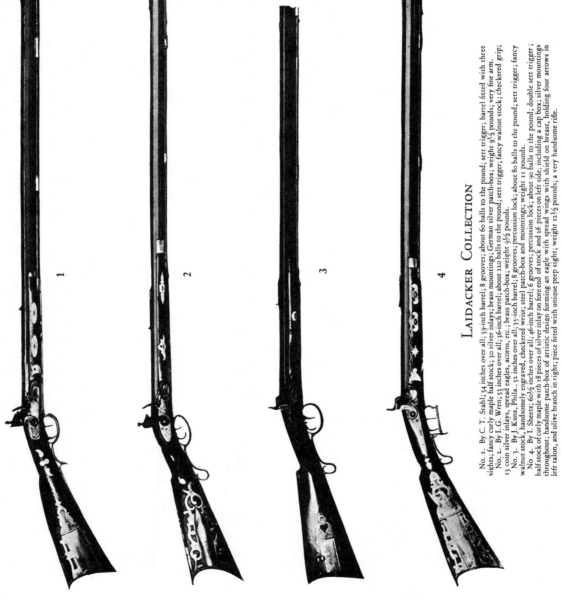

LAIDACKER COLLECTION

No. 1. By C. T. Stahl; 54 inches over all; 39-inch barrel; 8 grooves; about 60 balls to the pound; sett trigger; barrel fitted with three sights; fancy curly maple half stock; 30 silver inlays; brass mountings; German silver patch-box; weight 9½ pounds; very fine arm.

No. 2. By I. G. Wren; 53 inches over all; 36-inch barrel; about 120 balls to the pound; sett trigger; fancy walnut stock; checkered grip; 13 coin silver inlays, spread eagles, acorns, etc.; brass patch-box; weight 9½ pounds.

No. 3. By J. Kunz, Phila . 52 inches over all; 35-inch barrel; 8 grooves; percussion lock; about 80 balls to the pound; sett trigger; fancy walnut stock, handsomely engraved, checkered wrist; steel patch-box and mountings; weight 11 pounds.

No. 4. By I. Sheetz; 60½ inches over all; 46-inch barrel; 6 grooves; percussion lock; about 90 balls to the pound; double sett trigger; half stock of curly maple with 18 pieces of silver inlay on fore end of stock and 16 pieces on left side, including a cap box; silver mountings throughout; handsome patch-box of artistic design forming an eagle with spread wings with shield on breast, holding four arrows in left talon, and olive branch in right; piece fitted with unique peep sight; weight 12½ pounds; a very handsome rifle.

(Plate 7)

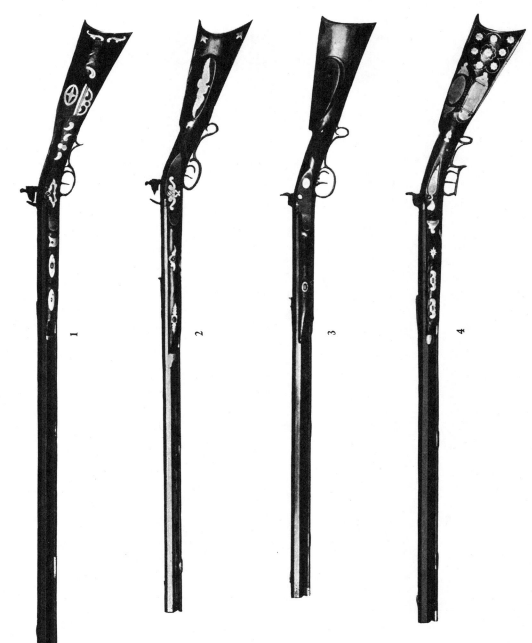

LAIDACKER COLLECTION

Reverse of rifles shown on preceding page.

(Plate 8)

1   2   3   4   5

LAIDACKER COLLECTION

No. 1. Unidentified; 60 inches over all; 44-inch barrel; 7 grooves; 60 balls to the pound; full curly maple stock, nicely carved; 2 wires for feather; brass patch-box; silver thumb-piece inlay; weight 8½ pounds; a very early arm.

No. 2. Unidentified; 58 inches over all; 44-inch barrel; straight cut; about 60 balls to the pound; full curly maple stock; well carved; 2 feather receptacles; brass patch-box; 21 silver inlays; weight 8½ pounds.

No. 3. Unidentified; 59 inches over all; 45-inch barrel; 60 balls to the pound; full curly maple stock; plain patch-box and mountings; a very old arm in good condition; weight 7 pounds.

No. 4. By D. Boyer; 58 inches over all; 42-inch barrel; 7 grooves; about 60 balls to the pound; full curly maple stock; handsomely carved on butt with large bunch of leaves; scrollwork toward wrist; raised work around side plate and around wrist; brass patch-box; brass mountings, including very broad trigger guard; 15 silver inlays; weight 14 pounds; a very beautiful rifle.

No. 5. By Miller; 57 inches over all; 41½-inch barrel; 120 balls to the pound; full curly maple stock, well carved, brass patch-box; 13 silver inlays; weight 10½ pounds.

(Plate 9)

The Evolution of the
American Rifle

Chapter Two

FROM sixteenth-century wheel-lock to eighteenth-century flint-lock Kentucky, the early American rifle was the result of an evolution dictated by rugged necessity.

To follow every link in the chain of change which finally dictated the outstanding and individual characteristics of the Kentucky rifle is impracticable, when four specimens will give the student of arms the salient steps in this development. Therefore the rifles shown in Plate 10 have been selected with great care as being representative of the several stages incident to the evolution of the American or Kentucky rifle.

No. 1 is a fine example of the German wheel-lock. It is well made and probably was produced about 1600. It weighs 9 pounds, is about .50 calibre, with seven deep grooves, and has one half-turn the entire length of barrel, which is 30½ inches long.

No. 2 was made by Andreas Staarman, Berlin. It is of the flint-lock type, short, clumsy, about .75 calibre, with one half-turn in the length of barrel, which is 25⅝ inches long. The barrel is deeply rifled with seven regular and seven narrow grooves. In outline it is vastly superior to the wheel-lock and approaches nearer to practical lines. The date of manufacture is probably about 1660.

No. 3 is the Edward Marshall Rifle, which accompanied this pioneer on his historic "Indian Walk," is the true hybrid German-Pennsylvania arm and links the old European weapon with the fully developed Kentucky. Its affinity to the Staarman rifle is apparent.

No. 4 is the fully developed American rifle. It is dated 1728 at the breech end of the barrel on the left side. This gun is 100 per cent American and is the earliest dated rifle which the author has yet seen. It is also **marked**

"H. T. 1739," which is scratched deeply on the stock, and bears other indications which suggest that it has seen military service. This rifle is 56 inches long over all, the length of the barrel being 44½ inches with a .44 calibre bore. It has a star on the cheek piece made of brass. A silver ornament on the small of the stock is made from a hammered Spanish coin. The patch box contains a mass of hardened grease.

From 1728, when the American rifle emerged in its truly American form, to the time more than a century later when percussion locks superseded flint ignition, some major and many minor variations in form were apparent with the different periods.

To obtain the other numerous specimens of American rifles embodying these changes, as herein shown, required much time and great labor.

From the beginning it was my aim to secure specimens from as many makers as possible. No distance was too great, no spot too remote. Figuratively, I have raked the Continent over for rifles and reliable data.

I have been most fortunate in having good friends who rendered me valuable assistance, and their efforts added to my own have made this work a possibility.

Included with these several plates are 206 Flint-lock Rifles, also 38 that were changed to percussion, and it seems only fair to class these as Flintlocks. When we add these 38 converted guns to the 206 originals it brings the total up to 244, and of these 240 were made by that many different smiths. I feel quite safe in saying that there are only four duplicate rifles shown in the entire set of plates. It was not intended to use any duplicates, but a few were included, and rather than spoil a good plate were allowed to remain.

But why go to so much trouble to get specimens, I have been asked, and to this query I have replied, "It is a case where seeing is believing." I am showing a list of 335 riflemakers of the flint-lock period. If I back this claim with a few rifles, there is apt to be a doubt as to the reliability of the claim I have made. If, on the other hand, I show a large percentage of the number claimed, it is a strong argument that my claims are well founded in fact. And this is not all, for it seems only fair that the works of our early riflemakers should be preserved whenever it is possible to do so. The old rifle was of inestimable value in America's development and its claim on common gratitude demands its preservation. By showing these numerous specimens, together with the plain statements of facts, a greater interest should result, and with this additional interest an appreciation that may eventually lead to a better preservation of the comparatively few remaining specimens. While I claim a list of 335 makers before 1840, I am well aware that this number, large though it is, by no means includes all. But

ANCESTRY OF THE KENTUCKY RIFLE

Firearms typical of four principal stages in the development which produced the Kentucky Rifle, with actual-size diagrams of bore sizes and rifling. Detailed descriptions of these weapons appear on pages 3 and 4.

(Plate 10)

FAMOUS RIFLES

Four rifles of known lineage illustrating types associated with the winning of America through four periods.

No. 1. Brown Bess English Musket; made in 1740; carried to the Northwest by Manuel Lisa in 1807. It is in a fair state of preservation.

No. 2. By John Shuler, Liverpool, Pa., 1850; superposed double-barrel rifle; both barrels rifled; property of the great plainsman, Jim Bridger, from whom it passed to a man named Clarke, who later was killed by Indians while piloting a wagon train from Missouri to the California gold fields in 1849.

No. 3. United States Springfield Rifle; calibre 50; property of the notorious Sioux Chief, Sitting Bull, and used by him at the memorable battle of the Little Big Horn in 1876, historically known as the Custer Massacre.

No. 4. Winchester Rifle, model of 1876; presented to the late Theodore Roosevelt by the Marquis de Mories, a French nobleman who was engaged in the meat packing business at Medora, South Dakota, while Roosevelt was operating his ranch at Chimney Buttes in the Little Missouri River bottoms. The Marquis was assassinated by a native in South Africa during the Boer War.

(Plate 11)

most assuredly a very large percentage are here recorded. Doubtless, there are rifles included on these plates and listed as unidentified whose makers' names are not recorded, and we can say with equal assurance that there are also numbers of these same unidentified pieces that were made by makers who are actually included on the list. To work out all these intricate features is out of the question.

And now a word as to historic rifles. Doubtless there are numbers of specimens shown in this work that are entitled to be classed as historic, but the proof in the great majority of instances is lacking and they are classed as mere specimens.

Someone has remarked, "If they could only talk!" Yes, if they could, what a revelation it would be, what tales of blood and adventure! What thrills! But they are mute things and their masters failed to record their deeds, and as these same masters whose hands guided them have been dust for a century or more there is no hope of learning their past history. Even tradition, meager at the outset, has dwindled with each succeeding generation until nothing remains. Yes, if they could only talk.

In the several rifles classed as historic, shown on these accompanying pages, we have been very careful in our conclusions. In each instance the claims presented were carefully weighed and found to be well sustained. We were compelled to reject quite a number that were offered in good faith as historic weapons. But as the claims seemed weak, it was thought best to reject them. They may have been *bona fide*, or they may not. More the regret if they were.

One rifle of known lineage is the Edward Marshall Rifle, referred to in connection with Plate 10 as the true hybrid, and which figured in the historic Indian walk occurring in 1737 as an outcome of the purchase of land from the Indians made by Thomas and John Penn.

This purchase or contract seems to have been made in the year 1734, the fulfilment of the agreement to terminate in a walk and the distance walked to govern the extent of the so-called purchase. The walk was to start from a point where Wrightstown now stands, in Bucks County. The length of time to be walked was one and one-half days, both the Indians and Whites to be represented at the walk, and the course to run in a northerly direction toward the Blue Mountains, with the Delaware River as an eastern boundary. Judging from the termination of this memorable affair, it was a studied plot on the part of the Penns to trick the Indians and take from them vastly more lands than the terms of the contract seemed to imply, and this in sad contrast with the ways of their illustrious father, William Penn, for we find that as early as the Fall of 1734, trial walks were secretly arranged, and in the following April these same trial walks were made. A record in

April shows where Timothy Smith was paid £5 and again six days later expense £2 11 s. for ye Indian walk expenses. It is a matter of record that trails were surveyed and paths blazed to determine the shortest course.

The services of the best walkers known were secured in these trails, in order that the greatest possible distance would be traveled. When the final walk occurred in 1737, three young men had been selected to start: Edward Marshall, Joseph Yates and Solomon Jennings; the prize to the one covering the greatest distance to be 500 acres of land, located where the present city of Allentown now stands. At the conclusion of this walk, Marshall had outdistanced his competitors and was declared the winner.

The Indians showed the greatest possible displeasure at the outcome of this transaction and openly declared that they had been badly treated and cheated by their White brethren.

The victory of Edward Marshall from his personal standpoint was a costly one, for while testifying before a Royal Court investigating committee in 1757, he stated that he had not received full payment for his services, and further declared that he had lost a wife and son, slain by the Indians in revenge for his part in the walk twenty years before.

Of considerable interest to the student of firearms evolution is the fact that the displacement of the wheel-lock by the flint-lock—the most important developmental step in the genealogy of the rifle—was accomplished only after a long period of propaganda against the flint-lock principle.

The flint-lock made its appearance in Holland after the close of the Thirty Years' War, when there were regiments in the armies of Denmark, Sweden and France equipped with wheel-locks.

With most of these countries either actively engaged in or threatened by hostilities, it was but natural that gunsmithing at that time should be a flourishing trade and that the smiths themselves should wield considerable influence. So when the gunsmiths saw the popularity of their complicated and expensive mechanisms threatened by the simple, inexpensive flint-lock, they moved heaven and earth to keep the flint-locks out of the European armies.

The opposition to the flint-lock took varied forms, from the derisive dubbing of it "the snap-haunce"—a supposed Dutch word meaning chicken thief—to statements contained in a book which was widely distributed that flint-locks were of uncertain operation, since most of the sparks spilled over the edge of the pan; which was true also of the wheel-lock.

The fight against the flint-lock culminated in an edict by Louis XIV forbidding soldiers to possess flint-locks on pain of death. In spite of propaganda and edicts, the flint-lock, however, survived and less than ten years later the French king was forced to repeal his anti-flint-lock law.

SMITHSONIAN COLLECTION
(Washington, D. C.)

No. 1. By Nathan Kile, Raccoon Creek, Jackson County, Ohio; 58 inches over all; 42-inch octagon barrel; calibre 36; full curly maple stock; brass butt plate, patch-box and trigger guard; sett trigger; wooden ramrod; silver plate set in top of barrel marked "N. Kile, 1817"; weight 10¾ pounds.

No. 2. By Jason L. Harris; 61 inches over all; 45-inch hexagon barrel; calibre 42; plain open sights; rear sight covered by home-made copper sun-shade 4 inches long; full walnut stock pinned to barrel; small cheek-piece; 3 metal inlays on left side of stock, of which 1 remains in place; small hole under stock in which a feather is stuck; on lower side of cheek three small staples carrying another feather; sett trigger; silver plate on top of barrel marked "Jason L. Harris for T. Deaton"; small bullet mold with rifle.

No. 3. Unidentified; long octagon barrel; calibre 45; brass-mounted; fancy patch-box, finely engraved. This rifle was once the property of an Indian by the name of Abram Antoine who was chief of the Stockbridge tribe of Oneida Indians, New York State. He was a bad man and killed many white people in his day with this rifle, in the vicinity of Morrisville, New York, from 1800 to 1822. The last man he killed was a Mr. Jacobs for which he was captured and hanged in 1823 in the village of Morrisville. His daughter, Mary, was hanged five miles from Morrisville, in the village of Peterboro, for murdering a man, before Antoine himself was killed. The rifle was broken when Antoine was captured. It was repaired by putting a rib under the barrel. It has been owned and used by many since Antoine was captured and hanged.

(Plate 12)

WILLIAM WALKER, TENNESSEE GUNSMITH

of the late flint-lock early percussion period, was born in Tuckaleeche Cove, at the foot of the Great Smoky Mountains in the year 1838. He was one of the most famous Hunters and Riflemen of his day. He shot a Leman rifle that weighed 14 pounds, the ball weighing ½ ounce. This gun, originally a flint-lock, he changed to percussion, and used the barrel as a guide in his own work.

In this same region there was another rifleman of the Walker type whose name was Matt Parltin, and naturally the rivalry between the two was strong. Finally a test for supremacy was the order of things, and a match was shot which resulted in a tie. They could not settle it at the targets and it was then proposed by the backers to decide matters in the woods on live game. Squirrels were numerous in the Tennessee Mountains in those days, and were chosen as the features for the contest. At the conclusion of the match another tie had been made, each having killed 39 without a miss. Walker's 40th shot was at a running squirrel. He scored and won the match. Walker died in the year 1919. There are people still living who will vouch for the correctness of this story.

(Plate 13)

The Kentucky and Game

CHAPTER THREE

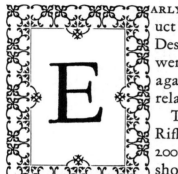ARLY American Kentucky Rifles were the direct product of the environment of the early American pioneer. Designed to meet the requirements of hunting which were far different from those of today, and for a warfare against redskins where the range of the shots was relatively short, it more than fulfilled its purpose.

Time and again, even in late years, the Kentucky Rifle has proved its accuracy up to and even beyond 200 yards—an extreme range in the early days of game shooting and redskin warfare. Game was then plentiful and taken at short distances. That the early pioneer was a skilled shot arose from the fact that occasionally his life depended upon downing an Indian, and also tended to the conservation of limited supplies of powder and lead. Also, marksmanship then was a generally accepted form of manly sport.

Hardly a history has been written wherein the part played by the pioneer's rifle in meat-getting has been overlooked. But histories upon such points are necessarily general rather than specific.

It is pertinent then, to consider in connection with any work on the Kentucky Rifle the vast amount of game which abounded almost in the door yard of the American frontiersman.

The "Annals of Early Philadelphia," by Watson; the writings of Colonel Henry W. Shoemaker, and material from other sources made it possible to present data on the abundance of game through three periods during which the flint-lock Kentucky was being developed and was actually in use. These facts form a background against which this rifle, so pre-eminently fitted to fill the backwoodsman's larder, unmistakably stands out as the logical weapon for the early settler.

From the "Annals of Early Philadelphia," we learn that by the close of the year 1682 more than twenty-three shiploads of passengers for the Penn

Colony had arrived since Spring, and that "in those times the Indians and the Swedes were kind and active to bring in and vend at moderate prices proper articles of subsistence. Wild fowl were in abundance. Wild pigeons were like clouds and often flew so low as to be knocked down with sticks. Wild turkeys sometimes were so immoderately fat and large as to have weighed forty-six pounds. Some turkeys of thirty pounds sold at one shilling; deer at two shillings."

The Annals continue: "The game for shooters much more abounded before the Revolution than since. Fishing and fowling were once subjects of great recreation and success. Wild pigeons used to be innumerable, so also blackbirds, reed birds and squirrels. As late as the year 1720, an act was passed, fining 5s. for shooting pigeons, doves or partridges, or other fowl (birds), in the streets of Philadelphia, or the gardens or orchards adjoining any house within the said city! In Penn's woods, westward of Broad street, used to be excellent pigeon shooting."

Passing to 1760, when the American type of rifle had emerged from the developmental stage, we come to Colonel Shoemaker's account of "The Great Slaughter."

Animal drives, similar to those once held in South Africa, were as plentiful in Central and Southern Pennsylvania as in the "Northerntier." They occurred in the remote backwoods districts where no written history was kept; accounts of them have well-nigh lapsed into oblivion. One of the greatest drives ever known took place about 1760, in the vicinity of Pomfret Castle, a fort for defense against the Indians, which had been constructed in 1756.

"Black Jack" Schwartz was the leader of this drive, which resulted in the death of more than forty panthers. Schwartz, or, as he is often called, "The wild hunter of the Juniata," must not be confounded with Captain Jack Armstrong, a trader, who was murdered by Indians in Jack's Narrows, in 1744. History has confused the two men, but as the wild hunter offered his command of sharpshooters to General Braddock in 1755, there can be no doubt that there were different persons.

Panthers and wolves had been troubling the more timid of the settlers, and a grand drive toward the center of a circle many miles in diameter was planned. A plot of ground was cleared into which the animals were driven.

In the outer edge of the circle fires were started, guns fired, bells rung, all manner of noises made. The hunters, men and boys, to the number of two hundred, gradually closed in on the center. When they reached the point where the killing was to be made, they found it crowded with yelping, growling, bellowing animals. Then the slaughter began, not ending

Laidacker Collection

No. 1. Unidentified; 61½ inches over all; 46-inch full octagon barrel; 8 deep grooves; 120 balls to the pound; full curly maple stock 9 inlays; brass patch-box; sett trigger; weight 11½ pounds; called the "Fish" gun on account of the mountings.

No. 2. Unidentified; 77 inches over all; 61½-inch half octagonal barrel; 8 deep grooves; about 40 balls to the pound; full walnut stock; no mountings, no butt plate; butt shows great wear, as if dragged over the ground; no trigger guard; weight 11½ pounds. The rifling is of a very odd nature. This rifle was known in the early days as "Long Tom, the Indian Killer."

No. 3. Unidentified; 71 inches over all; 56-inch full octagon barrel; 8 deep grooves; 60 balls to the pound; full wild cherry stock which has the appearance of not having been completed; German silver mountings; round patch-box, hand-made lock; weight 10½ pounds.

No. 4. By J. J. Henry & Son, Boulton; name stamped on barrel and lock plate; 68 inches over all; 53-inch full octagonal barrel; 6 deep grooves; 60 balls to the pound; full curly maple stock with long wrist and very heavy drop; plain brass patch-box; weight 7½ pounds.

(Plate 14)

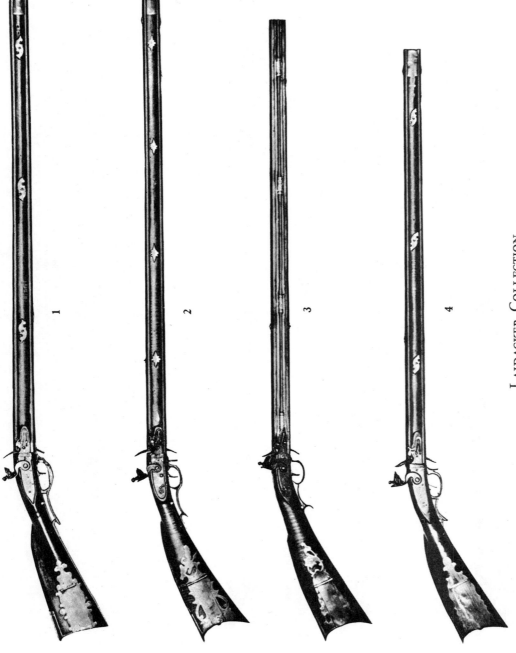

LAIDACKER COLLECTION

No. 1. By Boyer (father of Daniel Boyer); double-barrel flint-lock rifle; 36 inches over all; 41-inch barrels revolving on common axes operated by split trigger guard; 7 grooves in one barrel, the other smooth; one hammer fires both barrels; about 80 balls to the pound full curly maple stock, brass-mounted, with 3 brass inlays and silver star on checkpiece; weight 10 pounds; shows great age and much service.

No. 2. By Mull; double-barrel; 57 inches over all; 41-inch barrels revolving on common axes, operated by stud ahead of trigger guard; one barrel 6 and the other 8 grooves; one spiral, the other straight cut; one hammer fires both barrels; about 110 balls to the pound; full curly maple stock with ramrod; brass patch-box and trimmings; 6 silver inlays; checkpiece supported with beautiful brass feather receptacles; under part of stock carved; weight 9½ pounds.

No. 3. By Gumpf, of Lancaster, Pa.; double-barrel; 54¾ inches over all; 39½-inch barrels revolving on common axes, operated by lever on left side; 7 grooves in one barrel, the other smooth; one hammer fires both barrels; about 90 balls to the pound; each side of barrel trimmed with brass full length; full curly maple stock with ramrod; brass patch-box and trimmings; 2 silver inlays; weight 10½ pounds; a rare arm.

No. 4. By D. Boyer; double-barrel; 53 inches over all; 38-inch barrels revolving on common axes, operated by finger-piece on split trigger guard; 7 grooves in one barrel, the other smooth; one hammer fires both barrels; about 90 balls to the pound; full curly maple stock brass patch-box and trimmings; 9 silver inlays; checkpiece supported with plain brass feather receptacles; all parts including locks are hand-made; weight 9½ pounds.

(Plate 15)

STRONG COLLECTION

No. 1. Unidentified; 57 inches over all; 42-inch half octagon barrel; full curly maple stock; brass patch-box in form of eagle; of about period of 1780. This patch-box design was quite common at the close of the Revolution.

No. 2. Unidentified; 55 inches over all; 40-inch full octagon barrel; full maple stock; brass patch-box in eagle design. A later specimen than No. 1.

No. 3. Unidentified; 59 inches over all; 44-inch full octagon barrel; full curly maple stock; brass mountings; brass patch-box; period of about 1790; the author has seen four rifles apparently from the maker of this arm.

Nos. 4, 5. Unidentified; 58½ inches over all; 41½-inch full octagon barrel; barrel engraved with the letters "C. D."; percussion lock converted from flint-lock; outline and finish of the rifle of the highest order.

(Plate 16)

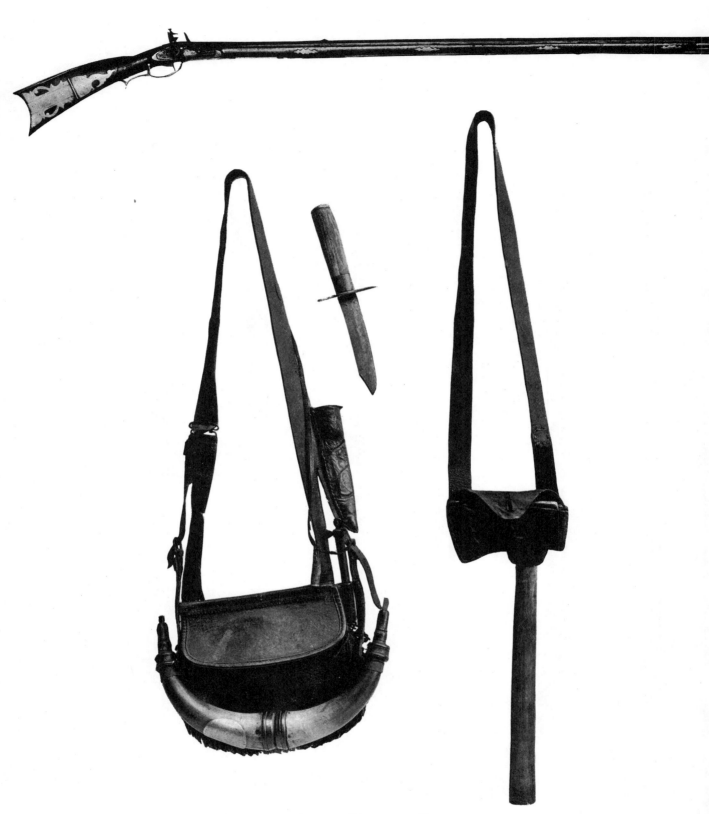

THE WEISER HUNTING OUTFIT

This hunting outfit was the property of G. W. Weiser, riflemaker of Northeastern Pennsylvania, who was also an expert rifle shot. In the bag were found several targets, shown on
Plate 71. They were made in the year 1839 by G. W. and J. Weiser, the latter evidently a relative, but not identified by surviving members of the family. The large target in the center is
inscribed with the numeral "100," which may or may not indicate the distance at which the
shots were fired. A descendant of Weiser says that they used to shoot at 60 yards off-hand and
at 100 yards muzzle rest. Whichever the position, the record for accuracy is admirable.

The rifle is a fine example of original flint-lock, by an unidentified maker. It is 58 inches
overall; 43-inch full octagon barrel and handsomely decorated; weight 10 pounds.

(Plate 17)

until the last animal had been slain. A group of buffalo broke through the guards at an early stage of the killing, and it is estimated that several hundred animals escaped in this way.

The recapitulation is as follows, the count having been made by Black Jack himself at the close of the carnage: 41 panthers, 109 wolves, 112 foxes, 114 mountain cats, 17 black bears, 1 white bear, 2 elk, 198 deer, 111 buffalo, 3 fishers, 1 otter, 12 gluttons, 3 beavers and upwards of 500 smaller animals. The proportion of panthers to the entire number killed is an interesting commentary on the early prevalence of these animals.

The choicest hides were taken, together with the buffalo tongues, and then the heap of carcasses, "as tall as the trees," was covered with rich pine and fired. This created such a stench that the settlers were compelled to vacate their cabins in the vicinity of the fort, three miles away.

There is a small mound that marks the spot of the slaughter, near the headwaters of (West) Mahantango Creek. When this was dug into some years ago, it was found filled with bones.

Black Jack's unpopularity with the Indians was added to when they learned of this animal drive. The red men, who killed only such animals as they actually needed for furs, and food, and were real conservationists, resented such a wholesale butchery. The story goes that the wild hunter was ambushed by Indians while on a hunting trip and killed.

Animal drives did not cease with Black Jack's death, but in some localities they were held annually, until game became practically exterminated. They were held in Northern Pennsylvania, which was settled at a much later date, until about 1830. After the great slaughter of Pomfret Castle many backwoodsmen appeared in full suits of panther skin. For several years they were known as the "Panther Boys," and in their old days they delighted to recount the "big hunt" to their descendants.

Among those said to have taken part in it were Jack Schwartz, Michael Dougherty, Felix Delehanty, Terence McGuire, Patt. Mitcheltree, brother of Hugh Mitcheltree, who was carried off by six Indians in 1756; Abraham Hart, Michael Flinn and Isaac Delaplain. The panther's uniform was abandoned because they became favorite targets for skulking Indians. The savages, infuriated by the arrogance of the white newcomers, spared persons falling into their power, occasionally, but gave no quarter to a "Panther Boy."

The great slaughter of animals kept alive ill feeling between the two races in the region of the Firestone Mountains, and probably a dozen settlers lost their lives because of it. However, they went on with their animal drives, as the hardy settlers loved to do what the Indians hated.

Of all the hunters contributing to the final extermination of the Pennsylvania lion, Aaron Hall, who died at the palatial mansion back of Unionville, Center County, in 1892, stands well up on the list. Between the years 1845 and 1869 he killed 50 panthers, principally in Center and Clearfield counties. As he began his career as a hunter on Wells and Tipton Runs, tributaries of the Juniata, he was often called the "lion hunter of the Juniata." On one occasion when visited by Hon. C. K. Sober, of Lewisburg, former State Game Commissioner, he had the hides of eleven panthers hanging up on his camp on Rock Run. In 1849 the last animal drive or "Ring Hunt" was held by the pioneers at Beech Creek, Clinton County. Several panthers, it is said, escaped through the human barrier.

Even as late as 1818 these slaughters, or "Circle Hunts," as they were called, were still held in communities where wild animals were so plentiful as to be a menace to the meager crops and herds of the pioneer farmer.

One of these drives, described some years ago by Orvin Decker, who was born in 1808, resulted in the killing in one day of 40 deer, 8 bear, 13 wolves, 1 panther and many foxes. The scene of this hunt in Bradford County still bears the name of Slaughter Hill.

OLD-TIME PENNSYLVANIA HUNTERS

Two locally noted Pennsylvania hunters. On the left, Martin Wagner, of Union County, who shot his first deer in 1855 with a flint-lock rifle. In 1910, he brought down a splendid buck in the same neighborhood. Mr. Wagner is eighty-three years old but asks no favors from younger companions when on a hunting trip. On the right is William H. French, shooting at a target with a record of five shots shown in the corner. He was accompanied by Seth Nelson, Jr., on a hunting trip through Clinton County.

At the top is a long graceful rifle, plainly finished, which was made by E. Boone, Oley Valley, Pa., a cousin of the famous Daniel Boone.

(Plate 18)

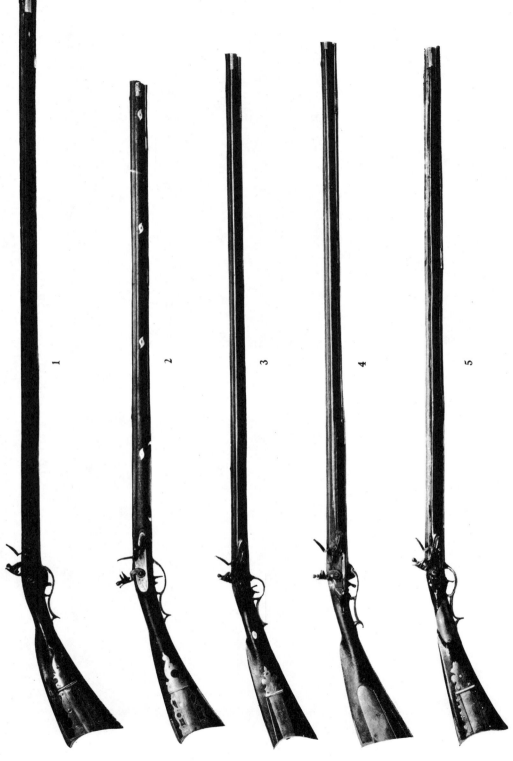

SNYDER COLLECTION

No. 1. Unidentified; 66 inches over all; 51-inch full octagon barrel; full maple stock; brass-mounted; brass patch-box; a most beautiful, early rifle.

No. 2. By A. Kiser; 57 inches over all; 42-inch full octagon barrel; full curly maple stock; brass-mounted; brass patch-box; very handsome.

No. 3. By P. and D. Moll, Hellertown, Pa.; 61½ inches over all; 46½-inch full octagon barrel; full maple stock; brass patch-box; splendid workmanship.

No. 4. By J. Daub, 61½ inches over all; 47½-inch full octagon barrel; full curly maple stock, hand-carved; plain brass patch-box; a very early rifle.

No. 5. Unidentified; 59½ inches over all; 44½-inch full octagon barrel; full maple stock; carved grip; brass patch-box; a fine old rifle.

(Plate 19)

The Rifle That Was Needed

CHAPTER FOUR

THE rifle manufactured for use in Central Europe in the latter part of the 17th and early part of the 18th Century failed utterly to meet the requirements of the American pioneer who at that time was setting forth on the conquest of a mighty wilderness. Germany, Austria and Switzerland all produced rifles, but they were large of bore, clumsy of construction, badly sighted, too unwieldy for long journeys and very hard to load. These undesirable features are only too evident in specimens on exhibition in museums and private collections and may be compared in the rifles shown in Plate No. 10. A radical departure from the models of the Fatherland was absolutely necessary, and stimulated by the complaints and criticisms of their customers, the early gunsmiths entered into a rivalry which resulted in the perfection of a new type of weapon destined to take its place in American history as the "Kentucky Rifle."

Just where or by whom this superb American rifle was first developed may never be known, but all authorities agree that it was produced somewhere in Eastern Pennsylvania. Some writers are explicit and name Lancaster as its birthplace and this theory seems to be more than mere conjecture.

Lancaster, for a long time, was the frontier settlement of Pennsylvania. It was founded in 1718 and called Hickory Town until 1730. Though a mere trading post with a few log cabins, it was, by reason of its geographical position, destined to become a place of great importance, for it lay at the very gate of a wilderness that seemed endless in extent, a region of apparently limitless possibilities and through which for more than twenty years emigration had proceeded on its westward march through Pennsylvania.

From early county records we learn that a very large percentage of immigrants who came to Pennsylvania after 1710 were Germans and Swiss, in many instances driven from the Fatherland through religious persecution.

These sturdy sons of toil, though largely agriculturists at home, included in their midst numerous craftsmen, skilled in the various trades, and conspicuous among these artisans were gunsmiths from both Germany and Switzerland, attracted to the New World by the great demand for fire-arms, a demand that not only seemed permanent but destined to become a leading industry in Colonial America. By reason of later developments, it is only fair to assume that these same gunsmiths were in reality skilled in the art of rifle making, and from many records we find that they were not long in establishing themselves in the village of Lancaster or its environs.

Included among such artisans were the Roessers, the Lemans, Ferree, Stenzel, Allbright, Folecht, LeFevre and doubtless others. The exact dates of their arrival are not known to a certainty, but by the year 1730 rifle making was a recognized industry, and it seems to be a well-authenticated fact that Peter Leman, the Swiss, was making rifles at the Leman Place, a few miles east of Lancaster, as early as 1721.

The new settlement of Lancaster was located about seventy miles due west from the more important town situated on the Delaware and called Philadelphia, where the great majority of emigrants first stood on American soil. Here they paused for a while, for they must arrange for their lands and secure supplies for the long, tedious journey over the rough Conestoga trail to Lancaster.

And what a journey this must have been. A mere winding packhorse trail that had been recently widened to accommodate the ox teams which carried the scanty belongings of the new homeseeker; here a small clearing and a log cabin; a mile or so farther on, another clearing with better improvements and bigger fields, with wilderness stretched between. A road tavern sheltered the weary travellers and furnished food for the animals that carried the burdens. Another cabin by the roadside was a rendezvous for hunters, the skins of deer, bear, wolves and panthers were stretched and drying in the cool autumn winds, and so mile by mile, such scenes spread before the eye for the greater part of the distance between Philadelphia and Lancaster two hundred years ago, and being witnessed by the early rifle maker on his way to the Conestoga, it is probable they acted as an inspiration, enabling him to see the possibilities of the region and the business he proposed to follow. Further and more intimate contact with his environment prepared him for the criticism of the old European rifle and the demand for a better and more economical rifle than had ever been produced—a new arm for new conditions.

The arrival at Lancaster of the first gunsmith undoubtedly created considerable interest. His services were in immediate demand, and it is safe to say that he was not long in acquiring a business which taxed to the full

AN EARLY LOG CABIN IN THE MOUNTAINS OF WESTERN TENNESSEE

(Plate 20)

HUNTING COSTUME OF OTHER DAYS

The coonskin cap, hunting shirt, leggins and moccasins marked the Backwoodsman. (Photo by Cline.

(Plate 21)

extent his limited resources. Patrons were numerous; rival smiths appeared and soon opened shops in the neighborhood. Business rivalry was keen then as now, and each strove for a reputation.

First came the repair work and, from examples of such repairs and alterations, it needs but little imagination to see in this work convincing proof that the old rifle of Central Europe would never meet the requirements of Colonial America. The early patrons included hunters, explorers, rangers and all sorts of adventurers usually found in a frontier town, and it is hardly necessary to add that they carried guns wherever they went.

These sturdy pioneers found a congenial meeting place at the log cabin rifle shops of early Lancaster and the talk naturally turned to a criticism of the arms on which they were dependent for their personal safety and for food.

The smith listened day by day to a constant pleading for a better rifle. The defects of the time-honored weapon of the Fatherland were pointed out by his visitors and suggestions made for their correction. He was told that the guns then in use were too big of bore and cost too much for the powder and lead, a matter of vital importance from a standpoint of economy. There was a steady complaint that the rifles were clumsy and ill-balanced, too heavy for a long journey, and that the trigger guards were both large and frail, becoming a perpetual annoyance. The sights were useless in a dark forest, and the loading methods were both slow and noisy.

These and other complaints, constantly made, must have at first surprised the rifle maker, and he may have resented at the outset the very criticisms which, as shown by subsequent developments, were responsible for radical changes in design. The weak parts of the old guns had been clearly set forth and it was demanded of the smith that he remedy the situation. Action was not long delayed. Competition was making itself felt. Rival smiths promised improvements and the race began.

There was a period of intense activity. Riflesmiths worked night and day, perhaps behind closed doors. Patrons with repair work had to take chances. Gossip drifted around that the smiths were secretly experimenting with new models, and soon it was a general topic of conversation. A few months later the climax was reached. A new rifle had been produced, differing from the old European type, unique in many respects and conforming very closely to public demand.

The new rifle had a longer barrel, one-third less diameter in bore. The trigger guard was smaller and more massive. There was no short iron rod and mallet required to start the bullet down the barrel. The ball was smaller in comparison to the bore than that used in the older gun, and was smeared with soft tallow. It was pushed down the barrel by a light iron rod. The front sight was slightly larger. The box in the stock was small and neat, its outlines more shapely, and was intended as a receptacle for greased bullets. This rifle shot well and was eagerly sought by purchasers.

But this creation was only a beginning, a model for the inventor's competitors to improve upon, and it is needless to say that they were not long in profiting from his genius. New rifles, all with similar characteristics, were soon in evidence. There had been no radical change from the first model, but there were changes necessary and they were soon made.

A better model appeared, bold in conception, and a long, graceful gun. The barrel was 40 inches in length and of .48 calibre. It carried a well-formed front sight of larger dimensions well set to the barrel. There was a brass hinged box on the side of the stock for hard grease. The trigger guard was strong and neat, and the rifle was equipped with a hickory ramrod. The workmanship was fair throughout and the rifle shot well. It was declared to be the best ever seen and the limit of perfection seemed to have been reached, but its triumph was short-lived.

Every smith was working out a model and it was a race to a finish. More rifles were offered, but for a while designs hung too closely to European lines to be classed as great improvements.

It was this keen and spirited competition between the gunsmiths of the early frontier that gives the individuality to so many specimens of the Kentucky type rifle. These weapons were handmade from front sight to butt plate and parts were interchangeable only by happenchance. The imagination of the smith had full and unhampered play, and as a result all expedients which might contribute to accuracy and effectiveness were tried from time to time. This explains to a great degree why two Kentucky rifles, even from the shop of the same maker are so rarely exact duplicates, and why such a wide range of diversities is apparent.

This period of experimentation during which the smiths not only followed their own ideas but embodied the suggestions of practical riflemen returning from frontier pilgrimages continued through a long period. Thus the retention of valuable departures from European types was assured as well as the abandonment of impractical features.

Then one day appeared a rifle so superior to any previous product in firearms that it was in a class by itself, and it can be truthfully said that for a hundred years it held its claim for superiority over any gun made in the world; in fact, it is a question if its accuracy has ever been surpassed in short range work.

The outlines of this rifle were graceful, the workmanship superb. It was strong without clumsiness. The barrel was full octagon and 42 inches long with about a .45 calibre. The upper small of the stock, which was of curly

Snyder Collection

No. 1. Unidentified; 60½ inches over all; 45½-inch half octagon barrel; full maple stock; brass patch-box; fine workmanship.

No. 2. By Barnhart, of Pennsylvania; 58 inches over all; 43½-inch full octagon barrel; full curly maple stock; brass mountings and inlay; brass patch-box; well made.

No. 3. Unidentified; 61½ inches over all; 48½-inch half octagon barrel; full curly maple stock; brass mountings; brass patch-box; a very high-class early rifle.

No. 4. By G. Feder; 61 inches over all; 46-inch full octagon barrel; full maple stock; brass patch-box; good work; this smith made a great many rifles.

No. 5. By Daniel Marker; 59 inches over all; 44-inch full octagon barrel; full curly maple stock; highly decorated; brass patch-box; Marker made a specialty of finely decorated rifles of splendid workmanship. Two of his rifles are known to the author.

(Plate 22)

SNYDER COLLECTION

No. 1. Unidentified; 55 inches over all; 41-inch full octagon barrels; double-barrel superposed rifle; one barrel rifled, one smooth bore; maple stock; brass patch-box; altered from flint lock; a rifle of rare beauty.

No. 2. Unidentified; 54 inches over all; 39-inch full octagon barrels; double-barrel superposed rifle; both barrels rifled; 60 balls to the pound: splendid workmanship.

No. 3. Unidentified; 54 inches over all; 39-inch full octagon barrels; double-barrel superposed rifle; one barrel rifled, one smooth bore; full curly maple stock, highly decorated; brass patch-box; a very rare piece.

No. 4. By Nathan Clause, of Pennsylvania; 51½ inches over all; 36½-inch full octagon barrels; double-barrel superposed rifle; one barrel rifled, one smooth; brass patch-box; a very handsome piece.

No. 5. By E. Brey 49 inches over all; 34-inch round barrels; double-barrel superposed rifle; one barrel rifled, one smooth; side hammer percussion; brass cap box; barrels are made of what is known as stub twist.

(Plate 23)

SNYDER COLLECTION

RARE UNITED STATES FLINT-LOCK SERVICE RIFLES, ALL IN PERFECT CONDITION

No. 1. Lock marked "Tryon, Philadelphia"; length over all, 57 inches; full octagon barrel, 40 inches; full stock.
No. 2. Barrel and lock marked "Tryon, Philadelphia"; length over all 57 inches; full octagon barrel, 40½ inches; full stock.
No. 3. Lock marked "Richmond, Virginia, 1821"; length over all, 55 inches; half octagon barrel, 40 inches; half stock, under-rib.
No. 4. Lock marked "Harper's Ferry, 1819"; length over all, 52½ inches; half octagon barrel, 37 inches; half stock, under-rib.
No. 5. Lock marked "Harper's Ferry, 1807"; length over all, 49 inches; half octagon barrel, 33½ inches; half stock, under-rib.

(Plate 24)

SNYDER COLLECTION

No. 1. Unidentified; double-barrel rifle, converted from flint-lock; right barrel smooth, left barrel rifled; called a side-by-side double rifle; very rare.

No. 2. By H. Carlisle; 57½ inches over all; 41½-inch full octagon barrel; converted from flint-lock.

No. 3. By Jasan; 57½ inches over all; 41½-inch full octagon barrel; converted from flint-lock of very early period.

No. 4. Unidentified; 55 inches over all; 40-inch octagon barrel; early period.

No. 5. By Ferree; 55 inches over all; 40-inch full octagon barrel; early Lancaster and very rare.

(Plate 25)

maple, carried a round silver plate neatly fitted to the wood. On the left side of the stock was a small, well-formed cheek piece in which was sunk a brass star. On the right side of the stock was a box five inches long by one and one-half inches wide, covered with a polished brass hinged lid and brass trimmings, all of artistic design. In this box there were neither flints nor bullets. Instead it was filled with round pieces of dressed buckskin about the size of a half dollar and heavily greased with soft tallow. The bullets used in this rifle were about 3/100 of an inch smaller than the bore and without the patch would roll down the barrel without ramming.

It is examples of this vintage Kentucky which are now so eagerly sought by collectors who know what is desirable, and most of these specimens, which are of infrequent occurrence, are of far greater importance than the more ornate examples of the later flint-lock period.

That these early rifles are so extremely rare is due undoubtedly to the terrifically hard usage to which frontier conditions of one hundred and fifty years ago subjected them. Such examples as have survived in good condition were in almost every instance, it is safe to assume, diverted into attic storage before the full toll of use and abuse had been taken of them. It is very doubtful whether very many of the extant early specimens saw any very considerable frontier service. The early rifle was of necessity a thoroughly practical arm, fulfilling specifically the needs of the men who were to place dependence for their lives upon it; for this reason it received the best of care possible under the conditions of its use, which explains the survival of such early specimens as are found from time to time.

The smith demonstrated his own handiwork. The long barrel, said he, takes less powder to the charge as it burns cleaner. The discharge makes less noise and the rifle can be held steadier. By the use of the greased pieces of buckskin, the rifle can be loaded in one-quarter of the time consumed in charging the guns of older make, and it will shoot with greater accuracy. The smith had solved the problem, and later tests by actual shooting abundantly proved his claims, which immediately appealed to the hard practical sense of the backwoodsman. In the new and distinctly American type of rifle the pioneer saw a weapon which would not only meet his demands for accuracy and which would be equally effective either upon hostile savages or game, but which would be economical in the consumption of ammunition which could be taken only in limited amounts into the wilderness.

Who first applied a patch to the ball will probably never be known, but it was a master stroke, the last link forged in the chain of evolution which brought forth a distinctly American rifle; an arm so entirely different from the rifle of Central Europe as to carry but a trace of similarity; a weapon of graceful lines and deadly precision; a new rifle embodying new ideas to meet new requirements.

Thus appeared, at an opportune time, the long, graceful hunting rifle of mid-Colonial days, the arm which stimulated adventure and turned a forbidding wilderness into a Happy Hunting Ground, furnishing the means of food and protection to the lonely settler who followed the hunter's trail and giving him security in times of danger.

Later this same rifle contributed enormously to the success of American arms in our wars with the Indians and foreign nations and was a mighty factor in shaping the destinies of our great American republic.

OLD TENNESSEE BLOCK HOUSE

Old block house, or fort, in Polk County, Tennessee, erected between 1830 and 1835, at the time of the removal of the Cherokee Indians by General Winfield Scott. This interesting old landmark was still standing in 1922.

(Plate 26)

OLD HENRY FACTORY ON BUSHKILL CREEK, BOULTON, PA.

(Plate 27)

Where and by Whom
The Kentucky Rifle Was Made

CHAPTER FIVE

HE most careful research has established beyond doubt that Pennsylvania was not only the birthplace of the American rifle, but that for many years thereafter it had a practical monopoly of the rifle industry. The location of the first rifle shop is a matter of argument and will doubtless remain legendary due to the loosely kept records of the early days and the destruction of family papers which would today be invaluable. Philadelphia has a claim to priority of manufacture, but there is nothing of record to support the theory, in fact the first reference the author has found is of a gunsmith having been located in Water Street. The fact that the rifle industry did not flourish in Philadelphia may be accounted for by reason of its being a Quaker settlement, whose people had little sympathy with firearms, and little or no use for them.

Another theory is that, while the Swiss and German emigrants were steadily pushing westward, a number of them preferred going up the Schuylkill to the Reading district, and still others at the same time were on their way up the Delaware River to the Lehigh region. Later on, both of these districts became famous for their rifles, but all known facts point to Lancaster as the great early rifle center, as it was also the schooling point for the skilled apprentices who later followed the emigrant trails south to the Carolinas and west to the Ohio River Country.

The Swiss emigrants who entered the wilderness of Pennsylvania in 1709, and settled where the city of Lancaster now stands, were riflemen, and Rupp, in his history of Lancaster County (pp. 74, 75), mentions that one of these emigrants, Martin Meylan, erected in 1719 what Rupp calls a boring mill to bore out gun barrels.

Philip LeFevre was another early gunsmith whose shop was located at Big Spring, Beaver Valley, about four miles from Lancaster, where he made guns (or rifles) from 1731 to 1766.

Matthew Roesser was making rifles in Lancaster before 1744 and Henry Albrecht was another riflesmith of the same period, in fact Lancaster County was a veritable beehive of riflemaking for more than one hundred years, and an idea of its importance can be formed from the claim, well authenticated, that, in the year 1815, there were in that county sixty gunsmiths.

Lancaster was not the only riflemaking center, however. The trade flourished wherever the German and Swiss tide of emigration spread.

Jacob Ferree, a son of Isaac Ferree, moved his family to Allegheny County about 1784 and took up a vast tract of land on Peters Creek, about twenty-four miles up the Monongahela River from Pittsburgh. There he erected a powder mill and gunsmith shop where his son Joel worked with him. Their rifles found a ready market in Doddridge County, Virginia, and in Kentucky and North Carolina.

The wife of Jacob Ferree was a fine shot, and at that early time had no rival in Allegheny County. It was she who tested the guns and powder which the skill of her husband produced.

As time passed and new settlements sprang up further to the south and west, the apprentices of the celebrated old riflesmiths, their period of service ended, drifted away from the Pennsylvania settlements and established their own shops nearer to the frontiers, where the demand for rifles still persisted.

The Carolinas, Virginia, the Ohio River Country, Kentucky, Tennessee and St. Louis all had their riflesmiths and some of the old shops and mills stand to this day in almost the same condition as when the smith was patiently working at a long-forgotten trade.

Who made the early American pistols is a question also often asked, and I feel safe in saying that this question can be easily answered. The pistols were with perhaps a few exceptions made by the rifle makers, these exceptions being in the instance of a Government contract. The early American pistols were generally made by pairs and carried in a double holster, no doubt made on order. Many of these were decorated, but a great many were plain. They varied in length, but barrels 8 or 10 inches long were the most numerous. They were large of bore, often reaching a .70 calibre; these pistols were as a rule smooth-bore; not infrequently the barrel was made of brass. P. and D. Moll seem to have specialized on brass barrels. In the careful examination of early pistols we find them bearing the names of the rifle makers, and so often, that I feel very safe in my conclusion that the

OLD HENRY RIFLE WORKS

Interior view of the old Henry rifle works at Boulton, Pa., showing the original grinding wheel with belt wheel attached. This was driven by waterpower and was in use for many years.

(Plate 28)

AN EARLY RIFLE SHOP

An early rifle shop in Eastern Tennessee, together with dam and flume, which operated the water-wheel and furnished power for the grinding machinery, etc. Here rifles were bored for smiths whose equipment was less complete.

(Plate 29)

rifle makers made most of the pistols, the names of the makers being cut on the barrels in the same manner as they were cut on the rifles.

There is much corroborative fact which points conclusively to the region around Lancaster as the birthplace of the Kentucky Rifle. Horace Kephart, who has given years of study and thought to the subject, writing in 1897, said:

"Your contributor is on the right track; but I fear some of his conclusions need revision. He says, for example:

" 'The rifle came to America from the Austro-German Tyrol about 1730, or possibly a year or two earlier. The first we know of the rifle, it was being made in Philadelphia by two gunsmiths named Decherd (or Dechert) and Leman, about 1732.'

"Now, the Swiss immigrants who entered the wilderness of Pennsylvania in 1709, and settled where the city of Lancaster subsequently arose, were riflemen. One of these, Martin Meylan, erected in 1719 what Rupp calls a boring mill, to bore out gun barrels ('History of Lancaster County,' pp. 74, 75). Lancaster soon became noted for its rifles and supplied the whole Appalachian border.

"The oldest rifle still preserved in America, of which I have heard—probably there are others older—is that used by Edward Marshall, who made the 'great walk' for the Penns in 1737. The following description of this venerable piece is taken from Davis' 'History of Bucks County, Pennsylvania,' 1876, pp. 507, 508:

"There was a famous rifle maker named Decherd, or Deckhard, at Lancaster during the Revolution. According to Ramsay's 'Annals of Tennessee,' p. 228, the trans-Allegheny backwoodsmen who defeated Ferguson at King's Mountain were mostly armed with the Deckhard rifle. He says in a footnote:

" 'This rifle was remarkable for the precision and distance of its shot. It was generally three feet six inches long, weighed about seven pounds, and ran about seventy bullets to the pound of lead. It was so-called from Deckhard, the maker, in Lancaster, Pa. One of them is now in the hands of the writer.'

"Either Ramsay refers to the dimensions of the barrel alone, or he has fallen across a very exceptional specimen of gun, for such diminutive arms were scarcely known at that time. Doddridge ('Notes on the Settlement of Virginia and Pennsylvania', '76 repr., p. 177), speaking from his own recollection of the period from 1763 to 1783, says:

" 'Rifles of former times were different from those of modern date; few of them carried more than forty-five bullets to the pound. Bullets of a less size were not thought sufficiently heavy for hunting or war.'

"The most celebrated rifle maker of revolutionary times was William Henry, of Lancaster. In 1744, when fifteen years of age, he was apprenticed to a Lancaster gunsmith named Martin Roeser, with whom he continued to the end of his term, in 1750, and commenced making rifles on his own account. Upon the breaking out of the French and Indian War he was appointed armorer to Braddock's expedition and ordered to Virginia. After the defeat of the expedition he returned to Lancaster and continued to supply the frontier and Indian trade with weapons. His son, William Henry, Jr., followed the same business, and executed contracts with the Government during the Revolution for many thousand stands of arms. In 1809 the younger Henry erected a gun factory near Nazareth, Pa., in which the business is still continued by his great-grandson (or was in 1890, when I obtained these particulars from John W. Jordan, a member of the family). The Henry rifle was famous throughout the western frontiers down to 1860, sharing with the Hawken in the esteem of the mountain men.

"The evidence that our national weapon was introduced into America by Swiss and Tyrolean mountaineers, sometime between 1683 and 1710, is circumstantial but exceedingly strong. Anyone interested in it may find the case presented in an article on 'The Rifle in Colonial Times,' which I published in the Magazine of American History, September, 1890. These same men, or other Germans, were the first rifle makers in this country, and most of the celebrated makers for a century and a half were German-Americans or their pupils."

It is fortunate for the students of the history of Kentucky Rifles that Kephart and other such enthusiasts recorded their conclusions on such vital questions as the place and date of origin of the essentially American weapon. These discussions, in an attempt at this late date to isolate such facts, become evidence of importance whether corroborative, or otherwise, of the conclusions of present day students which have been reached independently; and lacking definite and indisputable historical record, the consensus of opinion among intelligent investigators who have considered the question from all angles becomes the deciding factor.

More testimony as to the place where the first Kentuckys were made comes from Cora A. Weber Lindsay, who, however, while naming Lancaster as the birthplace of the American Rifle, identifies the French Huguenots as the originators of the arm. In "Shooting and Fishing" in 1897, she says:

"The history of Pennsylvania's early settlers has been to some extent written up; its German, Swiss, Dutch, Irish, Welsh and French settlers given their respective places in her annals. The Pennsylvania German, outnumbering all other nationalities, has gained a world-renowned reputation

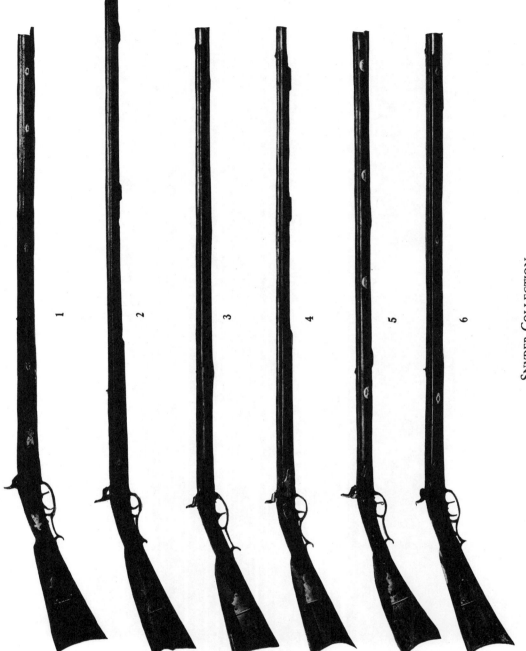

Snyder Collection

No. 1. By I. Haeffer; 57 inches over all; 42-inch full octagon barrel; altered from flintlock to percussion.
No. 2. Unidentified; 63 inches over all; 48-inch full octagon barrel; altered from flintlock to percussion.
No. 3. Unidentified; 59½ inches over all; 44½-inch full octagon barrel; altered from flintlock to percussion.
No. 4. By J. and W. Henry; 59 inches over all; 44-inch octagon barrel; altered from flintlock to percussion.
No. 5. By Dieschbach, of Pennsylvania; 59 inches over all; 44-inch octagon barrel; altered from flintlock to percussion.
No. 6. "Lancaster, Pa.," marked on barrel; 58½ inches over all; 43½-inch full octagon barrel; altered from flint-lock to percussion.

(Plate 30)

RIFLING GUIDE AND INDEX

Enlarged reproduction of rifling guide and index used by John Selvidge, Bradley County, Tennessee. No. 1 shows the two index fingers which turn the guide. No. 2 is the index and is stationary, being mounted in the bench. No. 3 is the spiral guide which turns the rifling rod. No. 4 is the frame which follows a slide on the bench and controls the guide.

(Plate 31)

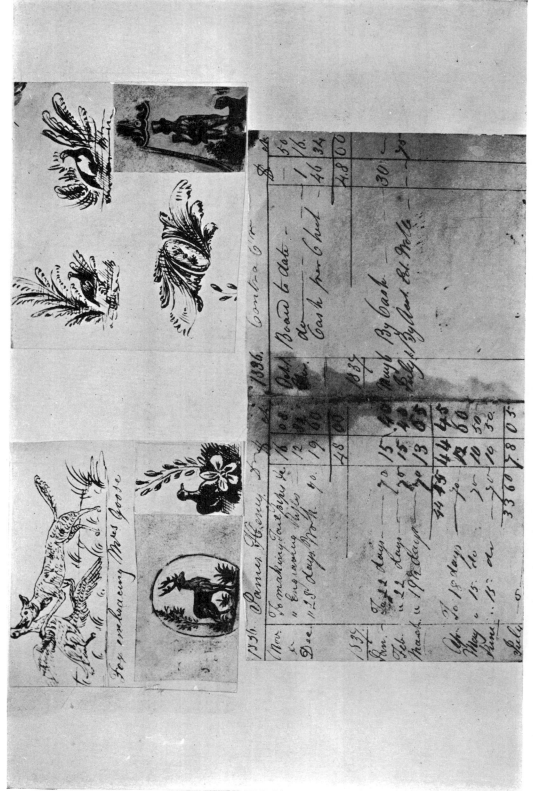

Billhead and account rendered by James Henry showing cost of engraving and ornamenting rifles.

(Plate 32)

Two Unusual Kentuckys

Nos. 1-2. By J. Roop, Bellefont; 55½ inches over all; 39-inch full octagon barrel; 36 balls to the pound; name on lock C. Baker; full curly maple stock; brass mountings; 47 silver inlays; converted from flint lock; one of the most elaborately decorated and beautifully made rifles in existence. Property A. G. Clyne, of Arkansas.

Nos. 3-4. Unidentified; 57 inches over all; 42-inch full octagon barrel; 42 calibre; full curly maple stock; brass-mounted and brass patch-box; 6 silver inlays; called the "Kopenhoven Rifle" from the fact of belonging to that famous pioneer family of Lycoming County, Pa.; now the property of Mrs. Coulter, of Philadelphia.

(Plate 33)

to the detriment of other nationalities which were in the minority—especially that of the French Huguenot colony, whose history became almost obliterated, submerged, interwoven with that of a German with whom they mingled ere the exodus, and when colonized within the Pequa Valley, speaking that language as fluently as a native-born German. To separate the two one cannot depend upon the names, which have changed. Hence that which belonged to the French Huguenot was attributed to a German gunsmith family by those not versed in the intricate histories of those different nationalities whose industry has made this State, aided by her natural resources, one of the wealthiest in the Union.

"The honor of having manufactured guns, which contributed in the supply of the entire Appalachian border with firearms, belongs also to the French Huguenots, who were the first to form a colony in Lancaster County, Pennsylvania. Of them it is said they were the best and thriftiest of the entire French, and whose emigration into other countries enriched those who welcomed them, and impoverished the land from whence they fled; a people who for centuries suffered from persecution under the tyranny of monarchical and popish despotism—'the patient de Huguenot,' whose enemies are said to have admitted their simple, pure and noble characteristics.

"Prominent among the Huguenots of France, prior to the revocation of the Edict of Nantes, 1685, were the LeFevre and Ferree families, who, upon the revocation, fled from thence into the Palatinate of Bavaria, met almost upon the eve of their arrival by the Germersheim Succession War; at Lindan eight members of the LeFevre family were massacred. Isaac, the only survivor, fled with the family of the Hon. Daniel Ferree to the village of Steenweller in the vicinity of the Black Forest, close to the border of the Grand Duchy of Baden. In less than two years thereafter the Hon. Daniel Ferree died, leaving a widow and six children, the youngest, Philip, an infant. In this strange country they remained for twenty-three years. In 1704 Isaac LeFevre, the only survivor of that family, married Catherine, the daughter of the widow, Madame Marie Warembier Ferree, and in 1708 this entire family emigrated to America on the ship Transport Globe, arriving at the port of New York, December 31, 1708, went to the Huguenot colony at Esopus, N. Y. (now Kingston), and in the fall of 1712, with other Huguenots from this colony, emigrated to Pennsylvania and settled a colony in Pequa Valley, now Lancaster County.

"Prior to leaving New York, on March 16, 1710, was born at Esopus, Philip LeFevre, the gunsmith of the Pennsylvania Huguenot colony. A grant of 10,000 acres of the Province of Pennsylvania from William Penn was made to the Palatinines, as these Huguenots were called (see Rupp's 'History of Lancaster County,' pub. 1844). Besides a grant of 2000 acres from William Penn and Queen Anne, Isaac LeFevre purchased 1500 acres in Strasburg township, Lancaster County (see Penna. Archives, 2d series, pp. 247, 334, 335, 529, 559, 587, 607, 609, 628, in vol. VI). On this land, four miles from Lancaster city, at a place called Big Spring, in Beaver Valley, Philip LeFevre, son of Isaac, made guns or rifles from 1731 to 1766 (see Rupp's 'History of Lancaster County,' pub. 1844, p. 98).

"Philip Ferree, born 1687, in the Palatinate, married Leah DuBois, May 10, 1712, at Esopus, N. Y. She was the daughter of Abraham DuBois, one of the twelve original patentees of New Paltz, N. Y., and Philip Ferree, the son of the Hon. Daniel Ferree and Madame Marie Warembier Ferree.

"Joel Ferree, son of Philip Ferree and Leah DuBois, born 1731, in the Huguenot colony, Lancaster, Pennsylvania, undoubtedly learned his trade with his relative, Philip LeFevre. He was a gunsmith who manufactured guns in Leacock township, Lancaster County, a few miles from the city of Lancaster. His shop was on the land granted his father by William Penn. In 1777, when the united colonies called for more arms, he extended his works, employed a larger force of men, and turned guns out for the Government at the rate of from thirty to forty per week (see Penna. Archives, 2d series, p. 583 Vol. I; see also same vol., p. 504). Gun locks were said to have been imported by a German.

"This French Huguenot family, from long residence in the Palatinate and in a German community in Pennsylvania, spoke German as fluently as a native born German, and only for their name would have been taken for that nationality. The Germans, refusing to use other than their own language for several generations, being in the majority, their rule was the inevitable; hence the French Huguenot colony was almost forgotten, having conformed to the Germans, after the manner of the Esopus French Huguenot colony, which became known and distinguished as the Dutch or Holland colony. Therefore, this French Huguenot family of gunsmiths is undoubtedly the family to which Baron Truro referred in 1885 when he addressed the Smithsonian Institution concerning the German family.

"Other members of this family, not engaged in making guns or rifles, erected gunpowder mills and manufactured gunpowder. Prior to the Revolutionary War Isaac LeFevre, a son of Joel LeFevre, had a mill on Wiconisco Creek, in Lykens Valley, Dauphin County, Pennsylvania. In 1777, Jacob Ferree, born August 8, 1750, son of Isaac Ferree, made gunpowder on French Creek in the employ of the Government (see Vol. I, Penna. Archives, p. 535), where their magazines were located.

"Jacob Ferree married twice; first his cousin, Rachel Ferree, the daughter of Joel Ferree, who made guns for the Revolutionary War. The eldest child of Jacob and Rachel Ferree was the famous Col. Joel Ferree in the War

JOHN SELVIDGE—RIFLESMITH

Portrait of John Selvidge, Bradley County, Tennessee, a widely known riflesmith about the year 1800. Under his picture is reproduced the wooden guide of his rifling bench.

(Plate 34)

Home of John Shell, Riflemaker, Leslie
County, Kentucky

(Plate 35)

of 1812; born January 26, 1771; died April, 1813. Jacob Ferree lost his first wife, Rachel, in 1781. In 1784 he married Alice Powel, and with his family came to Allegheny County that same year, and took up a vast tract of land on Peters Creek, about twenty-four miles up the Monongahela River from Pittsburgh. There he erected a powder mill and gunsmith shop, where his son Joel assisted him. These guns found ready market in Doddridge County, Virginia; in Kentucky and North Carolina, where the Ferree and LeFevre families founded settlements; the one in Surrey County in 1754, by the Jones, Gardner and Ferree family, the two first families having married into the Ferree family; in Kentucky the Steeles, Griffiths, Critchfields, Marlotts and Ferrees, the four former having married into the Ferree family. In Doddridge and other counties in Virginia, Maryland, Massachusetts and New Hampshire, went this family of French gunsmiths.

"The wife of Jacob Ferree, née Alice Powel, was a fine shot, and at that early date had no rival in Allegheny County, Pennsylvania. It was she who tested the guns and powder which the skill of her husband produced. Isaac Ferree, their son, also a gunsmith born in Allegheny County, Pennsylvania, January 9, 1786, was armorer to the First Pennsylvania Regiment, stationed at Baton Rouge, La., from 1818 to 1822, where he died from malignant fever, which was so fatal within the garrison at that period. His two sons, Joel Thornton and George Spencer Ferree, made rifles in Allegheny County, Pennsylvania, up to 1840, the last gunsmiths in this family. The Archives of Pennsylvania tell that they not only knew the mechanism of the American rifle, but how and when to use it.

"The honor of having manufactured the first American rifles belongs to the French Huguenot who settled the colony in Lancaster County, Pennsylvania. Your correspondent, Horace Kephart, writes that the Austro-German Tyrol rifle was made in Philadelphia about 1730 or 1732 by Leman & Lescher. Leman or Leaman is the corruption of the French LeMont, while Lescher was originally LeChaar. In 1715 or 1717 these two families settled in the French Huguenot colony; not Swiss or German, but French.

"To the Huguenot colony in Pequa Valley, Lancaster County, Pennsylvania, America is also indebted for another gunmaker, who is no less a person than the celebrated William Henry, of that place, whom Horace Kephart mentioned in his article, published in this journal January 7.

"The progenitor of the Henry family was a Robert Henry, a Scotchman, who emigrated to America in 1722 with his wife May and three sons—John, Robert and James. They first settled on a tract of 300 acres of land located on Doe Run, a tributary to the Brandywine in Chester County (see Penna. Archives, 3d series, vol. XIX, p. 728) in 1724-5.

"Thomas Lewis, the original patentee of the land, entered complaint in the land office, and the Henry family was forced to remove from Doe Run. It is presumable that they, at this period, went to the Huguenot colony in Pequa Valley, as John Henry, the father of the foregoing William Henry, married the daughter of Hugh DeVenny, French Huguenot of the Pequa colony. The issue of this marriage was five sons and several daughters, William Henry being the eldest. This gunsmith was not only the armorer to Braddock, but was a member of the general congress and treasurer of Lancaster County, Pennsylvania (see Vol. I of Notes and Queries by State Librarian William H. Engle). William Henry was a member of the Council of Safety from Lancaster County in 1777, and was in all probability the Lieutenant and Colonel William Henry of the Revolutionary War."

Horace Kephart, replying to Mrs. Lindsay's claim, said:

"Appreciating fully Mrs. Lindsay's researches, I can yet see nothing in the evidence she has produced that substantiates her claim that 'the honor of having manufactured the first American rifles belongs to the French Huguenot who settled the colony in Lancaster County, Pennsylvania. The most that her records show is simply this: that Philip LeFevre, descended from a French exile, but born in the German Palatinate, and bred in the German colony of Lancaster, made 'guns' from 1731 to 1766 in Lancaster. But she does not claim that these guns were rifles. Of course it is well known that smooth-bore guns were made in this country before LeFevre's time. It does not even appear that LeFevre was the first gunmaker in Lancaster County. I had already quoted Rupp to the effect that Martin Meylin, a Swiss, erected a boring mill to bore out gun barrels in this county as early as 1719, or twelve years before LeFevre began. Rupp mentions Philip LeFevre and John Vondersmith as later gunsmiths. Matthew Roeser was making guns in Lancaster before 1744, and Henry Albright (i. e., Albrecht) about the same time, while there were plenty of others engaged in the business in Lancaster town before the Revolution. So LeFevre had many competitors.

"Mrs. Lindsay confounds me with your talented correspondent R., who stated that a Tyrolese named Leman, together with one Decherd, or Deckhard, was making rifles in Philadelphia in 1732. Mrs. Lindsay—on what authority she does not state—twists these names into LeMont and LeChaar (?), a process to which any etymologist familiar with Pennsylvania names of the last century will surely demur. Leman is merely an anglicized spelling of Lehmann. LeMont becomes Lamont and retains its proper accent. The derivation of Decherd from LeChaar is evidently careless. The name is good enough German as it stands.

Snyder Collection

No. 1. By H. Mauger; 57 inches over all; 43-inch full octagon barrel; full maple stock; brass patch-box; fine workmanship.

No. 2. Unidentified; 56½ inches over all; 43-inch full octagon barrel; full maple stock; brass patch-box.

No. 3. By Leman, Lancaster, Pa.; 57 inches over all; 43-inch full octagon barrel, full maple stock; brass patch-box; an early rifle.

No. 4. Unidentified; 57½ inches over all; 43-inch half octagon barrel; full maple stock; brass patch-box; a very early make.

No. 5. Unidentified; 56 inches over all; 43-inch full octagon barrel; full maple stock; brass patch-box, a very fine rifle.

No. 6. By Drepperd, Lancaster, Pa.; 62 inches over all; 46-inch full octagon barrel; full maple stock; no patch-box a very plain and very early rifle.

(Plate 36)

DILLIN COLLECTION

Nos. 1-2. By J. Philpy; 59 inches over all; 44-inch half octagon barrel; 40 balls to the pound; full maple stock; brass patch-box; an oddly designed piece; weight 10¼ pounds.

Nos. 3-4. Unidentified; 58 inches over all; 43-inch full octagon barrel; 32 balls to the pound; full maple stock; brass-mounted; brass patch-box; weight 8 pounds; a very fine specimen.

Nos. 5-6. By J. Berstro, Buffalo, N. Y., 1835; 58½ inches over all; 43½-inch full octagon barrel; 120 balls to the pound; full maple stock; brass-mounted; brass patch-box; silver inlays; well made.

(Plate 37)

"I hold no brief for any race; and my conclusion that America owes her national weapon to German-speaking immigrants is based entirely upon historical evidence. All historians have ascribed the invention of the rifle to a German. It is a well-known fact that the grooved barrel was a practical, every-day weapon among German, Swiss and Tyrolese mountaineers for two or three centuries before it became much more than a curiosity elsewhere in Europe. It is also a fact that the rifle was not used in America until the German immigration set in; that it was first made here in the German-speaking counties of Pennsylvania, and that its use spread along precisely the same lines as the expansion of these German colonists. It is not strange, then, if we find the first American rifle maker was a Teuton, whether Swiss, Austrian or German proper. It would be indeed strange if he should prove to be a Frenchman or an Englishman, since the rifle at the beginning of the eighteenth century was all but unknown in France and England."

The historian Buell contributes to the available facts concerning the manufacture of early rifles some data as to the later distribution of gunsmithing activities. In his *Frontier Lawyer in Tennessee*, after fixing Lancaster as the birthplace of the Kentucky rifle and the Swiss emigrants as the first gunsmiths to make it he says:

"After 1760, makers who had learned the art at Lancaster branched out for themselves and set up shops all along the frontiers of Pennsylvania and the Southern colonies.

"The New England people never took to the rifle in those days, and when the Revolution broke out there was not a rifle-shop in existence anywhere east of the Hudson River. In 1768 Sir William Johnson induced several skilled gunsmiths to migrate from Lancaster, and they set up shops at Esopus, Schenectady, Johnstown and Canajoharie. But the main spread of rifle manufacture from Lancaster was south and southwest. By the outbreak of the Revolution there were rifle-shops at Baltimore, Cumberland, Alexandria, Winchester, Richmond, Hillsborough, Charlotte, Camden, Salisbury and Augusta, whose product rivaled in reputation that of Lancaster itself. The frontiersmen were armed with them almost universally, and many had found their way into the hands of the Indians belonging to the tribes most closely in communication with white traders—the Iroquois, Delawares, Shawnees, Wyandots, Miamis, Catawbas and Cherokees. The maker of Jackson's rifle, Youmans (spelled also Yeomans in some of the old documents), was among the most prominent and successful on the whole frontier, and his name was a guarantee of excellence."

In view of the data at hand, there would seem to be no doubt the early smiths of Lancaster gave the world the first Kentucky rifles. Referring to the rifle in New England, it is the general opinion that the rifle was rarely used in New England in Colonial times and this was the view held by the author for a long time, but the letter reproduced in Plate No. 38 seems to contradict the theory.

Stamford,
Sept. 29, 1776.

Sir:

    I send by the bearer, Mr. Isaac Rue, Three Rifle guns that do not answer the Character of Rifles; they carry as wild as any smooth Barrel gun. As you was so good as to offer your service in getting them done in the best manner, I take the Liberty of sending them to your care, not doubting but you will have them rectified so as to answer the character given to the best of Rifles. It will suit me better that they shall carry a ball of a larger size than they now carry, but not so large as will occasion the gun to spring when fired which will infallibly make them throw the ball wild. Would have a neat mould made to each gun. Let the ball be quite round and not over large for the bore, so as to be difficult to ram down. I find they don't carry so well as when they ram down lighter. Should be glad to have neat worms to each gun, and whatever charge you are at, will cheerfully repay as soon as I have your amt. and can get an opportunity to send it. Pray send me with the guns 12 L. of the best Pistol Powder. Don't suffer the guns to be turned off until they have been proved by firing at some object at a reasonable distance. Would have the moulds made of brass. The bearer informs me there is a Lancaster Gun Smith that lives in Water Street who is one of the best workmen in Rifle guns. If so you will be under no necessity of sending them to Lancaster.

I am your most humble servant,

(Signed) JOHN LLOYD.

    P. S. Pray let the Locks be repaired in the best manner. Be sure that they fire well. Have paid the Transportation of the guns.

    This letter, which was dated at Stamford (Connecticut), proves that at least there were some users of the rifle at that time, and in view of the fact that the rifle had been the standard arm of the hunters of Pennsylvania, Virginia and other colonies for thirty to fifty years, it seems unreasonable to assume that it had not been introduced into New England and been in more or less general use prior to the Revolution.

Above: One of the very few early New England-made rifles known—the as Allen. A more detailed description accompanies Plate 42.

Below: Letter proving that the rifle —distinct from the musket—was used in New England during Revolutionary times. For full text of letter see page 26.

(Plate 38)

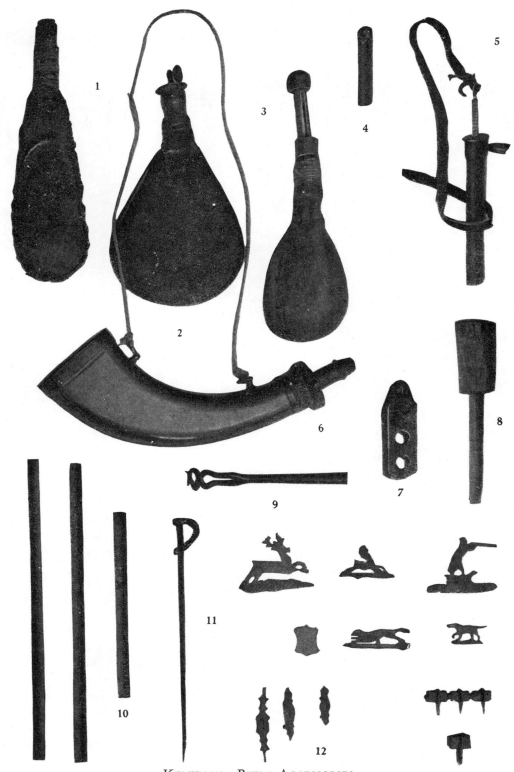

KENTUCKY RIFLE ACCESSORIES

Nos. 1, 2, 3. Bullet pouches. No. 3. Showing peculiar split stopper.
No.   4. Cast-iron charger.
No.   5. Graduated charger.
No.   6. Powder horn brass trimmings.
No.   7. Loading block for patched ball.
No.   8. Bullet starter.
No.   9. Worm.
No. 10. Three-sectioned hickory rod for starting bullets well down the barrel.
No. 11. Priming wire, or frizzen pick.
No. 12. Ornamental inlays.
No. 13. Cast sights used by late makers of percussion Kentuckys.

(Plate 39)

Materials Used

CHAPTER SIX

HE number of parts necessary in the assembly of a Kentucky Rifle varies from 44 to 50. These include barrel, stock, pins, screws, springs, in fact every detail necessary in the fabrication of the gun. The United States Regulation Springfield Rifle is made up of 109 parts and offers quite a contrast. The iron in the barrels of the old hand-made American rifles is soft and tough, and, in early days, those of domestic manufacture were the product of the charcoal furnace. The stock, invariably running to the end of the muzzle, in flint-lock days was made, wherever possible, of curly maple, cut from both the sugar and red maple tree, one tree in about fifteen being of sufficient curl to answer the demand of the smith, whose taste demanded fine wood. Occasionally a rifle was stocked with cherry, and after 1830 black walnut was sometimes used. In the South, where the sugar maple is not found, red maple and once in a while apple wood were used.

The ramrod was invariably worked out of split hickory, which is America's finest wood. It was usually striped barber-pole fashion, the stripes being wide and of a brownish tint which was probably stained with aqua fortis.

The patch box, trigger guard, side plate, rod pipes or thimbles, front sight and butt plate were, with rare exceptions, made of brass. Occasionally these details were made of German silver and in rare cases of iron. The front sight, side plate, butt plate and trigger guard were cast and file dressed. The ornaments were nearly always silver or brass, the former in preponderance.

Every hunter carried a priming wire, a reproduction of which is shown on Plate 39, No. 11. This was often carried in two small staples at bottom of cheek rest and sometimes in the hunting bag. Occasionally a feather was carried instead of the wire, or possibly both were kept in the kit, as both have been found, and there is no certain information as to the purpose of the feather. In the examination of powder horns, the author has found the priming pick and the cork of the horn made as one, a sharp pin, about 1½ inches long, being driven tight into the inner end of the horn plug, making the stopper answer two purposes.

The locks of the early rifles were largely home-made though later many were imported from England and Germany. Those of domestic manufacture were very plain but well made, and comprised about thirty per cent of the locks used.

The springs were beautifully tempered and showed that the early smiths were masters of the art.

The stocks, as a rule, were stained with soot and oil, well rubbed, though sometimes a varnish of a quality not unlike that used by the early Italian violin makers, and known the world over as Cremonese varnish, was carefully applied. This is an oil varnish and exceptionally good.

There were stocks made from plain maple, artificially grained. This was done by tightly wrapping a tarred string around the stock and burning it off. This would leave dark traces in the wood which were a substitute for the curly grain, so much desired. There were several makers who were conspicuous for this practice, among whom were the Leamans of Lancaster, and P. and D. Moll.

Often the riflesmith would simply stain the stock and rub it to a high gloss finish.

The flints were imported from England.

The obscurity which covers most of the data concerning the Kentucky Rifle has rendered the task of isolating authentic details of their manufacture an extremely difficult one. So facts must be drawn largely from two sources: the testimony of men who are personally conversant with the methods used in the manufacture of the percussion rifles which followed the flint-lock type and in which the earlier gunsmithing methods persisted in modified form, and the less frequently encountered details to be culled from contemporary records.

One such account, which reflects not only the customs and practices of the early American gunsmith, but also the atmosphere of the infant Republic, is of especial interest. It outlines the methods used in the Whitesides factory at Abingdon, Va., and is made available by Dr. O. W. Ferguson, of Illinois.

The story is told in the words of Milton Warren, of Abingdon, who was apprenticed to John M. Whitesides, of Abingdon (then Wolf Hills), a gunmaker of the old school, a very fine artisan of methods as primitive as those of the Colonial craftsmen who perfected the Kentucky rifle. He had

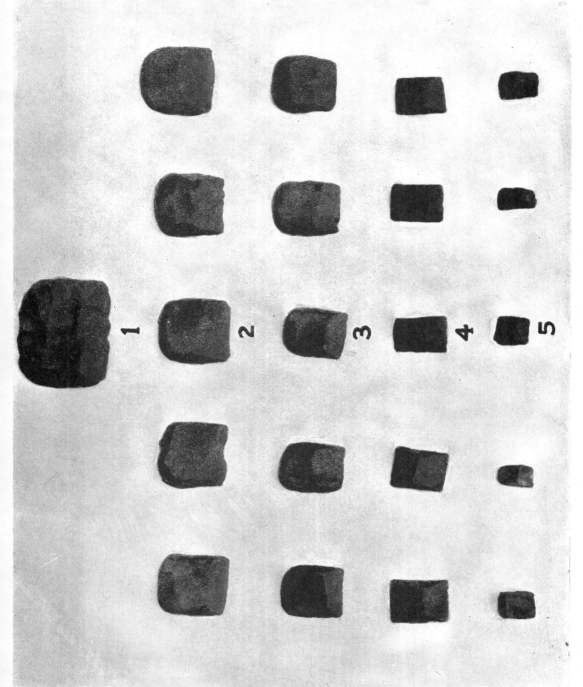

STANDARD SIZES OF FLINTS

Five sizes of flints were made, each for a particular type of arm. They are shown in the above plate three-quarter size and were for purposes: No. 1, Cannon Flint; No. 2, Large Musket; No. 3, Small Musket, or Shot Gun; No. 4, Rifle and Duelling Pistol; No. 5, Small Pocket Pistol.

(Plate 40)

Snyder Collection

No. 1. By Tryon, Philadelphia, Pa., under contract with United States about 1815; length over all, 57 inches; 41½-inch full octagon barrel.

No. 2. By H. Deringer, Philadelphia, Pa., under contract with the United States; length over all, 51 inches; 36½-inch half octagon barrel.

No. 3. Unidentified; 48½ inches over all; 33½-inch full octagon barrels; double-barrel superposed rifle; one barrel rifled, one smooth; side hammer percussion; brass patch-box; very rare and beautiful specimen.

No. 4. Unidentified; 43½ inches over all; 28½-inch barrels; three barrel rifle; two barrels rifled, one smooth; curly maple stock; brass patch-box; converted from flint-lock; a very rare piece.

No. 5. By J. Kuntz, Philadelphia, Pa.; 53 inches over all; 38-inch full octagon barrels, double-barrel, side by side; full maple stock; no patch-box.

No. 6. By Deringer, Philadelphia, Pa.; 57 inches over all; 42-inch full octagon barrel; 45 calibre; half maple stock; no patch-box; rigged with brass sighting tube with aperture and front pin-head sights; weight 20 pounds; a typical shooting match rifle of about 1830; converted from flint-lock.

(Plate 41)

A GROUP OF NOTABLE RIFLES

Nos. 1-2. By Silas Allen, Shrewsbury, Mass.; 56 inches over all; fine workmanship; very rare. (Offerman Collection.)
Nos. 3-4. Unidentified; 59 inches over all; 44-inch octagon barrel; 40 balls to the pound; full curly maple stock, inlaid with 25 pieces of silver; one of the best specimens of the highly decorated type in existence; altered from flintlock to percussion. (Price Collection.)
Nos. 5-6. By J. Hoffman, Lancaster, Pa.; superposed double-barreled rifle; one barrel rifled, the other smooth; two hammers; two ramrods; a very superior arm both in outline and workmanship; Civil War period. (Offerman Collection.)

(Plate 42)

SNYDER COLLECTION

Five unidentified rifles, three of which are very beautiful.

(Plate 43)

a penchant for wire scroll inlaying of his gun stocks and fancy embellishments of barrels and locks.

The region where Mr. Whitesides lived and worked is rich in historical interest. It was settled largely by Scotch and Irish who reached it by way of Carolina and Virginia, and conveyed with them the skill to make and handle the gun together with its tradition.

Here is Milton Warren's story:

"You would probably call Abingdon an old-fashioned community; the people were very much alike and had never changed their methods of living very much. It was considered extravagant to buy anything that could be raised at home. The men chopped down the timber, cleared the ground and raised little patches of corn, tobacco and vegetables. There were enough sheep to supply wool for clothing, which was home made. The women carded, spun and wove the wool into cloth and handy cutters and sewers made it into wearing apparel for all of us. There were rifles in every home —the man who was too poor to own one was considered destitute. We all hunted, shooting matches were regular functions and hunting and shooting stories were standard fireside diversions. I am afraid that many of us took more pride in hitting what we shot at than in turning out a full day's work. Mr. Whitesides had been an axe-maker, capable of forging his dozen every day, and he was famous for the quality of his axes, but there seemed to have been something in him which he could not hammer into an axe; and being a very fine shot with a rifle and not finding one to suit his fancy, he made one, which was so good that his neighbors wanted duplicates of it and he began making them on orders.

"It took about a week to make a good, plain rifle, of which time two days would be spent on the stock. Besides rifles, we made a great many under-hammer boot-leg pistols. They are simple things and one could be made in a day.

"This is how we made our guns:

"Mr. Whitesides owned, on Smith's Creek, a little water-power sash sawmill (a straight saw set in a rectangular frame or 'sash,' working up and down on an eccentric, through a log). The same power was also used to run a crude lathe and a large grindstone on which rifle barrels were finished.

"At 'Old Shady,' over the mountains about fifteen miles, there was an iron mine and smelter worked by three or four men. The ore was smelted in a charcoal furnace, run into chunks of suitable size for ready handling and drawn out on a big anvil with a trip hammer into rods, bars and such shapes as local smiths demanded, and then peddled around and sold to them. It was good iron and it worked fine.

"While we carried a few guns in stock, they were usually made to specifications as to length of barrel, weight, ornamentation, etc. Not infrequently the order would be to 'make a gun just like' the one used by some famous marksman in the vicinity.

"For the barrel a bar of iron of the right length, width and thickness would be selected, and half of its length, at welding heat, turned around a core rod somewhat larger than the ultimate bore desired. The core was then withdrawn and the other half treated in the same way, the whole being worked into rough octagonal form. Next a rod slightly smaller than the final calibre was used and the barrel finished as nearly perfect as possible.

"During the welding process the smith used a hammer while his helper wielded a sledge. If the whole barrel had been welded at one heating the rod could not have been removed; as it was, sometimes it welded fast and had to be cut out with a cold chisel and the blemish worked over.

"We did not bother much with flatters or shaping devices of any kind—just trusted to hand and eye—yet when the barrels left the anvil they were very straight and regular, requiring but little grinding.

"Charcoal was used exclusively for forge fire; in fact, we did not know that stone coal could be used for such welding as we did.

"The bore of the barrel was sized with a cutting bit or reamer, on a hand brace—just began at one end and worked through to the other with the same motion that a carpenter uses in boring holes in wood. The lathe could not be used for this purpose because it was only belt-geared and did not run steady enough—it would have broken the reamer. Anyway the hole in the barrel was so true that it only required a little work to smooth it out. Of course, now and then, a barrel showed flaws and sometimes these did not develop until it was rifled. We just threw it away, made some remarks to the mountains, took a drink of spring water and welded another barrel.

"In straightening a barrel a fine thread was passed through it and attached to a light hickory bow to hold it taut. There was no difficulty in seeing the shadow where the thread did not touch. The crook was located by touching the place with a little saliva, placed on the anvil and tapped lightly until the thread touched and the process repeated until barrel and thread were in contact from end to end.

"Straightening always began in the middle of the barrel, just as in welding, the old man saying that he would 'chase the d—d rascals out at the ends,' and it was about as easy for him to take the kinks out of a rifle barrel as it is for a boy to make shavings with a sharp knife and a pine stick.

"The barrel was now centered by inserting a plug in each end, taken to the grindstone and fastened into a frame so adjusted that it allowed the center of the barrel to come within one-half of its desired diameter to the

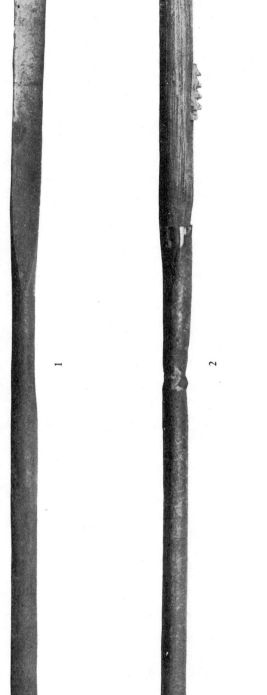

Tools Used in Rifling

No. 1. Bit for boring channel for ramrod. No. 2. Rifling tool showing cutter inserted in hickory rod. No. 3. Short bit for roughing out the bore after welding. No. 4. Long bit for smoothing bore in rifle barrels, with hickory guard on off side of cutter to prevent borings from scratching barrel.

(Plate 44)

BARREL BORING MACHINE

Original barrel boring machine of John Selvidge, Bradley County, Tennessee. A barrel is shown clamped to the bench with tool and machine for operating same in position for boring. (Photo by Cline.)

(Plate 45)

stone. It was worked back and forth until the stone no longer cut when it was shifted to the next octagon and so on until all were ground and the whole was bound to be evenly finished and all the octagons alike. Inequalities were removed by draw filing and hand polishing.

"The barrel, now ready for rifling, was taken to the rifling machine, or bench, as we called it, a contrivance simple enough in its working but not easy to describe.

"It consisted of a hard wooden bar of cherry, three inches in diameter by four and one-half feet long, with four deep radial grooves, each making one turn in four feet, extending from end to end. To the proximal end of this bar was fastened a loosely revolving handle and to its far end a chuck for holding a steel rifling rod. The wooden bar passed through a ten-inch dialed headpiece whose circumference was divided by deep rectangular notches into eight equal parts, while from its round central opening there passed into each of the four grooves on the bar an iron lug to hold it in place. This arrangement was set on a frame in smoothly working longitudinal guides.

"The barrel was clamped into the frame with its axis in direct line with that of the spiral wooden bar. Into a piece of tough hickory wood, rounded to closely fit the bore of the barrel, a piece of thin, very hard, sharply toothed steel was set to act as a saw or cutter. This section of wood was now connected with a rigid steel rod the length of the barrel and fastened in the chuck.

"The cutter, kept well oiled, was pushed back and forth, the guides on the central bar carrying it around spirally, until it no longer bit, when the dial was turned one notch and then another until all of the right rifle grooves had been well started.

"The saw was now taken out of its bed and elevated by having a shim of paper placed under it and the work done over and over until the rifles were as deep as desired. With sharp saws and good working iron, a neat job could be done in about two hours. Burrs were smoothed off and the calibre polished with lead plugs and fine emery powder.

"Sometimes a lug was brazed on to the barrel for the tube, but more frequently a cylindrical drum was used, this being the cheaper way.

"Barrels were browned with a mixture of aqua fortis, blue vitriol, tincture of iron and water. Almost anything that will rust iron will brown a barrel, but to get a good job it must be rubbed down smooth between coats.

"Tubes were made by drawing them out on an anvil, filing them to shape and drilling with different-sized drills, finally finishing with a very fine tapered reamer. During the earlier years of my apprenticeship we made all tubes by hand, but later bought them and could fit one for fifty cents, whereas for the others we charged six bits.

"All of our locks were made by hand—mostly the back action kind—possibly because they are a trifle easier to make, but probably they just happened to be the style on the Holston.

"The lock plate was hammered out on the anvil, filed into accurate shape; the springs—which were made from old whip saws, swords and bayonets mostly—laid on, the holes marked and drilled and screwed in place with hand-made screws and with the tumbler and hammer all made on the anvil and filing vise, the lock was ready for the gun.

"Small holes were made with the lathe, all larger ones with a bow drill.

"For stocking material we went to the mountains and got close-grained rock maple—the trees that grow on thin rocky soil are always closer grained and curlier than those that grow in open ground on heavy soil. Sometimes we used walnut, now and then cherry, and occasionally a customer would bring his own stock blank of apple wood. A cherry crotch makes a beautiful stock and apple finishes up very smooth and stays where you put it; it also takes inlaying well, but both apple and cherry depend upon their grain for beauty, while curly maple can be finished with various stains and is just about the prettiest wood in the world. We always mention a gun as 'her' and name them 'Betsy,' 'Samanthy' and 'Jane.'

"Lumber was sawn into two-inch planks on the sash mill and a pile of it was always stacked up in the corner of the shop seasoning. It was entirely air-dried and it took about four years to properly ripen a gun stock blank.

"Yes, I guess we could have split out the lumber and hewed it down to dimension; I know we could, for there were men in the mountains who could take a broadaxe and scutch out puncheons for floors and school seats so smooth that there would not be a mark showing.

"The wynde was taken out of the stock blank with a plane, centered all round with a marking gauge and the butt plate put on, after which barrel and trimmings were let into the wood—all with gouges, chisels and rifflers of our own making—and the stock worked down to form with drawer knife and rasp and sandpaper until it was ready for staining. This was accomplished by freely brushing the wood with strong aqua fortis, then holding it over a fire until it was pretty deeply scorched, after which it was rubbed down to a smooth surface, the hard ridges of the wood barely showing, and finally treated with a light coat of alkanet root in oil, after which it was varnished with shellac in alcohol or rubbed with oil—the more coats of the latter the better.

"When first turned out the wood was just a trifle glary, but after the gun had been used a while and rubbed down many, many times it became as smooth as satin and as richly blended as tortoise shell.

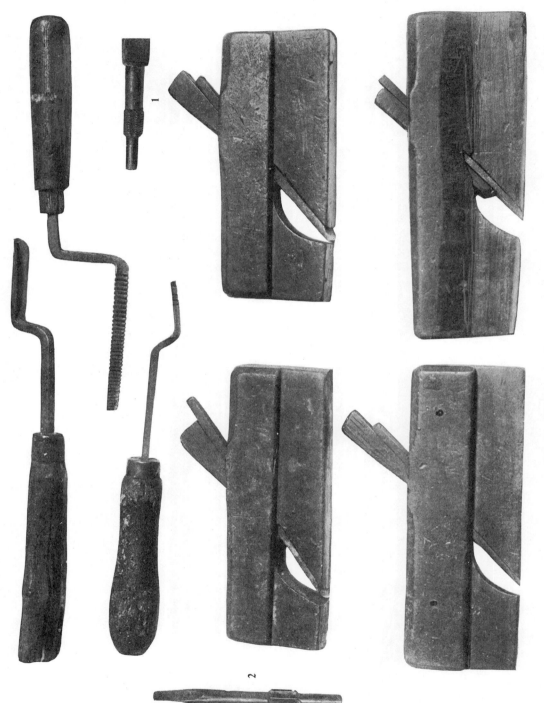

Tools Used in Rifle Making

The tools shown in this plate were used in making rifles by John Selvidge, Bradley County, Tennessee. No. 1 is a tool for threading the barrel for the breech plug. No. 2 was used in preparing the breech for the threading tool. Reproductions are one-third size. The remaining seven pieces are all stocking tools and are made of persimmon wood. They are reproduced in half size.

(Plate 46)

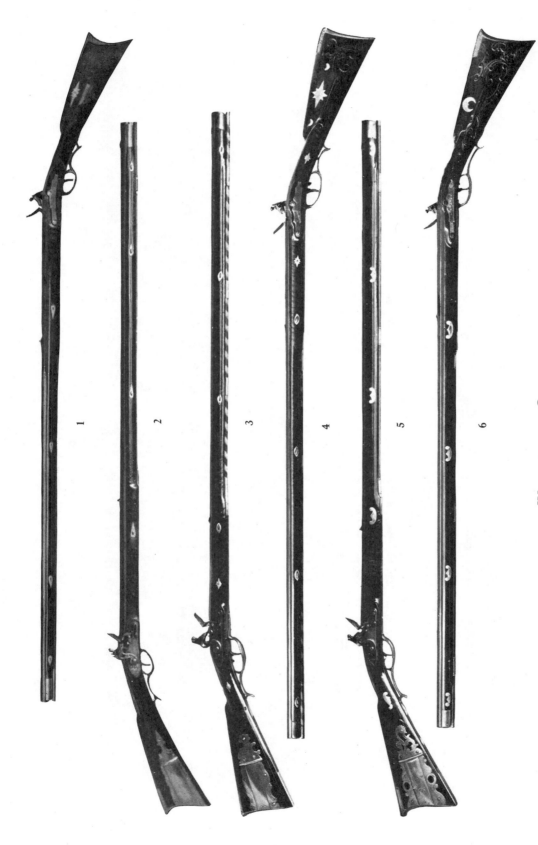

WOODMANSEE COLLECTION

Nos. 1-2. By J. Palm; 59 inches over all; 44-inch half octagon barrel; .50 calibre; maker's name in silver inlay on barrel; engraved flint-lock by Jos. Goulcher; full curly maple stock, brass-mounted, with 10 silver inlays.

Nos. 3-4. By P. B. Haedler; 61 inches over all; 46-inch octagon barrel; .50 calibre; full curly maple stock, brass mounted, with raised carving and 16 silver inlays; plain hand-made flint-lock.

Nos. 5-6. By A. Ernst; 59½ inches over all; 44-inch octagon barrel; .45 calibre; hand-made, engraved flint-lock; full curly maple stock, brass mounted, with raised carving and 12 silver inlays.

(Plate 47)

"My boss was something of an artist in making designs for the scroll wire inlaying he delighted in. He simply drew a pattern of anything he fancied on the stock and sunk very finely tapered chisels and specially shaped gouges into it and into these marks drove sharp-edged strips of silver or brass and filed it down flush with the surface and when finished this method of ornamentation gave beautiful results.

"For the common run of guns everything was of iron, butt plate, trigger guards, trigger plate, thimbles, escutcheons and all, but for the fancy ones we worked out from sheets of German silver, brass and silver various designs for inlays and bought guards and butt plates (I think from Pittsburgh). Buckhorn sights were standard equipment on all rifles with a silver bead in front.

"After the gun was finished the old man would say, 'Well, Milt, she's finished, but she ain't wuth a d— if she won't shoot straight; let's try her.' He was by all odds the best rifle shot I have ever known and no gun ever suited him unless it was capable of driving a tack three times out of five at fifty yards.

"Our guns were all nicely finished; they were symmetrical and pleasing to the eye; they felt good in the hand and at the shoulder, and they shot where they were held. The men who bought them could hold them right. It is too bad that progress and civilization have eliminated both man and gun."

Mr. Warren's description of the finishing of a newly rifled barrel, while giving an excellent insight into the methods used by gunsmiths who produced rifles in their own shops from raw materials, will be found at variance with those set forth in a later chapter by Mr. Cline. Doubtless both Mr. Cline and Mr. Warren are right. Different periods are being discussed, Mr. Cline's remarks applying quite plainly to the flint-lock period while Mr. Warren's are quite as evidently applicable to the percussion period.

At this late date and in the absence of definite records which preserve all of the vast technical detail which went into the making of a Kentucky rifle, we may consider ourselves more than fortunate in having at hand as much material as is available, even though it occasionally presents some seeming contradictions.

It must be borne in mind also that riflesmiths of different and often widely separated localities of necessity differed in the manufacturing processes they followed; for instance, there is small doubt from the best information obtainable that the early Lancaster smiths never employed emery flour as an abrasive; yet it is equally certain that many gunsmiths of the later generations systematically employed emery and oil in their polishing processes.

There are several fundamentals in the production of the Kentucky rifle to which all processes of every period attest. Without exception this type of weapon was the product of honest material worked up, sometimes laboriously and under handicap, by artisans who were the product of a vanished apprentice system in which the workman took pride in his product.

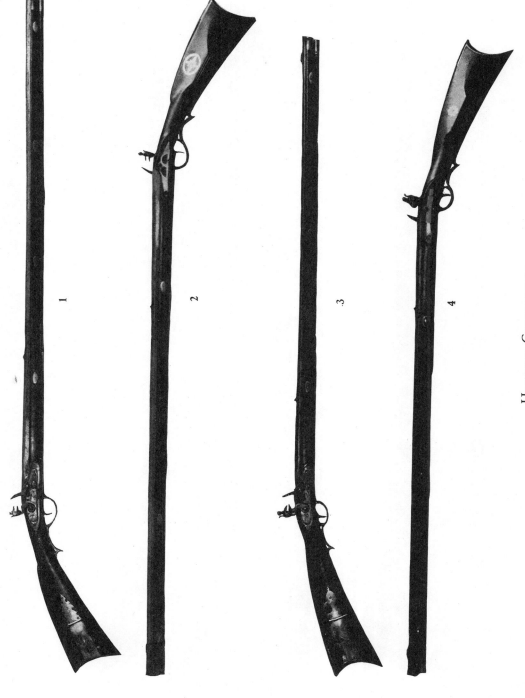

HUNTER COLLECTION

Nos. 1-2. Unidentified; 58 inches over all; 43-inch full octagon barrel; straight cut; 50 calibre; full maple stock; brass mountings and inlays; brass patch-box; weight 8½ pounds.

Nos. 3-4. By James Goulcher; 54½ inches over all; 39½-inch full octagon barrel; full maple stock; brass mountings; brass patch-box; weight 7½ pounds; as both barrel and lock are marked with the name of the smith there can be no doubt this is a genuine Goulcher rifle.

(Plate 48)

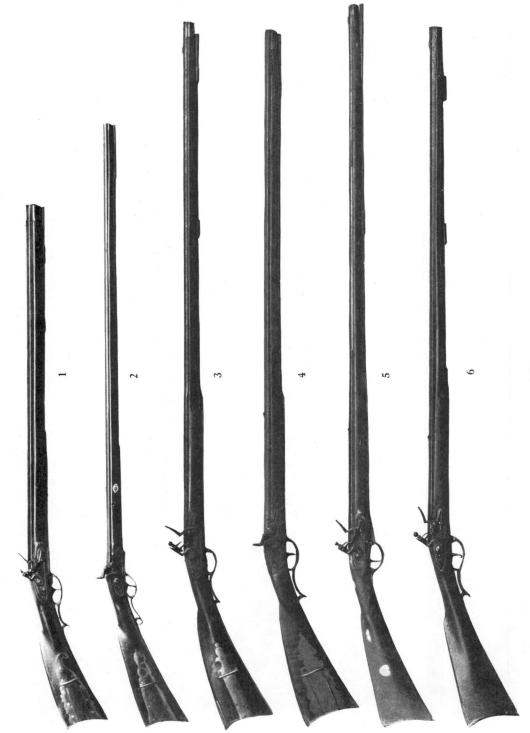

SNYDER COLLECTION

Six very old rifles, none of which show any marks which make identification possible. The two rifles with percussion hammers were originally flint-locks.

(Plate 49)

Characteristics of the Early Rifle

CHAPTER SEVEN

FTER the American rifle had assumed its form and become what it is only fair to term a standardized arm, its general character was never materially changed and the patterns of the earliest known examples are strikingly similar to the specimens of the latest flint-lock period. The general outlines of the early arms compare very closely with rifles of a later date, but there are minor differences which can always be depended upon to distinguish first period arms from those of later make. Both the lower and upper stock of the very early rifles, in most instances, show more or less carving. The scroll work was apt to be elaborate, and both carved designs and scroll were as a rule the work of a master hand. As time passed this class of work gradually disappeared until by 1780 it had nearly died out. Again the early rifle had but few metal decorations. The characteristic star on the cheek piece was, however, in evidence, and is undoubtedly of American origin—figuratively speaking, being born with the rifle. A small setting of silver on the upper small of the stock was also a feature.

Before 1750 about one-half of the rifles were made with barrels full octagon from the breech to the lower thimble and round from the thimble to the muzzle; from 1750 to 1780 there were still a percentage of barrels finished in the same way, but after 1780 practically all rifles were fitted with full-octagon barrels.

The highly decorated rifle followed the period of the carved stock, the earliest reference to such a decorated arm noted by the author being dated 1777. Decorations vary greatly both in general outline, workmanship and artistic conception. Rifles by the same maker are apt to carry brass or silver inlays so similar in outline as to make their identification possible. Again, there is a noticeable difference between rifles made in the North and those manufactured in the South. The northern rifle of the later period was very

35

elaborately decorated, while those of the South were beautiful in workmanship and outline, but very plain, often without a patch box. The finish was lighter in color than that turned out by the Pennsylvania smiths.

Two very fine specimens of the southern type of rifles are shown in Plate 74. One, the Alexander Clege rifle used at the battle of King's Mountain during the Revolution, represents the heavy sett-trigger type. The other is the Simon Kenton rifle, a typical southern arm of the single trigger hunting type.

The tendency of the early smiths was toward a straight, or as it is now called, a shotgun butt, and in some instances there is but a suggestion of the crescent so frequently found after 1800. However, even in the very early period there were notable exceptions, for we find some rifles with the crescent quite defined, but it is doubtful if the butt plate ever ran to the extreme crescent shape in early flint-lock days. This design reached its full development after 1840, when the stock was made thinner and the crescent more pronounced, particularly at the toe.

As already stated, the early smith was little given to silver or brass trappings. His product was plain but beautiful. There were times, however, when he broke the rule and etched upon the stock or patch box the bust of an Indian. Occasionally he cut this design from metal and inlaid it neatly to the stock. This custom was rarely followed by the later makers. It was a practice of the Molls, and on the stock of a rifle made by M. Roesser in 1746 the Indian is shown with a heart drawn on his chest, no doubt suggesting a target, or aiming spot. This rifle is very beautifully made and is of the type known as the small wrist. A full description is given elsewhere.

The first American rifle makers almost without exception colored their rifle stocks very dark, finishing them as a rule with soot and oil. They were rubbed to high polish and a few of the early rifles were varnished. Not until later was varnish generally used.

One of the most beautiful rifles which have been brought to the attention of the writer, both in outline and finish, was made before 1750.

Perhaps the most striking characteristic of the American rifle is its calibre. In designing the new weapon the early American smith made many departures from the European rifle, but the widest variance was in the size of the bore. A glance at the several muzzles shown in the illustrations will clearly show the great change which was made. (See Plate 10.)

The rifles of Central Europe of those days were of an average .65 calibre as reckoned by our modern standard of calibration. The American riflesmiths so reduced the bore that a .45 calibre would seem to be the average, a reduction of about 25%. Such a reduction meant vastly more than setting a fashion. It was an economic necessity. The difference in weight of lead

1

2

3

4

Huston Collection

No. 1. Unidentified; 56 inches over all; 41½-inch barrel; 18 balls to the pound; straight cut; full curly maple stock; 20 silver inlays; weight 9 pounds; fine workmanship.

No. 2. By M. Martin; 59 inches over all; 44-inch full octagon barrel; 34 balls to the pound; full curly maple stock, with 8 silver inlays, weight 9½ pounds; excellent work.

No. 3. By H. Eckler; 53 inches over all; 38-inch barrel; 7 grooves; about 30 balls to the pound; full maple stock; a well-made gun.

No. 4. By Yocum; 57 inches over all; 42-inch full octagon barrel; 8 grooves; about 18 balls to the pound; sett trigger; full curly maple stock; 19 silver and 3 brass inlays; weight 12½ pounds; a very handsome piece.

(Plate 50)

1   2   3   4

WOODMANSEE COLLECTION

No. 1. By Frederick Tell; 59½ inches over all; 44-inch octagon barrel; 45 calibre; hand-made brass plate flint-lock full curly maple stock; brass-mounted, with raised carving, 8 brass inlays and 2 of silver.

No. 2. By M. Shell; 59½ inches over all; 44-inch octagon barrel; about 45 calibre; smooth bore; hand-made, engraved flint-lock; full curly maple stock; brass-mounted, with raised carving, 6 silver inlays, and brass wire inlay work in scroll.

No. 3. By Frederick Tell; 59 inches over all; 43½-inch octagon barrel; about 48 calibre; smooth bore; hand-made brass plate flint-lock; full curly maple stock; brass-mounted, with raised carving and 10 silver inlays.

No. 4. By John Armstrong; 58½ inches over all; 43-inch octagon barrel; 40 calibre; hand-made flint-lock; full curly maple stock; brass-mounted, with raised carving and 12 silver inlays.

(Plate 51)

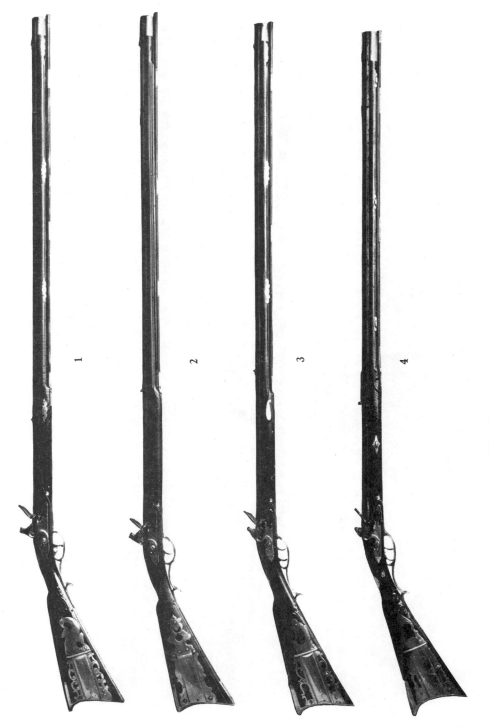

WOODMANSEE COLLECTION

Reverse of rifles shown on preceding page.

(Plate 52)

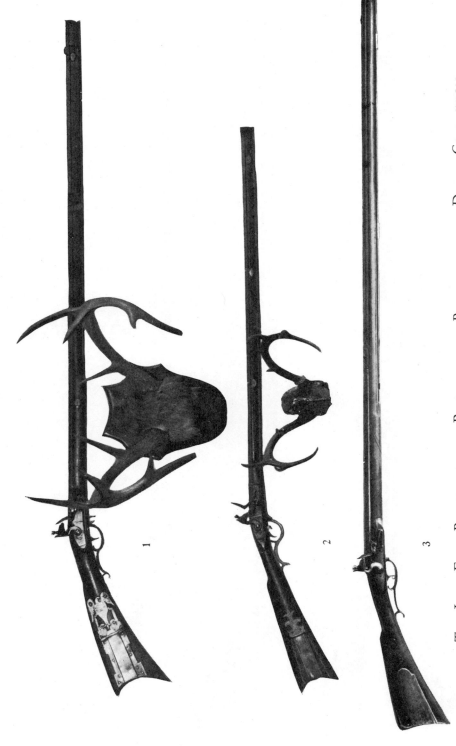

The John Fries Rifle and two Pennsylvania Rifles from the Dillin Collection

No. 1. Rifle marked Christ, period about 1810, notable for elaborate Patch Box
No. 2. Boy's rifle, maker unknown.
No. 3. Rifle of early period, belonging to John Fries, leader of Fries' Rebellion in Bucks and parts of Northampton Counties, Pennsylvania, in 1798.

(Plate 53)

was a most important factor. A pound of that metal run into bullets for a .70-calibre gun would turn out sixteen, whereas the same amount of lead run for a .45 calibre would make forty-eight. The difference in the amount of powder required for a charge would also be great, and in a country where money was scarce and the use of the gun frequent, economy was of the first importance. Then, too, consider the hunter starting on a trip which would consume weeks, or in many instances months. With the smaller calibre rifle he was enabled to carry three times the ammunition which he could pack for the larger bore gun. All things considered, it is easily understood why the American demanded a rifle suitable to his needs.

The American rifle, or Kentucky rifle, once standardized, was a fixed model as long as the big game remained. When a region was safe from Indian raids and depleted of its large wild animals the hunter turned his attention to the turkey and squirrel. Again the smith reduced the bore and produced what is called the Squirrel or Turkey Rifle.

While the Kentucky rifle in the main followed the conventional lines of its fellows in most particulars, barrel length was a variable dimension.

The length of the American flint-lock rifle seems to have been a matter decided upon by the owner. Without doubt the riflesmith made his suggestions and argued from his experience with other customers as salesmen do today, but it is fair to suppose that, as now, the prospective purchaser had in mind about the type of arm he required, and as the rifle was made to his order it had to fulfill his requirements. For this reason, perhaps, if for no other, the length of the early rifles varies from the extreme of about seventy-seven inches over all to the short, stocky gun measuring a scant fifty-one inches from butt plate to muzzle.

Specimens representing the entire flint period, from the earliest to the latest, are shown in Plate No. 54, and are so placed as to show the comparative lengths. There may have been a few rifles longer than those shown, or a few shorter, but they would only further emphasize the wide difference which existed. Feet and inches are indicated on the scale at the extreme left of the pieces, but, due to the fact that the rifles stand at a slant, they are actually about one inch longer than is shown by the measuring stick.

No. 1 on the extreme left is a weapon of rather plain workmanship, period of 1790.

No. 2 is a very early production of Isaac Haines.

No. 3 is a most beautiful rifle bearing a carved Indian on the stock.

No. 6 is the Kauffman Indian Rifle (Old Killdeer) elsewhere described.

No. 7 is the Matthew Roesser, dated 1746. It also has the Indian carved on the stock.

No. 8 is a duplicate of the Kauffman rifle. It is in excellent condition and has been repeatedly shot in recent years.

No. 13 is by James Wood and is a fine specimen of his work.

No. 14 is dated 1728 and is shown in Plate No. 10, with its description.

No. 16 is the Leman rifle, a very late specimen of flint-lock.

All the rifles shown are in their original form and constitute a most interesting group.

The plate showing the different lengths of rifle also gives an excellent idea of the thickness of stocks, the under ornamentation of trigger guards and the thimble forms.

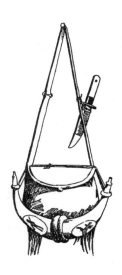

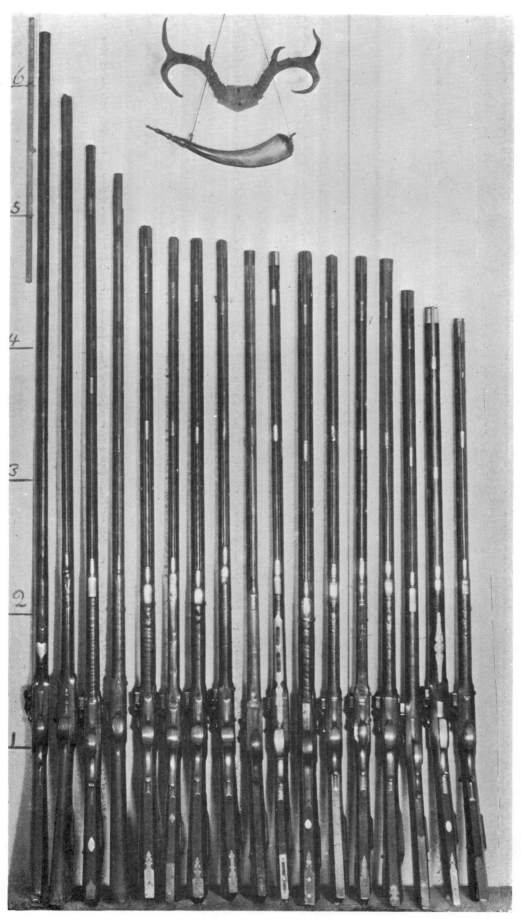

Varying lengths of rifles.   Scale in feet is shown at side.
From Dillin Collection
(See text, pages 37-38.)

(Plate 54)

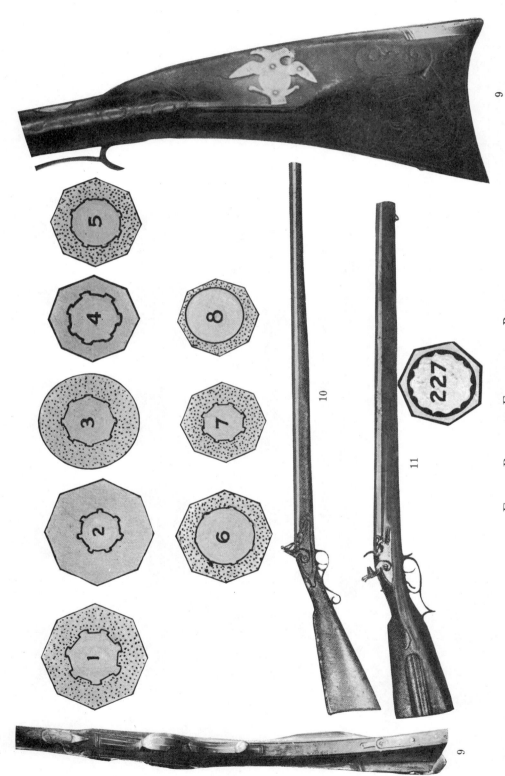

Exact Bores of Flint-lock Rifles

No. 1. By William Pannabecker, about 1810. No. 2. By H. F. Leman, about 1810. No. 3. By Thomas P. Cherrington, about 1840.
No. 4. Maker unknown, about 1770. No. 5. By James Woods, about 1820. No. 6. Maker unknown; early rifle, rifling nearly gone.
No. 7. By J. H. Berstro, 1815. No. 8. Maker unknown, bore ruined in an attempt to convert rifle into smooth bore. No. 9. Two
views of stock of an early rifle carrying as decorations the British Lion, the German Eagle and the American Indian. No. 10. Early
flint-lock rifle by Yomens. No. 11. Swiss flint-lock rifle with exact size of bore and style of rifling.

(Plate 55)

Flint-lock Barrels

Chapter Eight

ALTHOUGH to the collector of firearms the shapely maple stock, the finely cut patch box cover and other ornamentation may make the stronger appeal in determining the degree of excellence of a Kentucky rifle, the secret of its success as the American pioneer weapon lay in the long, heavy barrel. In bore and rifling it was frequently as characteristically distinct from other flint-lock types as in design and balance. The rifle of "The Dark and Bloody Ground," while unmistakably distinct as a class from weapons of European sporting and American military design, presented many variations in barrel dimensions.

The two chief divisions into which Kentucky rifle barrels naturally fall are "rifled barrels," which were the accepted form, and "smooth-bores," the latter in reality a misnomer, yet, in general use, being applied to any arm which to all appearances was a rifle but which lacked the actual rifling. It is probable that 95 per cent of the so-called "smooth-bores" had originally been rifled and rebored for shot after the accuracy life of the rifled tube had gone. They then became small-bore shotguns, but were frequently used by hunters, who fired patch and ball from them with deadly effect. The real "smooth-bores" constituting the remaining 5 per cent were seldom encountered in original barrels.

The occurrence of so-called "smooth-bores" now and again among examples of Kentucky rifles is traceable, to a degree, also to the practice of some gunsmiths in isolated communities of purchasing barrels bored to calibre from other smiths specializing in barrel making. The theory is advanced, and seems reasonable, that the gunsmiths of the past, like those of today, made and sold different grades of guns, and that for reasons of economy or because of personal preference, some barrels were sold as they came from the manufacturer, bored to calibre but not rifled.

Beyond this division, Kentucky barrels are to be classified according to whether the rifling proved to be "straight cut," "spiral" or "gain-twist." Moreover, within these classifications, Kentucky rifle barrels exhibit a surprisingly wide range of bore diameters.

Considering the original "smooth-bore" type of barrel, an exhaustive research covering several hundred of these so-called smooth-bore rifles disclosed but six specimens which could be certainly classified as original smooth-bore guns. Two of these were supplied with the regulation patch box, the others lacking this feature. All had regular rifle sights. When in doubt as to the original condition of the gun, a lead core was cast in the bore, and an examination of same with a magnifying glass easily determined its original status.

Mr. John Laidacker has informed the author that in the late flintlock period an old man in the Lehigh district rigged up a portable machine with which to bore out and smooth the worn-out rifle barrels. He traveled about the country soliciting work of this character. Mr. Laidacker was fortunate in securing the tools he used in this profession.

The smooth-bore, when used as a hunting arm, was frequently loaded with two balls, and in view of its heavy barrel, a large charge of powder was used. This gave great penetration and made it a very formidable weapon. In 1891 the writer came upon an old hunter with one of these guns on a deer range in Southern Pennsylvania. He had just shot a three-pronged buck. Two balls had passed through the neck. The job was complete.

The Straight-Cut

This method in all probability represents the earliest form of rifling. The original idea of cutting a number of deep grooves through the bore of a gun was doubtless for the purpose of making loading easier, for by removing about one-half of the surface of the bore, a tight ball could be driven down much easier than when a ball of similar diameter was forced through a barrel without rifling. The American straight-cut was as a rule large of bore and the barrel considerably thinner than that used for the spiral rifling. Such a rifle carried six grooves as against seven used in the spiral. It was cut deep and the gun supplied with a patch box, its general appearance being identical with the spiral-cut rifle. A considerable number of these straight-cuts were made, perhaps 15 per cent of the total number manufactured.

It seems somewhat strange, in view of the fact that the straight-cut was inferior to the spiral-grooved rifle, that so great a number should have been turned out, but a credible explanation is that it was a combination weapon. When used with patch and ball they had sufficient accuracy for big game hunting. They were often used with two balls like a smooth-bore and the hunter who was low in marksmanship undoubtedly preferred them. In addition, they would fire shot admirably, and this was a feature for consideration. It has been established for a certainty that the hunter who carried a straight-cut almost invariably carried in his hunting bag a small leather pouch that held about three-quarters of a pound of shot, generally of large size, BB to No. 4. This he used in emergencies. For instance, if his prospects were good for fox or turkey, he put in a load of shot, sometimes on top of the ball, the weight of the barrel with its corresponding strength making it perfectly safe for this double load.

The straight-cut rifle is an early arm. Such as have been examined apparently were made prior to 1800. Further the American straight-cut was not made with sett triggers.

The Spiral Rifling

This type of rifling is too well known to call for detailed description. Just when the principle of rotary flight was applied to the rifle is shrouded in mystery. As already stated, it probably followed the straight cut. It may have been an accident in boring or it may have been the outcome of a well-conceived idea. At all events its application was a master-stroke.

The earliest specimens of spiral rifling which have come under the notice of the writer are the wheel-lock guns shown in Plate I. These three rifles are of very early manufacture and were originally in a private collection in Philadelphia. On the death of the owner they were disposed of at public sale, unfortunately before full measurements could be secured.

The barrels of No. 1 and No. 3 were about 30 inches in length, of about .60 calibre with a three-quarter turn in the full length. Each barrel had seven lands and seven deep grooves, well cut, lands and grooves being of equal width. No. 2 was fitted with a barrel about 36 inches long, apparently of about .70 calibre, with 8 grooves, and rifling similar to No. 1 and No. 3. Rifle No. 1 had no rear sight and the barrel was half octagon; rifles No. 2 and No. 3 were full octagon. The date of manufacture of rifle No. 2 was given as 1525 and that of No. 3 as 1585, such information being credited to an English authority, who probably based his opinion on the style of workmanship and general characteristics of the pieces. They are evidently very old, of German workmanship and of wonderful handiwork. Another arm in the same collection was an Arab model, long, slender and highly decorated, a flintlock of the snap-haunce type, a six-groove, straight-cut rifle. This is the only rifled Arab gun of which the writer knows.

The Gain Twist

In an examination of a large number of early American rifles not a single specimen of rifle with gain twist has been found. In early percussion days this type of rifling was in vogue to a limited extent, but prior to 1840 it is safe to say that it was very rarely, if ever, in use.

The sizes of bores in American flint-lock rifles offers an interesting field for research. Captain William De V. Foulke has made a study of the calibres of the early American rifles and the author is much indebted to him for the following data on the subject:

The American rifle is a direct descendant of the German Jaeger rifle, and the imprint of its paternity is plain in many early examples; in fact, it was well on in the nineteenth century before it was outgrown and cast aside. In Germany the influence of the large, smooth Shoreth military arms was still asserting itself in the size of the bores adopted for the rifle at the time the American rifle came into being. In America the distances the hunter or soldier had to carry his rifle and the ammunition for it, as well as his distance from his base of supplies, all tended to demand the most efficient arm using the lightest charge which would kill game or stop an enemy.

This was secured by increasing the length of the barrel to one hundred or more calibres, which gave the maximum speed to the round ball then in universal use, and a round ball is most accurate and deadly when driven at high speed.

There was no standard size to which the rifle was bored, nor did it remain very long the original size. Rust from constant exposure to the weather, and the funneling of the muzzle by wear of the rod in loading and wiping, forced a quite frequent freshing out of the bore with a consequent enlargement each time, necessitating the use of a thicker patch, or that the moulds should be cherried out.

The smallest flint-lock rifle bore was probably about one hundred and fifty to the pound of lead, the largest (except wall pieces) about eight to the pound. General George Washington had some of these latter made for long-range sharpshooting and concerning them he says in a letter which is still in existence: "Firing from a rest good marksmen hit a sheet of note paper three out of five shots at a distance of eighty rods." (Note paper was then about 8 x 10 inches in size.)

The smallest American muzzle-loading rifle known to the writer used a ball of four hundred to the pound. With this rifle a deer was killed in West Virginia across the Elk River at a point where that stream is seven to eight rods wide.

The size of a round-ball rifle is spoken of as so many balls to the pound. A rifle which gauged, say, eighty to the pound, might use a ball 81, 82, 83 or 84 to the pound, depending on the thickness of the patch used with it, hence a nominal size of the bore meant only that of a ball fitting the bore bare, without the patch.

FIVE RIFLES OF VARYING LENGTHS

No. 1. Long Pennsylvania rifled gun, period about 1815.
No. 2. Early Pennsylvania rifle changed to percussion.
No. 3. Longest known gun, 82 inches long, upper stock missing, about 42 calibre, rifled.
No. 4. Pennsylvania rifle of unusual appearance, from Dillin collection.
No. 5. Boy's Kentucky rifle.

(Plate 56)

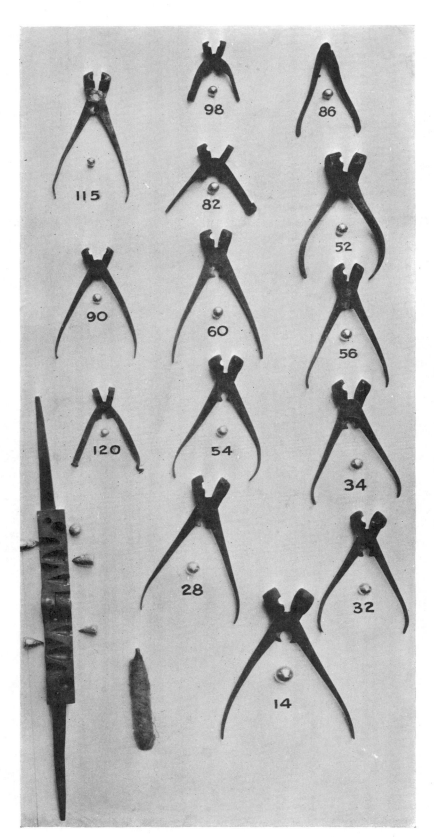

Bullet Moulds and Bullets

Bullet Moulds (one-third actual size) together with bullets cast from same. Numeral under each bullet designates the number of balls to the pound which represented bore or calibre of the rifle. In the lower left centre of the plate is shown a swab for cleaning the rifle bore after each shot. The rod wormer is tightly wound with unspun flax, well-greased, and attached to the ramrod by a screw.

(Plate 57)

Here follow the micrometer measurements of the gauge used by George Schalk, of Pottsville, Pa., 1824-1892. Schalk was one of America's best riflesmiths and was a maker of many famous rifles. He was a most careful man and hence his gauge may be accepted as correct.

No. of balls to pound	Measurement in inches and decimals of inch	No. of balls to pound	Measurement in inches and decimals of inch	No. of balls to pound	Measurement in inches and decimals of inch
5	1.15	25	.585	110	.350
6	.954	26	.575	120	.340
7	.900	27	.572	130	.332
8	.861	28	.559	140	.324
9	.823	29	.549	150	.318
10	.790	30	.533	150	.310
11	.760	32	.530	170	.305
12	.748	34	.519	180	.298
13	.727	36	.506	190	.292
14	.708	38	.491	200	.290
15	.695	40	.485	210	.288
16	.682	44	.474	220	.284
17	.665	48	.463	230	.282
18	.647	52	.453	240	.280
19	.637	56	.442	250	.278
20	.628	64	.416	260	.274
21	.618	70	.400	270	.2715
22	.609	80	.388	280	.269
23	.601	90	.383		
24	.588	100	.364		

An unusually good description from which may be visualized the rifling shop of the early smith is available through the courtesy of Walter M. Cline, of Tennessee.

In the manufacture of the hand-made rifle the first step was the barrel. The gunsmith of pioneer days having no boring machine, the barrel had to be welded or forged out of a flat bar of iron. This iron came from the early furnaces which were charcoal furnaces and the iron was no doubt hammered iron. A bar was selected which would be of the weight desired by the customer when finished. The bar selected was placed in the forge and the end brought to a welding heat; as the bar was brought to the anvil the smith's helper or striker, as he was usually called, laid the point of a tapered rod, with the other end turned up like the calk on a horseshoe, on the end of the bar. A weld was made around this rod, which was then knocked out by striking the calked end. The bar was then heated again and a weld again made of perhaps only a half an inch; the rod again knocked out. This was repeated until the barrel was finished. Forty-eight inches was the standard length. It usually required a half day to weld a barrel. The barrel was now ready for boring, having a hole that the bit would follow. The first boring was made with what was called the short bit. This was made by the smith squaring a piece of steel and welding it to a rod, then heating it and placing it in a vise, giving it a twist and tempering it. This bit being the size to make the finished bore to use so many balls to the pound of lead as per order of customer. Some gunsmiths had water power for boring, others had to do it by hand with the crudest of home-made machinery; after this boring, it was reamed out with the long bit. The cutting edge of this bit was a thin piece of steel welded on to one side of a squared end of the rod or shaft of the bit. On the other side was an oval piece of well-seasoned hickory to prevent any cutting injuring the barrel. This boring left the barrel highly polished and perfectly smooth. The barrel was now straightened by stretching a silk thread through the barrel, and by looking through the crooked places they could be detected and straightened by striking with the hammer. The barrel was now ready for rifling.

On the smith's work bench was the rifle guide. This was a cylinder of wood about fifty-four inches long in which were spiral-cut grooves, one turn in forty-eight inches. This was in a framework of wood having an index through which the spiral-grooved cylinder revolved when the frame was moved back and forward on the bench, the index being stationary with fingers which engaged the grooves. A rifling rod with a hollow end in which was fastened a short hickory rod was fastened to the end of the spiral-grooved cylinder. The saw for cutting the grooves in the barrel was set in the hickory rod. The barrel was aligned with the rifle guide, the rod run through the barrel until the hickory rod extended through the barrel. The smith's helper now held an awl on the hickory rod, when the smith taking hold of the handles on the frame pulled it towards him. This made a mark to set the saw so that it would have the proper angle with the spiral grooves. The saw was now set in the wood with a special chisel. A cut was now made by pulling the guide along the bench, the spiral-cut cylinder revolving through the index, the rod following. It required about one hundred cuts to cut a groove, an eight-rifled barrel requiring approximately eight hundred cuts to complete. The barrel was perfect and required no smoothing out. The barrel was then ground or left just as it came from the forge, as sometimes the customer wanted just the hammered barrel.

A breech pin was put in with hand-made tools, as were all other fittings. The trigger guard and triggers were forged out, as was many times the lock. The stock was usually made from curly maple or walnut and after a stock pattern. This stock was made with hand-made tools. Planes for cutting different parts of the stock were made by the smith, persimmon wood being used for the block of the planes. The rifle was then sighted and targeted.

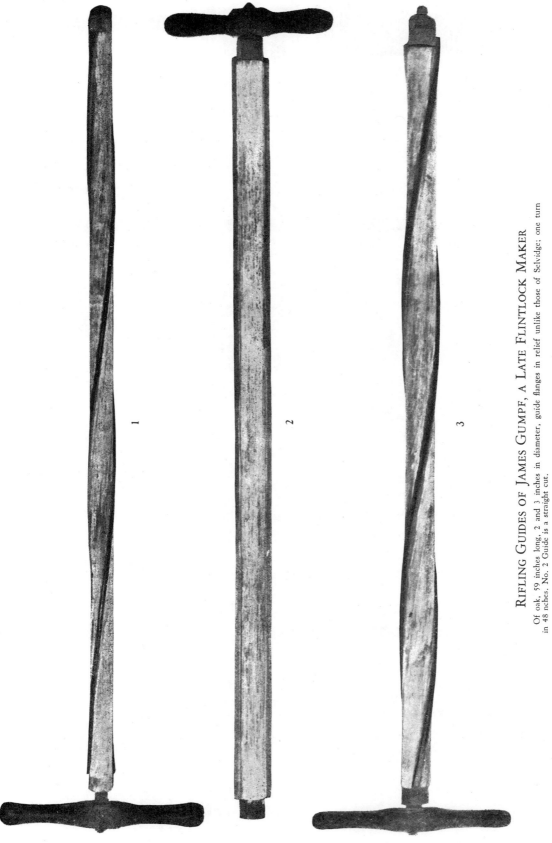

RIFLING GUIDES OF JAMES GUMPF, A LATE FLINTLOCK MAKER

Of oak, 59 inches long, 2 and 3 inches in diameter, guide flanges in relief unlike those of Selvidge; one turn in 48 inches. No. 2 Guide is a straight cut.

(Plate 58)

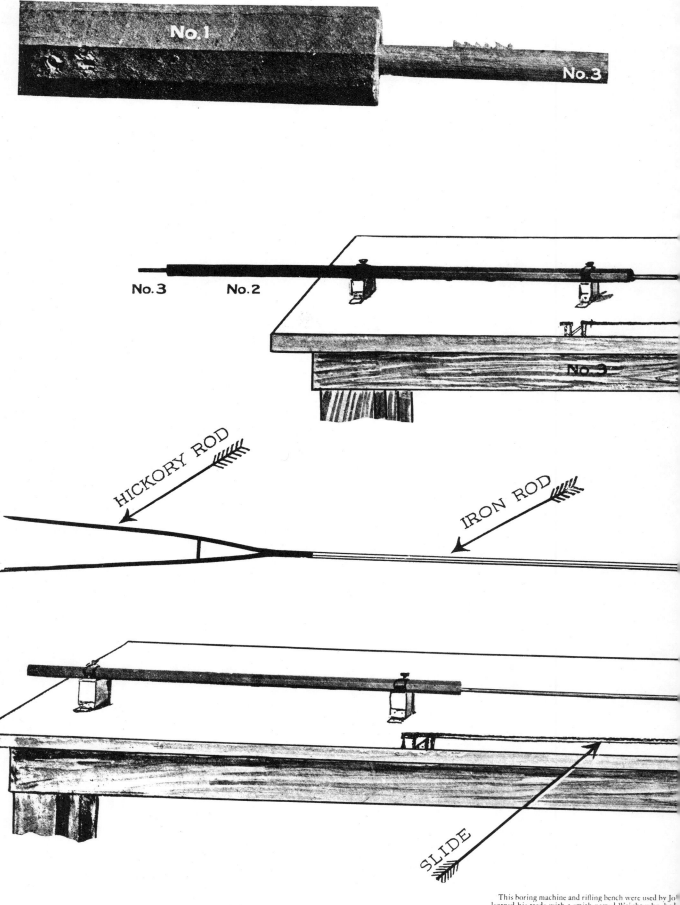

No. 1

No. 3

No. 3 No. 2

No. 3

HICKORY ROD

IRON ROD

SLIDE

This boring machine and rifling bench were used by Jo⬛
learned his trade with a smith named Wright who had ⬛
Selvidge went to Tennessee about the year 1800. He h⬛
apprenticeship in 1845. Later Wolf married Selvidge's d⬛
for years as the greatest offhand rifle shot in Eastern Te⬛
This old rifling bench is equipped with three different ⬛
turn in 48 inches was the recognized standard. The ben⬛

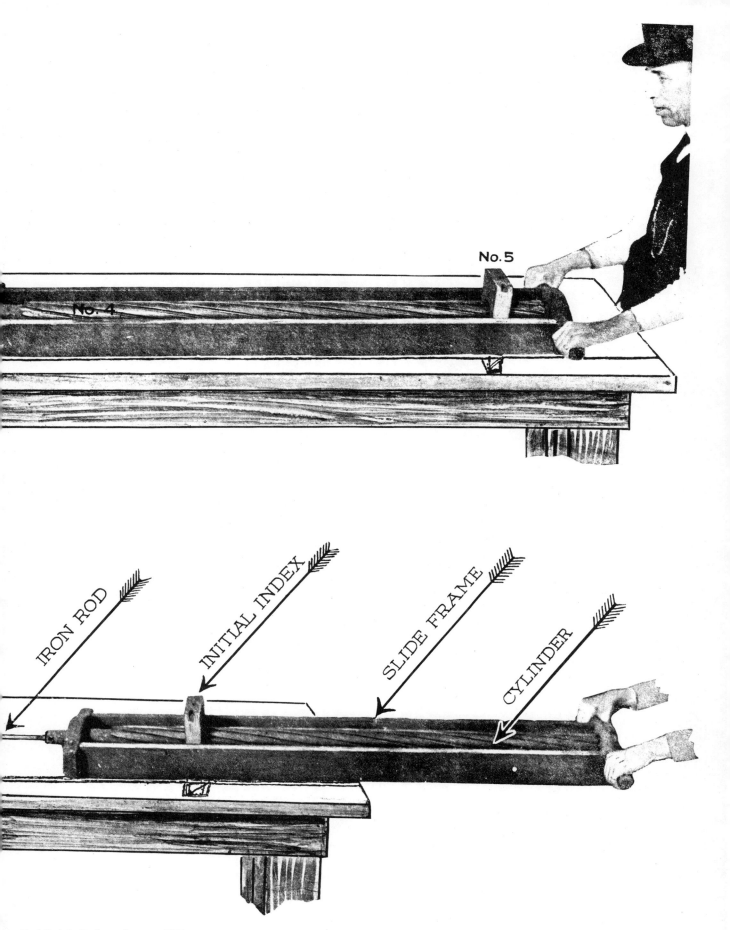

No. 5

No. 4

IRON ROD

INITIAL INDEX

SLIDE FRAME

CYLINDER

op at Harris Creek, Bradley County, Tennessee. Selvidge
tice of the Yomens, of Charlotte, North Carolina. John
eridith Wolf, who was born in 1832, and who began his
rking at his trade at the age of 91 years. He was known

resenting as many different pitches of rifling, though one
d is of the type used by the pioneer smiths.

McComb and Company
Dr to the Estate of John Henry deceased.

1773

August.	To 6 Rifles at £7. each		£42. 0. 0
Septr 6.	To bushing a Gun		4.
16.	To repairing a Fusee		4.
21.	To a Ramrod for a fusee		1.
October 16th	To Stocking a fusee		1.
	To a Lock for Do & Straitning		19.
23.	To Straitning a fusee		3.
Decemr 22.	To Setting a Pair of Sheets & grinding		5.
	To Grinding one pair Do.		2. 6

1774

Feby. 19th	To a Cock for a Lock		8.
	To a Sett for a Rifle		2.
	Bushing a fusee a Lock & Jaw		7.
	Tumbler Pin for Do.		1.
April 24th	Cleaning a Lock		3.
	Ramrod		1.
May 8"	Cleaning three Rifles		15.
	Cow Pin Jata & Moles		9.
24	Repairing a Rifle		1. 2.
June 4th	Straitning a fusee		3.
4th	Tumbler for a fusee & Straitning		4.
10.	To Stocking 2 fusees & repairing Do.		2. 10.
	To repairing one ditto		2. 6
July 8th	To Stocking a Rifle		1. 5.
	To a Sett of Mounting		1.
	To Cutting a Rifle		16.
	To a Lock for Do.		16.
	To a Lock for another Rifle		16. 0
22.	To Stocking a Rifle		1. 5.
	To a Sett of Mounting & bushing		1.
25.	To Cleaning a Rifle		5. 6
26.	To hardning 2 hammers		4.
	To Repairing a Lock		3. 6
27.	To Stocking a Rifle		1. 5.
	To a Sett of Mounting £1. to a Lock 16. 2 Sctes for Do. 4.s		2.
			62 .19 .0

INVOICE 150 YEARS OLD

An original bill rendered by the estate of John Henry, Boulton, Pa., for
material and labor furnished to McComb & Company. A valuable document
which shows costs one hundred and fifty years ago.

(Plate 60)

Who Rifled the Rifles

CHAPTER NINE

ROM time to time the question is raised as to whether the early riflesmiths rifled the barrels of the guns which they turned out, or employed the services of another smith to accomplish this very important work for them. At this late day it is a difficult question to answer in any way except by a study of the conditions surrounding the smith. If the narrative of Mr. Milton Warren which appears in a preceding chapter is taken as a basis of theory, or if the relics of old rifle shops showing well-preserved rifling benches were types of every rifle smithy, the assumption would naturally be that each smith rifled his own barrels.

On the other hand, the author was informed by the late Philip de Turk, of Reading, Pa., that he distinctly recollected that somewhere in the Reading district there was a man by the name of Johnson, who had a rifling plant and did work for other smiths. L. K. Siner, the well-known gunsmith who still conducts a business at the old Krider Gun Store, Second and Walnut Streets, Philadelphia, also says that his father well remembered that barrels were taken to the Nippes factory on Mill Creek, about eight miles west of the city, to be rifled.

The records of John Henry, one of the most celebrated rifle makers of Lancaster, Pa., show that he also rifled barrels for others, and while each of the foregoing instances relate to the later period of the flintlock it is fair to suppose that in the earlier days, one smith may have depended upon another for his rifling.

The pioneer smith undoubtedly rifled his own barrels. His isolated situation would argue against his sending barrels a great distance. The very fact that in learning his trade he became familiar with this process would make him independent. The time consumed in a journey to the nearest smith would be greater by far than that required for rifling. Only the smith making an occasional rifle would be likely to entrust such work to another and it is most probable that in each period every smith with any considerable business had his own rifling bench.

As a matter of information, there follow the items of a bill in connection with the estate of John Henry:

Lancaster, Pa., Dec. 1774.

George Rathfong, debtor to the Estate of John Henry, deceased.

1774

	£	s	d
Dec. 20, To finishing 2 smooth rifles............£4		10 s	o d
To cash.........................3		o	o

1775
March 16 ditto............................6		o	o
April 16 ditto.............................3		o	o
April 29 ditto.............................3		o	o
May 5 ditto..............................o		10	o
Aug. 10 ditto.............................6		o	o
Dec. 2 ditto..............................1		10	6

1776
Feb. 17 ditto.............................9			
" " to 39 Musket Scalps @ 3⅙ pair........6		16	o
June 12 To cutting a smooth rifle...............o		10	o
July 8 To cutting a rifle.......................o		10	o
July 24 To cash.............................8		11	o
Aug. 14 To cash.............................3		o	o
Aug. 23 To cash.............................6		o	o
Sept. 9 To cash.............................4		10	o

1777
Feb. 8 To cash.............................3		15	o
	70	17	o

Note: A Pennsylvania £ was $2.62.

The author has spent much time in the search for information bearing on this subject and has met with a fair degree of success. Twelve rifling benches have been located at this late date, nine of which are in Pennsylvania, but, strange to relate, none of which were found in Lancaster County. No two of these machines are exactly alike.

In view of the fact that so many rifling benches have been found so long after their disuse, there is more than a strong suggestion that a very large percentage of the old smiths rifled their own barrels with their own equipment.

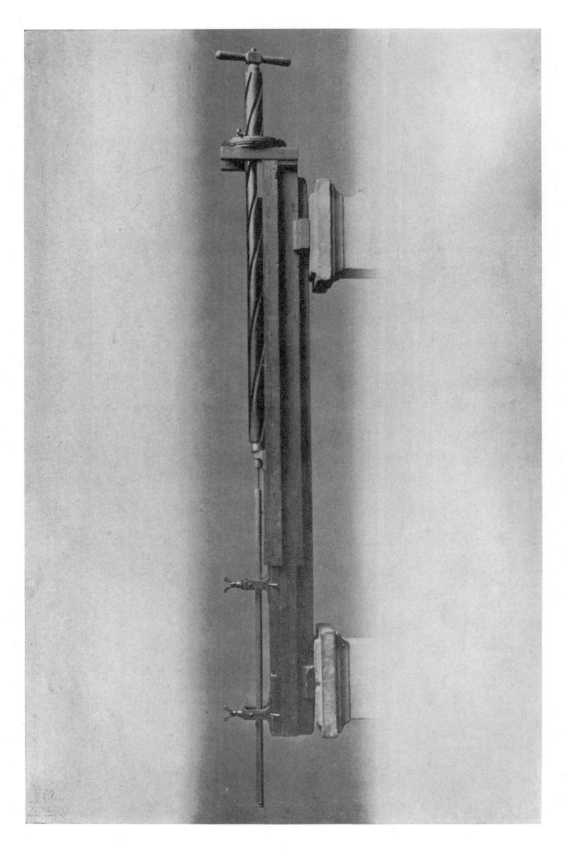

A Fine Specimen of Rifling Bench

Rifling bench in use in Virginia from 1800 to about 1820. A very fine example of the bench during the late flintlock period. Now the property of Dr. O. W. Ferguson, of Illinois.

(Plate 61)

RIFLING A BARREL

Outside the Henry rifle works at Boulton, Pa. Charles Henry, the last of the great family of riflemakers, is giving a demonstration to the author of the method pursued in rifling a barrel. (Photograph taken November 18, 1921.)

(Plate 62)

It was the good fortune of the author to be able to visit the old gun factory at Boulton, Northampton County, Pa., located on the east bank of Bushkill Creek, and historically known as the Henry Rifle Works. This old mill was built by William Henry, Jr., whose father was William Henry, a pioneer rifle maker of Lancaster, Pa. The factory was completed in the year 1813, and the business of making firearms was continued until the eighties. Since then the plant has been in disuse, and stands today as a monument to what was once a leading American industry, and here it is in order to add that it is a question if another similar example of an early rifle works can be found anywhere in the United States of America. The old mill, notwithstanding its age and the lack of interest that generally follows disuse, is in a very fair state of preservation. An interior view will also show a few remainders of the early rifle industry, as there are still remaining parts of machinery, features of the water power that drove this machinery, rifle stocks in crude form; the grindstone that was used in shaping the barrels is still there, and upon the time-dimmed surface of the walls may be seen records of measurements, together with the names or initials of workmen who helped make Boulton famous as a firearms center.

These and a few remaining mechanical features are the distinguishing parts that remain within the walls of this historic old landmark of the Bushkill.

But this quaint old factory is not the only object of interest that has defied the ravages of time. Thus the story is only part told. When William Henry acquired this extensive tract of land by the Bushkill, upon which he built his rifle works, he at once began improvements. The log cabin that stood on the west bank of the creek and nearly opposite the factory site was remodeled, and also a commodious stone house was built. Later on after his marriage, William Henry, 3rd, chose the log cabin as his place of abode. This pioneer cabin, built in 1794, was a settler's home of the better type, four rooms and back kitchen. The big fireplace with its crane and iron kettle completed the interior. Outside, the improvements consisted of what might be termed regulation log buildings of the early settler, these buildings being surrounded by a high picket fence that would afford the protection necessary to his flocks against prowling wolves that might swoop down from the nearby mountains and take a heavy toll of the settler's scanty supply.

Within a few steps of the cabin door, a beautiful spring of pure cold water bubbled forth from the rocks, while the great oaks and hemlocks afforded an abundance of shade. This spring is of the never-failing class, and at this writing still flows as it did more than a hundred years ago, while the great trees standing as protectors against storm and heat add a charm to the scenic features of the landscape.

William Henry was no doubt contented with his home and primitive surroundings, but with the prosperity that crowned his business efforts, new conditions arose. The Henrys had become important factors in the business world, celebrated as makers of firearms and known all over the settled parts of North America.

With this expansion of trade, social features became matters of concern. Traders came from far-away parts to place orders. Men of affairs came for consultation, and all must be entertained. The log cabin with its latch string ever on the outside would no longer measure up to the requirements of an ever-increasing social obligation that an expanding business would naturally create, and something must be done. Action was not long delayed. The Henry home was made bigger and better and filled requirements for a time, when new conditions were injected into the situation and more room was necessary. So new houses were added. These latter dwellings were not log cabins, but substantial mansions of the early nineteenth century type. They also were built on the west bank of the Bushkill and close to the old homestead, as already described. And it is a remarkable fact that these four houses still stand in a beautiful state of preservation, and more remarkable is the fact that at this writing each house is the home of a family bearing the name of Henry, the lineal descendants of the Honorable William Henry, of Lancaster, patriot, statesman, inventor and riflemaker.

The Pioneer and His Rifle

CHAPTER TEN

O THE American pioneer, the Kentucky rifle was dependable not alone as a means of defense, a meat-getter and a fire lighter, but was also the prime factor about which centered the sport and recreation indulged in by the frontiersman. In fact, much of the skill which stood the pioneer in such good stead when beating off a hostile attack or keeping a full larder, was predicated largely upon the training he acquired in the shooting matches.

More thoroughly to understand the use of the Kentucky rifle, a description of the methods of loading is not out of place.

The difference between loading a flint-lock rifle and the method employed with an ordinary percussion gun is not very great, differing mainly in the variance of the cap and nipple and the flint and pan. However, it is interesting to reconstruct conditions surrounding the early American hunter who has just fired a shot from his single-barrel rifle and who wishes to reload. Firing has left the pan open, the frizzen pushed forward, the hammer down. The first procedure is the swabbing of the bore. The worm, which is tightly wrapped with greased linen tow, is withdrawn from the patch box or leather hunting bag; the ramrod is drawn from its position under the barrel and the worm screwed to the small end of the rod. The butt of the rifle is pushed well to the left and in front, the left hand grasping the muzzle. The swab, held loosely in the right hand so that it will turn with the rifling, is pushed up and down the barrel. This is repeated two or three times and the rod is withdrawn and laid against a convenient tree or held between the knees. The rifle is now drawn squarely in front and held vertical by the left hand. The hunter places his lips over the muzzle and blows down the bore to clear the channel between barrel and pan. If the channel is clear he knows that he will not have use for the pick. If it is clogged it must be forced open.

Next the rifle butt is put back to the left with the left arm thrown around the rifle a foot below the muzzle. The powder horn and bag hanging on the right side are pushed forward by the right hand. The left hand seizes the measure which hangs to the bag or horn and with the right hand the horn is raised to the lips and the plug or stopper is drawn with the teeth. The left hand holds the measure; the right hand pours the powder. When the measure is full it is passed to the right hand and while the rifle is held by the left hand, the right pours the powder down the bore. Now a round, greased patch of linen or leather is withdrawn from the pouch and placed squarely across the muzzle with the fingers of the right hand and held in place with the thumb of the left while a ball is taken from the pouch and placed in the center of the patch. The head of the rod which has been raised with the right hand is brought to bear squarely on the ball, which is forced under pressure down the bore until it rests on the powder charge. The rod is then withdrawn and the worm and swab removed unless more shooting is soon expected, in which case the rod is not cleared or replaced in the thimbles.

The rifle being loaded, priming follows. The piece is laid across the left arm and the frizzen pushed forward. If a grain or two of powder is found in the pan, no picking of the channel is necessary; if no powder is found care to clear the channel must be exercised by use of the pick. The pan is now filled from a small horn containing very fine grain powder which insures quick and certain ignition.

The foregoing description of loading may be considered as the rule, but there were exceptions. Some hunters carried balls already patched for quick action, and elsewhere in this book will be found an illustration showing three balls fitted to a flat strip of wood. Again it was customary for some hunters to make the patch while loading. A piece of greased patch cloth was drawn across the muzzle, the ball properly placed in it and started into the bore about 7/16 of an inch with a short rod. The left hand then grasped the cloth, which was held tight in an upright position, and a sharp knife in the right hand cut it off even with the muzzle, the patch being sufficiently large to fold well over the ball and prevent mutilation from the rod in seating it on the powder. While this is a good way to patch a ball it is apt to work an injury to the muzzle of the rifle.

Patches can be cut round, square or as above described. The square patch was not often used, though it gave good results if carefully centered, but any patch not centered to the bore will give an erratic delivery of the ball, invariably a wild shot to the right.

The accepted process of loading may seem laborious and slow, but it was accomplished in about twenty seconds by an expert of the muzzle-

RELICS OF AN ANCIENT MATCH

Targets found in an old hunting bag in Northeastern Pennsylvania, which are relics of flint-lock days. They came from the same region where the Weiser targets shown on another page were found. No name, date or distance could be discovered.

(Plate 63)

The Turkey Shoot

Reproduction of an early Pennsylvania sketch of a Turkey Shoot at a country tavern. The rifleman is in position for an off-hand shot at the bird, seen in the background. As a rule at such shoots, the distance was 100 yards, the head of the turkey alone being exposed. In this sketch the whole bird is shown, which would suggest that the distance was 200 yards, which was the customary range when the entire bird was the target. (From very early woodcut.)

(Plate 64)

loading days and the author has seen a flint-lock properly loaded, aimed and fired in twenty-seven seconds. It is claimed that on the battlefront our old-time riflemen carried their patches between the fingers of the left hand to insure quick action.

The flint was good for about fifty shots and cost about two cents. As a rule they were imported from England. To properly flint a gun, the flint is clamped between two pieces of leather in the jaws of the hammer. The custom of clamping flints with cloth was frowned upon because the cloth was likely to ignite. The use of sheet lead as found in certain heavier military arms was impracticable in connection with the lighter Kentucky type hammers.

Concerning the loading of the flint-lock in battle, it has often been stated that the American rifleman carried his patches between his fingers while in action on the battlefront and that he also carried bullets in his mouth at the same time. Now, while we are not able to fully confirm these statements, I must say that in either instance an advantage would have resulted if the loading could have been done a little more quickly, as rapidity in loading a muzzle loader was a feature not to be overlooked. In viewing these claims from all angles it seems only fair to say that the statements as above noted were in all probability correct.

Now as to targets used in muzzle-loading days—

Several forms of targets were used by the American rifleman in shooting matches and the distances shot were from a minimum of 20 yards to a maximum of 100 yards, rarely beyond that distance. The targets generally used were blocks of wood, often split and charred, upon which cross lines were marked. Sometimes, if available, pieces of cardboard were substituted. Tack heads were also a favorite mark for shooting at twenty yards. Positions were offhand, muzzle rest and prone from the elbows. The latter position was in vogue, the author having seen a powder horn upon which was engraved the figure of a rifleman shooting from this position. He was pictured in a high hat and held his feet in the air.

In addition to these recognized positions, some riflemen shot from the back position, a posture which was to be perpetuated in American shooting even down to nineteenth-century Creedmoor, while others shot while lying on their sides. Still other demonstrations of marksmanship, as recorded in Force's American Archives, set forth that the frontier rifleman frequently ran twenty or thirty steps, halted suddenly to fire and was very skilful in hitting his marks.

Many demonstrations of these shooting positions, according to Force, were given to the Colonists when the mountain men, called to the colors, began arriving at the Colonial camps in the early revolutionary days.

These demonstrations undoubtedly laid the foundation for the development of that high degree of skill with the rifle which reached its height nationally immediately following the War for Independence.

The 20-yard match at tack heads was offhand; at 40, 60, 75 and 100 yards contestants were permitted either muzzle rest or prone position according to prearranged rules.

Group shooting was mostly from muzzle rest. In such contest, three to five shots were, as a rule, fired. At the conclusion of the string a wooden peg was inserted in each bullet hole and a piece of cord stretched around each peg. Later the cord was measured and the marksman with the shortest cord won. This was called string measure.

Another and very popular form of target was a live turkey. Sometimes the bird was tied to a stake about 200 yards from the marksman, the full body exposed. Again the turkey was tied only 100 yards away, but the body was protected, the head and neck alone being visible. This contest was always shot offhand. A reproduction of an old print in Plate No. 64 gives an idea of such a match.

Occasionally the relative skill of riflemen was put to the test on live game in the woods, each contestant shooting from an offhand position. Squirrel were usually selected for targets in such a contest.

Let us set imagination to work upon established facts concerning the frontier rifleman and his methods and turn back the years to a picture of a typical rifle match.

It was a pleasant day in early December when two young men were seen riding eastward over the Pack Horse Trail. Both carried saddle bags swung across the backs of their well-groomed horses, and each carried a short German rifle, strapped across his back in a manner for quick action. When the cross trail was reached, about three miles east, they dismounted and hitched their horses to a sapling that stood by the roadside. At the junction of these trails and only a few yards back was a rather crude log house and outbuildings, the home and gun shop of a French Huguenot, named Ferree. The house and yard were enclosed by a strong picket fence, made from split chestnut and pointed at the tops. Directly in front of the house and just outside the picket fence a high sign-board stated that Ferree made and sold rifled guns, and also carried a stock of wolf and bear traps. This spacious board served a double purpose, for it contained numerous notices pertaining to the affairs of the settlers. A few minutes' talk with the smith, then one of the young men took from a saddle bag a large roll of coarse paper. This he unrolled and proceeded to post upon the sign-board, with some wooden pegs cut for the purpose. It was to notify the people that a shooting match was to take place, and read about as follows:

HUNTERS
And Others Look This Way

The Great Shooting Match Will Take Place on

DECEMBER 15th and 16th, 1727

AT THE PLACE OF
DANIEL YEOMANS BY THE BIG CREEK

FIRST PRIZE

Is a BIG FAT OX for the First Day
Second Day, a SNAP-HAUNCE GUN
With a Long Barl

Distance 15 rods. A charge of two shillings for each man. Only one shot for each two shillings.

There will be more prizes, such as traps, robes, knives and skins at less charges.

Hunters coming from a long distance can be kept for one shilling a day. Horses at one-half shilling. *Plenty to eat and drink for all that come.*

Lead, powder and flints to be sold. Bear and wolf traps to sell.

ANYONE GOING BACK TO SETTLEMENTS MUST TELL EVERY MAN TO COME TO THE MATCH

The notice of this great event was soon conveyed to the most remote parts of the settlements, from the Blue Ridge to the Delaware, and the coming event was eagerly discussed. It was well understood that it was to be no ordinary rifle shoot; it was to be an event of unusual importance. New rifles and new ideas would figure in the event. Late in the afternoon of December 14th contestants began to arrive. They came by horseback, on foot and a few by wagon. They came from all directions, and many from distant points. Great fires blazed about several big iron pots, and the savory odor of stewing venison was well calculated to sharpen the appetites of the hungry visitors. Long tables, made from hewn logs, were set up in a temporary shelter arranged to meet the needs of the visiting riflemen. A hearty supper of venison and corn bread, and a day of strenuous work was over.

On the following morning, and perhaps one hour before the break of day, there was great activity about the rifle camp. Contestants began coming in, and when the match was called at nine o'clock, the crowd was so large that additional targets were arranged to meet what promised to be an actual necessity; then the promoters of the match felt that a great success was assured.

Down at the log barn a huge ox stood in his stall, representing the first prize. A basketful of split pine blocks, about six inches square and charred black, were being offered at two shillings each; one shot to each block, with the number of blocks to each entrant limited to three; the contestant placing a ball nearest to center of the cross lines, these to be located in such a position on the charred block as desired by the contestant, to be declared the winner. All preliminaries having been completed, the management announced that the match was open. Six men at once purchased blocks; then there was a protracted lull, and every persuasion failed to induce the contestants to enter.

Of the six persons referred to, it was noticed that five were gunsmiths or represented smiths. It was also noted that they carried rifles of the new small-bore, long-barreled type, so much talked about.

"Come on, boys," exclaimed the management, "and buy your blocks and let's start to shoot," but there was no response.

A great silence prevailed, but this silence was a mere calm before a storm, for suddenly a mighty protest went up against the use of some new rifles which, it was claimed, had been brought into the shoot.

"No, sir," exclaimed half a dozen at a time, "we will not risk our shillings against them long-barreled, small-ball rifles," and no amount of persuasion could change their views.

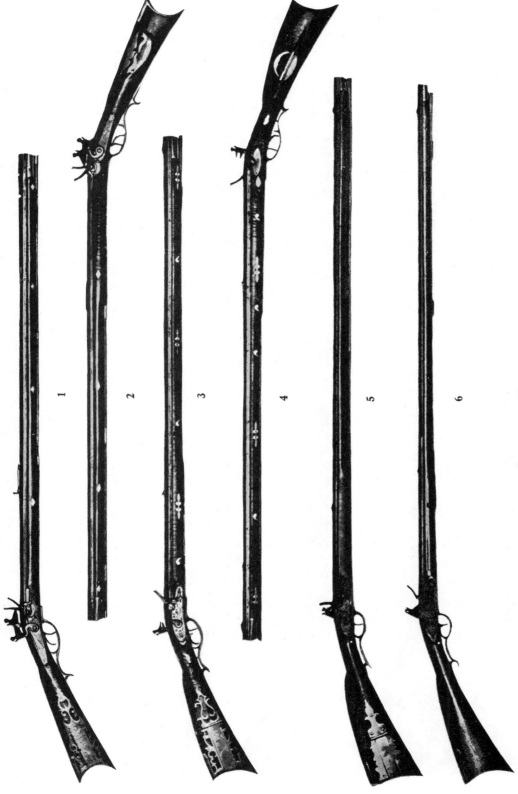

LAIDACKER COLLECTION

Nos. 1-2. By S. Smith; single-barrel flint-lock rifle firing two shots from one barrel; 56 inches over all; 41½-inch barrel; 8 grooves; about 120 balls to the pound; full curly maple stock; brass patch-box; 13 silver inlays; made about 1805; in fine condition; weight 9½ pounds; very rare piece.

Nos. 3-4. Schickellimy's* rifle; maker unidentified; 57 inches over all; 42½-inch barrel; 7 grooves; about 60 balls to the pound; double sett trigger; full curly maple stock; handsome curl through whole length; brass patch-box with 7 decorations; 24 pieces of silver inlay of artistic design; weight 11½ pounds.

No. 5. By Starr; 62 inches over all; 46½-inch barrel; full maple stock, well carved; high comb, slender wrist; plain patch-box; weight 9 pounds; a well-made early piece.

No. 6. By "G. S."; 61½ inches over all; 46-inch half octagonal barrel (turned down from original full octagon barrel); full maple stock, nicely carved; high comb, slender wrist; no patch-box; weight 6 pounds; well made; early period.

*Mr. J. G. Laidacker, the owner of this rifle, says that upon his purchase of this rifle he was credibly informed that the piece was made for Conrad Wiser who later traded the rifle to the Indian Chief Schickellimy for the "Isle of Q" in the Susquehanna River.

(Plate 65)

SNYDER COLLECTION

No. 1. Unidentified; 66 inches over all; 51-inch full octagon barrel; full maple stock; iron patch-box and mountings; weight 11½ pounds; an early and very rare rifle.

No. 2. By A. Kiser; 57 inches over all; 42-inch full octagon barrel; 60 balls to the pound; full maple stock; brass patch-box; a very good piece.

No. 3. Unidentified; 61 inches over all; 46-inch full octagon barrel; 60 balls to the pound; full maple stock; brass patch-box, opening from the side; weight 9¼ pounds.

No. 4. By P. Palm; 60 inches over all; 45-inch full octagon barrel; full maple stock; brass mountings; silver inlay; brass patch-box; heavy match rifle, marked No. 4 on barrel; superb workmanship.

No. 5. Unidentified; 60 inches over all; 44½-inch full octagon barrel; side hammer; full curly maple stock, highly decorated; brass patch-box.

(Plate 66)

Then the management realized that something must be done, or the event would be a failure. But it was not long until an agreement was reached. The five riflemen with the long rifles must stand twenty paces farther back; they must shoot at eighty yards as against sixty for the shorter European type. When the loading of rifles was in progress, the five men with the long rifles were the center of attraction. They were perhaps Peter Leaman, Peter Gonter, Matthias Roesser, Joel Ferree and Stenzel, or perhaps Albright or Philip Lefevre, Volvert or possibly Franck—we cannot say who, but both traditional and historical evidence seems to point toward these early smiths as above mentioned. At all events there were five long guns, and they were on trial, to be judged by their work.

As the loading progressed, an intense interest centered on all rifles of this new type, but especially so with two having hinged brass boxes in the stocks.

"Them boxes don't have flints in," exclaimed an onlooker. "No, no," came from several other voices.

These two riflemen, having poured a charge of powder down the long, slender barrels, opened the brass hinged boxes from the stock, and from one came a square greased piece of linen. From the other was taken a round piece of dressed buckskin. These, in each instance, were laid square in the center of the muzzles of the rifle, a ball placed in the center, the head of the hickory rod placed on the ball, and with a couple of downward strokes, the round leaden missile slid down the rifled barrel and rested on the powder charge, some fine powder poured into the pan, and the load was complete.

By this time the excited onlookers nearly swept the two riflemen from their feet in order to get a better view of their mysterious weapons. Fortunately, the order came to commence firing, and immediately the contestants assumed their positions at the shooting benches, which were well arranged for rest work, benches that conformed to the specifications of match conditions.

The first to be called were those shooting at sixty yards, and it took perhaps three hours to finish this stage of the match, as many of the contestants shot the limit of three blocks, one shot to each block for center. When the eighty-rod relay was called, the five riflemen previously cited responded promptly, fully realizing that they were not only the center of attraction, but also that great things were expected of them. By their acts they would be known in the future.

This ordeal was nerve-racking in the extreme, and had its effect on possibly two of the number. But when the last shot was fired, word came down the targets that twelve hits had been made in fifteen shots fired. A dead stillness pervaded the camp. Every participant knew that all records were broken.

Never in history had it been done before, but there was still one remaining hope for the less fortunate riflemen: the prizes would be won by the bullets that hit nearest the cross center lines, and possibly these shots were not centered well; but, alas, the measurements brought little comfort, for it was found that the three bullets nearest the center were credited to the long rifles, and the giant ox was won by the rifleman who used a greasy buckskin patch.

Just who he was we are unable to say, and it is regrettable. With the close of the first day's shoot came a mighty protest from the host of unfortunates whose skill was so greatly handicapped by the inaccuracy of their weapons. So great was this protest that the management was obliged to announce that on the following day no long-barreled rifle would be allowed to enter the contest, and although the long rifles were eliminated from the second stage of the match, their triumph was complete. Their superiority of accuracy was never questioned; but were they a practical weapon, would the small ball with its light powder charge stop a deer, or bear, or would it merely inflict a wound?

There was a division of opinion on this point, with the majority clinging to the belief that the new rifle with its 40 balls to the pound was too light for a hunting arm. Strictly a target rifle, they said. However, a test on the wolf drive that was to follow would be of great interest; and the results of the drive demonstrated the entire practicability of the new rifles which under actual hunting conditions proved worthy of the confidence of their makers.

How few people of the present generation realize the problems that confronted the pioneer in his conquest of the American wilderness that seemed endless in extent! Dangers, difficulties and inconveniences were all his, but a long immunity from civilized environment made him a man of iron and qualified him for the arduous duties of his calling.

Of the numerous inconveniences ever endured by the American pioneer in his wanderings through the wilderness or even when in full enjoyment of his cabin comforts, that of kindling and conserving fire was a matter of no small concern, for it must be borne in mind that matches as we know them today were unknown in pioneer times and are a comparatively modern idea.

In Colonial America, as in Europe, the flint and steel were used in generating the spark to be fanned into flame. In producing a spark by flint and steel two methods were in general use.

The first seems to have been the steel ring or clasp. This form was operated by simply grasping the steel in one hand and striking it violently against a chunk of flint held by the other. The scraping of the metal against the flint would throw a volume of sparks downward into a quantity of linen tow or lint that had been so arranged as to receive them—thus forming a coal.

The second method that seems to have been of a much later origin was a feature embracing the lock principle of the flint-gun, the lock proper being nearly identical. There was no powder used, but instead a box-like receptacle filled with a highly inflammable material called "tinder" was so arranged that the shower of sparks fell into this receptacle, creating a live coal. This contrivance was called a tinder box. When a fire was once established on the cabin hearth it was, as a rule, kept constantly burning. Fire wood was everywhere in abundance and labor was not a consideration with the settler.

His methods of keeping a fire overnight were very simple. Half an hour before retiring a few chunks of hardwood were placed against the back log. When these were reduced to live coals they were scraped together well up against the back log, then with the fire shovel a covering of ashes to the depth of two or three inches would insure a good bed of coals for the next morning; but in this connection I will say there were families that possessed no means for producing fire and when a fire was to be started they would take a tin pan or other metal holder and go to a neighbor and borrow (as they termed it) a bunch of live coals, carry them home to build a fire; and here I must add that within the past twoscore years there were people yet living who could recall witnessing such events as above described. An old lady once told me of a great forest fire in Eastern Pennsylvania that was started by a colored girl carelessly dropping coals from her fire pan while going from the neighbors to her cabin home. This occurrence was perhaps as late as 1830.

The tinder box was a rather expensive article and not often possessed by the poorer class of settlers. Now, so much for the flint and steel, so much for the tinder box with its several refinements; but the American pioneer was by no means baffled even though he possessed neither of these fire-producing features of the fatherland. For so long as his old reliable flint-gun hung on its wooden hooks by the fireside he was possessed of an infallible fire producer, be it either rifle or smooth-bore it made no difference. His method of getting results for the same can be told in the following words: when the gun was found to be empty the hammer was brought to full cock, the frizzen steel pushed forward and the pan left fully exposed. Then the pioneer took from his hunting bag a small wad of unspun flax, or tow as it was called. From this he made a small tight wad just large enough to fill the pan. He then poured from his horn-pan a few grains of powder upon this flaxen wad. The frizzen was then clamped back to its place, the trigger pulled, then a flash, and the flax wad was burnt into a glowing coal. This coal was quickly dropped into a bunch of dry matter prepared for the occasion, and easily fanned to a flame.

The hunter and explorer used the flint-gun exclusively for fire starting. If his gun was loaded, he simply made a tight plug with a long shank, then poured the powder from the pan of the rifle and inserted the slender plug tight into the touch hole and used the flax pad, as above described. When the coal was removed the plug was pulled out, the pan refilled with powder, and the arm was again ready for action. In using the flint-arm for such purposes as here described, great care had to be exercised to prevent accidents. Sometimes guns were improperly examined and contained a charge when thought empty. A badly scared family or a mutilated wall or ceiling was apt to follow the mistake, and here I must add that to this day there are old log houses still standing in Pennsylvania in which unmistakable evidence of this form of accident is plainly visible in the vicinity of the old open fireplace. A load of shot through the board ceiling, or perhaps a bullet hole in the mantel, bears mute testimony to an accident of the long ago.

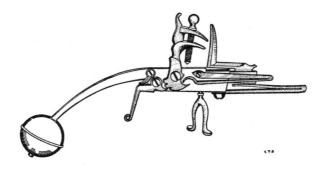

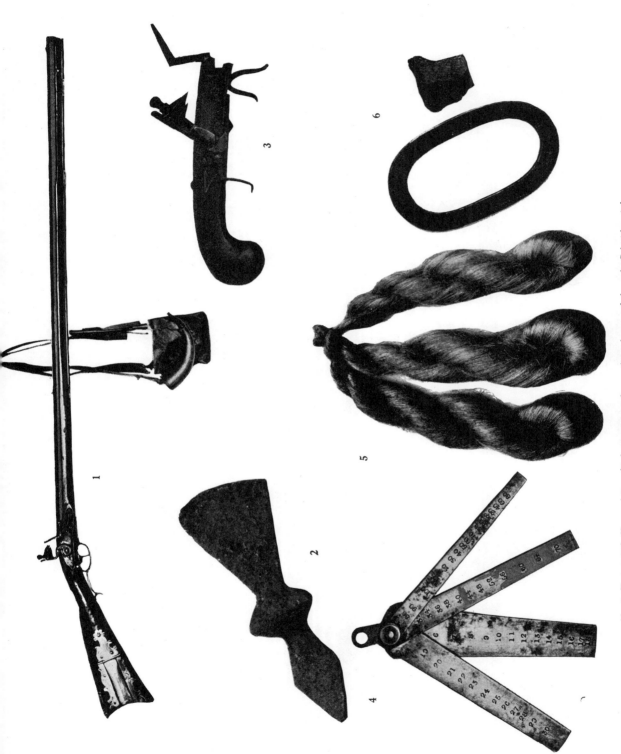

No. 1. Trescott Rifle Horn and Bag; this bag contains 2 brass military buttons of the early Colonial period.
No. 2 is a very early Tomahawk made for the Indian trader, by early rifle smiths. It is made of soft iron, in 2 pieces and welded together. This Tomahawk was found not many years ago in the Blue Mountain district of Pennsylvania, in the woods and almost on the surface. It is a rare piece.
No. 3 is a flint-lock for starting fire. Very fine lint is placed in the receptacle in front of the hammer, the sparks falling in form a coal which is easily fanned into flames.
No. 4. Barrel gauge by George Schalk.
No. 5. Unspun flax, used for swabbing bore.
No. 6. Flint and steel firestriker.

(Plate 67)

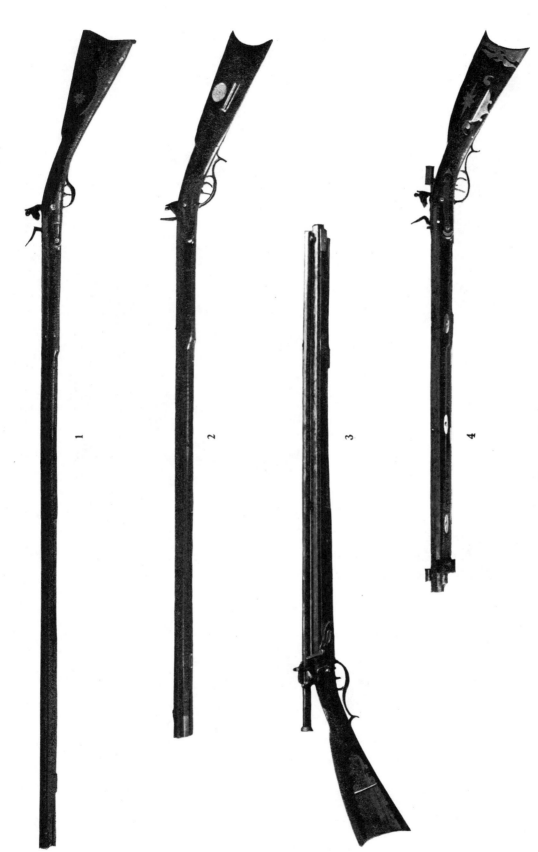

1   2   3   4

DILLIN COLLECTION

No. 1. By Isaac Haines; 71½ inches over all; 56½-inch half octagon barrel; 40 balls to the pound; full maple stock, on which lion is carved; weight 9½ pounds; excellent workmanship; a very early rifle, possibly before 1740.

No. 2. By S. Spangler; 60½ inches over all; 45½-inch full octagon barrel; 60 balls to the pound; sett triggers; weight 11¼ pounds; a splendid specimen of the heavy hunting type.

No. 3. By J. Beck; 53 inches over all; 38-inch full octagon barrel; rigged with long brass tubes, mounted with peep and globe sights; a typical match rifle, period of 1800.

No. 4. By Thomas Cherrington, Cattawissa, Pa.; 48 inches over all; 38¼-inch full octagon barrel; equipped with piston bullet starter, such as was used by Schalk Pope and other renowned riflesmiths; also has peep and globe sights; weight 12¾ pounds; wonderful specimen of the late flint-lock period.

(Plate 68)

Triggers and Sights of
Flint-lock Days

CHAPTER ELEVEN

THE early American hunter invariably used plain open sights, both front and rear, fixed to the barrel by a grooved slide which permitted of horizontal adjustment. The sights were so set that the rifle actually shot a trifle high up to at least fifty yards. Somewhere between fifty and one hundred yards the ball reached its maximum height and at one hundred yards the force of gravity caused a drop of about three inches. Thus it was a point-blank gun up to one hundred yards. The pin head was the standard front sight for match shooting, a variety of devices being used for rear sights. One is a small drum-like appliance, mounted on a post screwed into the small of the stock. To raise or lower this sight it was only necessary to turn the screw end of the post. The drum was one and one-half inches long, closed at both ends by discs, punctured in line by a fine opening. A second type shows a plain piece of metal about the size of a half-dollar, mounted on a post and pierced with a tiny hole for a peep. A third was a hood both front and rear, the rear hood being about one and one-quarter inches long, divided in the centre by a circular plate containing a peep hole to act in conjunction with the front pin head. The rear hood was enclosed in a clamp, fitted with a screw in the top and wooden wedges underneath by which the vertical elevation was regulated.

Other match rifles were rigged with open sights and sunshades such as appear on the Kauffman rifle in Plate No. 78. These gave a very good definition and were used by many riflemen.

The examination of numerous specimens of flint-lock rifles used in shooting matches has failed to give any proof that the early riflemen were using actual telescopic sights. There was, however, a very popular device consisting of a long tube made of brass or iron, and extending the full length of the barrel. It was, as a rule, from three-eighths to five-eighths inches in diameter, clamped to a sliding base at each end to permit of horizontal adjustment, and in many of the heavy match rifles the rear slide was in the form of an arm which extended back to near the end of the tube and supported it. Directly under this arm at the rear, which is flat, there is set vertically in the breech tang a screw, so drilled that, by the insertion of an iron pin, it may be turned to regulate the elevation of the piece. The tube was fitted with an eye cup containing the peep-hole and at the fore or muzzle end there was a small, well-formed pin head sight set to a little below point-blank aim. No glass was used in the tube, and while in reality there is no magnifying power in this tubular feature, it served a good purpose by causing an intense concentration upon the object aimed at, and a clearer definition.

The Continental Congress, in 1776, authorized the purchase of telescopes for rifles, but it is doubtful if they were telescopes in a literal sense. It is far more likely that they were the tubular sights spoken of above which were in use up to the concluding days of the flint-lock rifle.

As a matter of general interest it may be mentioned that telescopes were occasionally used on percussion rifles during the Civil War. These appliances were long, slender tubes with a very small field but rather high magnification.

Wind gauges, as we now understand them, were rarely used. During the past ten years and after a careful inspection of probably six hundred early American rifles, only two instances have been found where wind gauges had been fitted to the rifle.

One of these rifles was a very beautiful arm of the regular hunting type that had been made about 1820. It had a hooded front sight with pin head. The octagon of the barrel which formed the base was highly polished and a long, well-cut arrow marked the center, on each side of which were five neatly cut lines about one-eighth of an inch long and one-sixteenth of an inch wide, similar to those used at the present time. In the centre of the hood at the base there was a slender, needle-like feature extending upward about one-eighth of an inch, forming the guide. There was no screw, the adjustment being made with a mallet and punch. This was a wind gauge from a modern standpoint, lacking only the slide base and screw.

Another specimen to come under observation is a flintlock of a late date fitted with what is literally a rear wind gauge. This sight is shown on Plate No. 72. This appliance is in the form of a brass drum, one and one-fourth inches long by three-fourths of an inch in diameter, and threaded at both ends. A brass cup is fitted tightly into each end reaching nearly to the center. An iron disc, pierced with a peep-hole, is set in the middle of the drum, being held in position by the two caps, in each of which is a central aperture of about one-quarter of an inch in diameter. The base has a slide and screw working on the exact principle of a modern rear wind gauge, the base being fixed to a square iron post which sits in the small of the stock and brings the sight very close to the eye. There are no graduated lines.

Both plain and sett triggers are found upon Kentucky rifles, this to a certain extent being determined by the age of the piece—since more sett triggers were found on the later types—but more often the type of trigger was decided by personal preference.

The primary use of the sett trigger is so well known to riflemen as to need no detailed description or explanation. It was evidently of very early origin, having been fitted to the cross bow, undoubtedly, far in advance of its use on the rifle of Central Europe. The oldest rifle ever seen by the author, and made (as determined by an English authority) about 1525, is equipped with this appliance, and its use was constant down to the time of the development of the American rifle. In spite of this fact, however, careful examination of many early specimens of the American arm shows that the sett trigger was rarely applied to that weapon prior to about 1770.

After the Revolution and until the end of flint-lock days, the sett trigger was very much in evidence, perhaps forty per cent of the total number of rifles made being so equipped.

In the early days it is not likely that the sett trigger was considered necessary, or even practical, by the American hunter, but later it seems entirely probable that the expert rifleman in his race for supremacy in marksmanship demanded, as he would today, the best appliance known to the riflesmith.

The hunters of the late flint-lock and the entire percussion period used many sett trigger rifles, some of them being supplied with the type of lock which cannot be fired unless the trigger is set. In using the sett trigger in the woods, the rifle was, as a rule, carried at full cock, and upon discovery of game the trigger was quickly set while the rifle was being brought to the shoulder.

Now a word as to trigger guards.

That the long American rifle came to meet new requirements we have already stated, and it seems very safe to add that of the numerous weak points that prevailed in the rifle of Central Europe—the arm from which our American rifle was evolved—there was none that was more pronounced than the feature known as trigger guard and none that called louder for a radical change of pattern. The trigger guard of Europe was so poorly adapted to meet the requirements of the American pioneer in his invasion of the wilderness that a change must have been quickly demanded. The old rifle has a guard, huge in proportion and weak in construction, a constant menace in the forest and which with rough usage would have fallen short of its purpose.

As proof that this change came early, we will simply call attention to the rifle shown in our illustration of the evolution, Plate No. 10. It is dated 1728, and we here find the low heavy guard in its full development. We also find it in the 1746 Roesser, and in each instance it combines strength and grace, in marked contrast to the time-honored monstrosity of the European rifle; thus it can be truthfully said that the cast brass, file-dressed trigger guard was the product of the early colonial gunsmith, and like the eight-pointed metal star ornament, was born with the American rifle and lasted until the end of the flint-lock period.

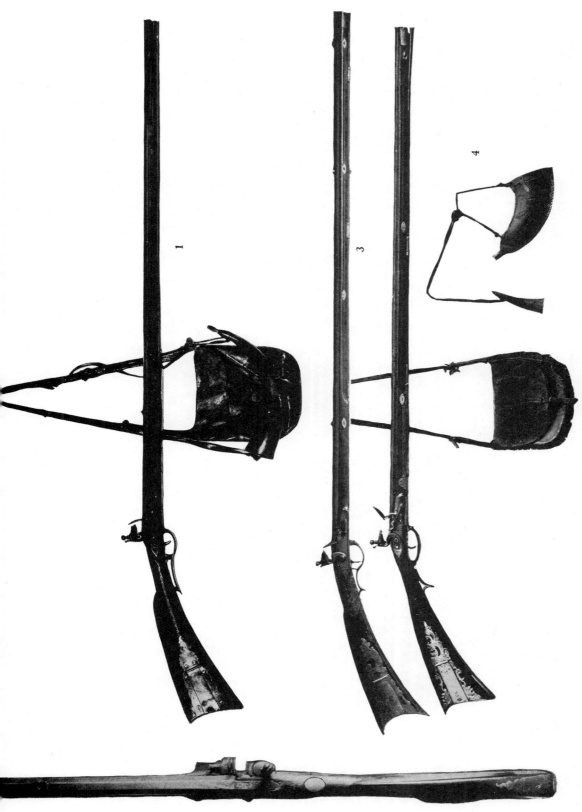

The Early Roesser and Two Later Rifles

No. 1. By Matthias Roesser, Lancaster, Pa.; dated 1746; 59 inches over all; 44-inch half octagon barrel; originally about .42 calibre; small wrist type; weight 8 pounds; bust of Indian engraved on upper butt plate; very handsome piece. (From the Dillin Collection.)

No. 2. Stock of Roesser rifle showing inlay bust of Indian, with heart on left chest suggestive of target.

No. 3. Unidentified; 56½ inches over all; 41½-inch full octagon barrel; .45 calibre; artistically decorated; period of about 1810. (From the Dillin Collection.)

No. 4. Unidentified; 54½ inches over all; 39½-inch full octagon barrel; weight 8¼ pounds; highly decorated; period of about 1800. (From the Van Rensselaer Collection.)

(Plate 69)

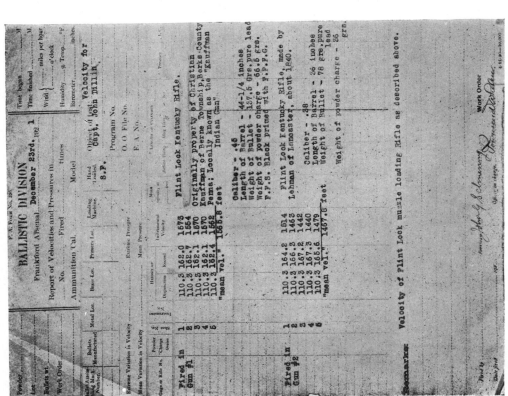

The Remington Arms Union Metallic Cartridge Company

INCORPORATED

FIREARMS AND AMMUNITION

REMINGTON ILION WORKS

ILION, N.Y.

Ilion, N. Y., September 20, 1917.

Mr. J. G. Dillin,

Dear Sir:-

As I stated in my letter to you dated September 10th, your small muzzle-loading rifle was shipped from Bridgeport September 12th and your two big rifles from Ilion September 10th. This in response to your post card of August 29th, requesting that these guns start back to you not later than September 12th.

I hope that all three guns reach you in time and also in good order. Kindly let me know in case they did not.

Due to the fact that we had to return these guns unexpectedly we were able to make velocity tests on the small rifle only. These were as follows:

Average velocity over 55 feet. . . . . . . 1305 ft. per second

Muzzle velocity. . . . . .1483 "

Muzzle energy. . . . . 239 ft. lbs.

Velocity at 100 yds. . . . . 850 ft. per second

Energy. . . . . 79 ft. lbs.

Velocity at 200 yds. . . . . 617 ft. per second

Energy. . . . . 41 ft. lbs.

The round balls .52 inch in diameter weigh 49 grains. Powder charge as given by the measure 22 grains of black powder.

The above information is highly interesting and is probably unique as we have no record of velocities having been measured for flint lock rifles.

Again thanking you for the courtesy of loaning us these guns, I am,

Very truly yours,

JDP:IEW

F. A. Form No. 290

BALLISTIC DIVISION

Frankford Arsenal   December 23rd, 192 1

Report of Velocities and Pressures in ......

Object of test: Velocity for Capt. John Dillin,

Flint Lock Kentucky Rifle.

Fired in Gun #1   Originally property of Christian Kauffman of Berne Township, Berks County Penna; Locally known as the "Kauffman Indian Gun"

Caliber - .45
Length of Barrel - 44-1/4 inches
Weight of Bullet - 137.5 Grs. pure lead
Weight of powder charge - 66.5 grs.
F.F.S. Black primed with F.F.F.G.

Shot No.			Instrumental Velocity
1	110.3	162.0	1673
2	110.3	162.7	1654
3	110.3	162.1	1570
4	110.3	162.4	1562
5			

"mean vel." 1565.8 feet

Fired in Gun #2   Flint Lock Kentucky Rifle, made by Lehman of Lancaster, about 1840.

Caliber - .38
Length of Barrel - 36 inches
Weight of Bullet - 78 grs. pure lead
Weight of powder charge - 35 grs.

Shot No.			Instrumental Velocity
1	110.3	164.2	1614
2	110.3	166.3	1463
3	110.3	167.2	1442
4	110.3	167.3	1440
5	110.3	166.6	1479

"mean vel." 1487.8 feet

Remarks: Velocity of Flint Lock muzzle loading Rifle as described above.

Velocity tests of flint-lock rifles. (See text.)

(Plate 70)

Powder, Bullets,
Velocities and Penetration

CHAPTER TWELVE

HE muzzle-loading rifle, carrying a round bullet of soft lead propelled by powder which was far from uniform in grade and which in fact gave different ballistics with almost every shot, cannot possibly compare in penetration with the modern, high-power rifle firing a jacketed pointed projectile or a solid bullet made of an alloy vastly harder than lead.

The powder with which the early flintlocks were charged was, until the establishment of powder mills in this country, a commodity coming from various sources, mostly French or British, with consequent variety in character. A small percentage was even home-made. Yet strange as it may seem, this powder, which even by early nineteenth-century standards was very poor, gave good accuracy at the ranges over which the pioneer shot.

While there are few if any available records of powder statistics prior to 1800, it is well established that a fair grade of powder was developed in this country during the first quarter of the nineteenth century, both by private and Government sources.

Under date of April 24, 1827, the commanding officer of Frankford Arsenal reported upon a series of tests made with several samples of black powder. The report reads:

"Arsenal, Frankford, April 24, 1827.

"It is with much pride and satisfaction I communicate to you the result of a series of experiments made upon several samples of powder which you furnished me for that purpose, together with that manufactured by Messrs. du Pont de Nemours & Co., of Brandywine.

"I say that I am proud to communicate these results, not only because they fully prove that our powder is the best in the world, but they enable me to do justice to the manufacturers, who from their care and enterprise have not only been able to compete with, but have actually, in a few years, outdone all Europe in this important article. This is a pretty bold assertion, but it is nevertheless true.

"I speak without prejudice, and although I have invariably given the preference to domestic articles, when of as good a quality and at as reasonable prices as foreign, still I have never boasted of so much patriotism as to give a high price for an inferior article because made at home.

"There is certainly no nation in the world whose manufactures, in general, have so justly become celebrated as Great Britain, and in no article, perhaps, more than in gunpowder. The French powder has been highly spoken of, but by experiments made upon what is called 'King's powder,' made expressly for the King of France and his court, and which is doubtless the best made in France, it has been found not to bear comparison with Pegou, Andrews & Wilkes, which is no doubt the best foreign powder ever introduced into this country.

"The annexed table will show the result of the experiments which were made upon an improved Eprovette for the proof of fine sporting powder. This Eprovette is nothing more than a small chamber capable of containing about the charge for a patent breech fowling-piece, placed in a vertical position so that the action of the powder is upwards; when loaded, a weight of about four pounds, attached to a lever, is let down so as to cover the chamber. To the movable end of the lever, a graduated ribbon is so attached that when explosion takes place the weight is thrown up, taking with it the ribbon, which passes through a small slide; the weight, of course, again falls to its place, but the ribbon is held by the slide at the point to which the force of the powder carried the weight.

GUNPOWDER TABLE

Description of Powder	1st Range in Degrees	2nd Range in Degrees	3rd Range in Degrees	Mean Range in Degrees	Remarks
Pegou, Andrews & Wilkes					
single seal	82	81	82	82	
double seal	95	84	95	91	
canister	110	105	105	107	
Edinburgh	93	93	93	93	
London*	78	82	82	81	
Du Pont de Nemours & Co.	112	115	119	115	Being a degree stronger than Pegou, Andrews & Wilkes' Canister.

*The London powder is said to be of an inferior quality to the Edinburgh.

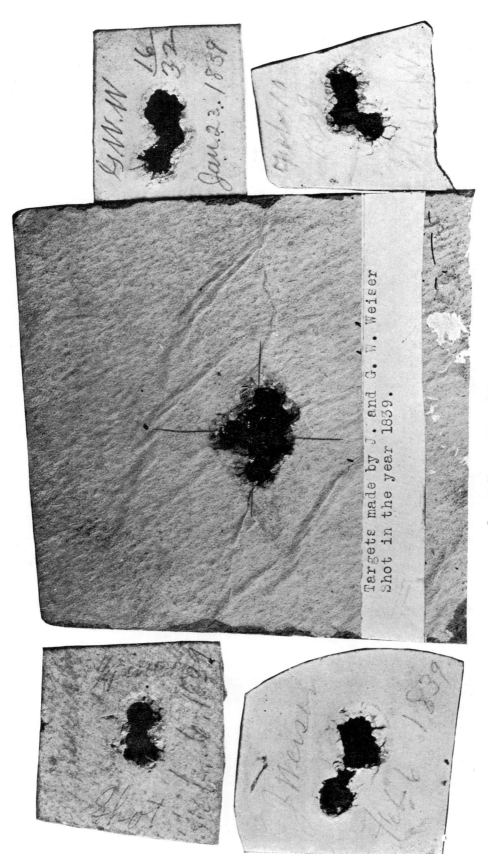

OTHER EARLY MATCH RELICS

(Plate 71)

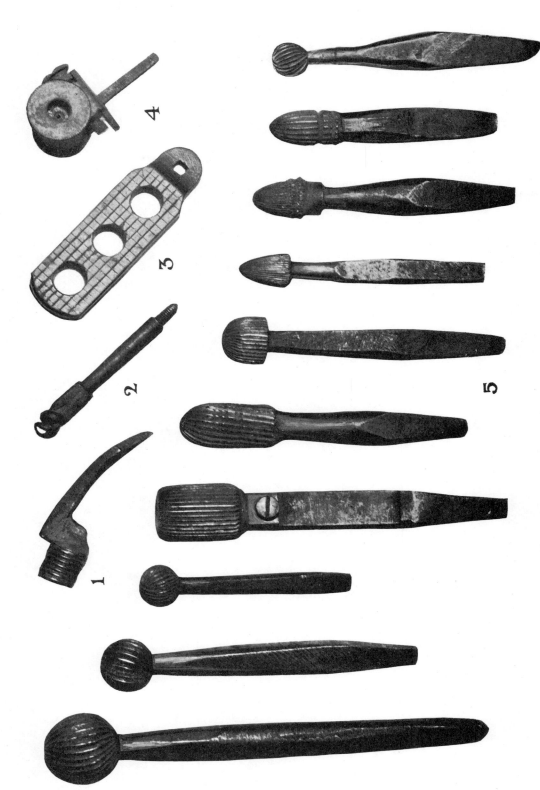

No. 1. Tang and breach plug of muzzle-loading rifle.
No. 2. Worm of ramrod used for swabbing bore.
No. 3. Loading block for patched ball. This block saves considerable time.
No. 4. Peep sight and wind gauge used on a flint-lock rifle.
No. 5. Cherries for making bullet moulds. The mould form is first made in duplicate. A cherry is then placed between the parts, which are then placed in a vise. As the cherry is turned with a brace the vise is tightened, sinking the cherry into the softer iron and forming the cup or mould into which the lead is poured.
(All illustrations three-quarter actual size.)

(Plate 72)

"By this it will be seen that du Pont's powder is eight degrees stronger than the best sample of foreign, namely, Pegou, Andrews & Wilkes.

"Having tested the strength, I shall now proceed to show the quickness of the different samples, as proved by a machine invented by Mr. A. du Pont. The manner of testing quickness upon this machine is both simple and satisfactory. It is nothing more than burning a train of twelve feet, or one hundred and forty-four inches, of each of the two samples to be tried; these trains are laid parallel to each other; and the board being graduated, you see plainly the comparative quickness of each sample. The following is the result of these experiments; du Pont taken as the standard, one hundred and forty-four.

GUNPOWDER TABLE

Description of Powder	Inches	Description of Powder	Inches	Difference in Favor of Du Pont's Inches
Du Pont's	144	Pegou, Andrews & Wilkes double seal	96	48
Du Pont's	144	canister	103	41
Du Pont's	144	Edinburgh	128	16
Du Pont's	144	London	102	42

"By this it will be seen that there exists a still greater difference in favour of du Pont's powder over the foreign, in point of quickness than in that of strength. When we consider the difference between one hundred and forty-four and one hundred and three, we will perceive that du Pont's powder burns nearly one-third faster than Pegou, Andrews & Wilkes' justly celebrated canister. The Edinburgh powder comes nearest du Pont's in point of quickness, burning as one hundred and twenty-eight to one hundred and forty-four, making a difference of one-ninth in favour of du Pont's; although it falls far short of Pegou, Andrews & Wilkes' in strength.

"I must also remark that the residuum in burning all these powders is much greater than in du Pont's, consequently the latter also possesses the quality of cleanliness in a greater degree than the others."

The round, soft-lead bullets of pioneer days, when alloys as applied to projectiles were practically unknown, were sometimes fired without a patch—the piece of greased linen or buckskin in which the ball was wrapped—but as a general rule the patch was used, and all available data would lead to the assumption that the patch as an indispensable accessory did not come into general use until its acceptance by American riflesmiths.

The early Swedish hunters are credited with a knowledge of the value of patching the ball, but there is no evidence to support the fact that such practice was in general use. It is also possible that the German rifle makers were aware of the principle of the patch but any certain information is lacking.

An examination of numerous German and Swiss rifles of early manufacture shows no evidence whatever that greased patches were used, the box in the stock in which the American invariably carried his grease, or greased patches, being found, with one exception, dry and absolutely free from any indication of grease, and there are the strongest suggestions that these boxes were merely used for storage of bullets, flints, and small tools. Again, the European rifles were nearly always supplied with iron ramrods instead of the wooden rod so necessary for proper loading with patch and ball. Such iron rods were not supplied with a worm for swabbing.

From specimens of early bullets that have occasionally been found—notably those recovered from the Kings Mountain battlefield with a consequent authentic dating of 1780, and two recovered from Indian graves in Tennessee—and also numerous bullet moulds as well as "cherries" used in cutting the moulds, a clear idea of the Kentucky rifle ball may be gained.

During the summer of 1922 two Indian graves were opened in the State of Tennessee. They were located on an island in the Tennessee River; near the center of each grave a bullet was found, as is here shown by photograph, and it is needless to say that these two balls came from the bodies of the Indians there buried. Lead oxidizes but does not disintegrate, hence the perfect preservation of these specimens. A remarkable feature is in the fact that both bullets seem to have been shot without a patch, as the lands of the rifle barrel are well cut into each ball. This would not likely have happened had a patch been used in a regular way. The following explanation is perhaps a correct one. Many of our early hunters had two moulds for their rifle: one for the ball that used a patch, this being smaller than the bore; another to cast a ball of groove-deep diameter. This latter ball was shot naked and used only when quick action was necessary, an emergency bullet in reality, for it could be seated on the powder in half the time required when the regular patch was used. As a matter of reason extreme accuracy could not be expected, but it was a proper ball for a desperate encounter. In the instance of these two bullets here shown, it is in order to call attention to the similarity in size, also to mention the fact that the mark of the rifling is exactly the same. All this seems to strongly suggest that both Indians were shot with the same rifle. We have photographed a measuring rule with the bullets. This will serve the purpose of showing their exact measure. It is regrettable that there are no records or even

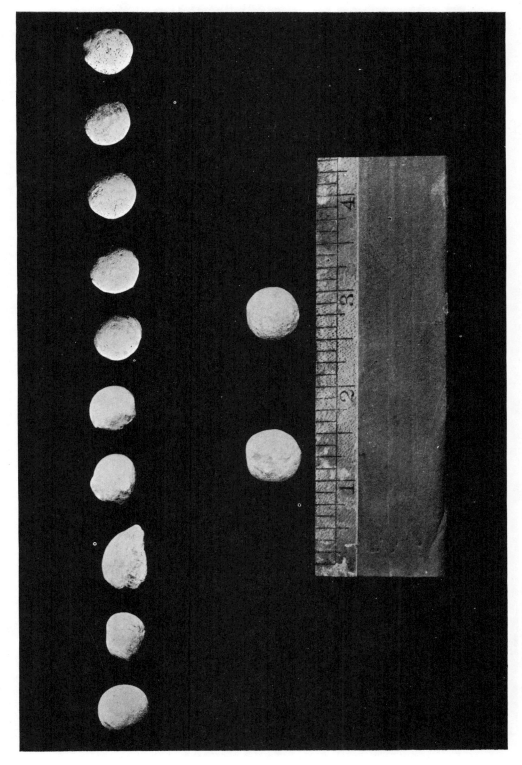

BULLETS OF THE AMERICAN PIONEER RIFLEMAN

Above: Ten bullets recovered from the battlefield of Kings Mountain.
Below: Two bullets recovered from Indian graves.

(Plate 73)

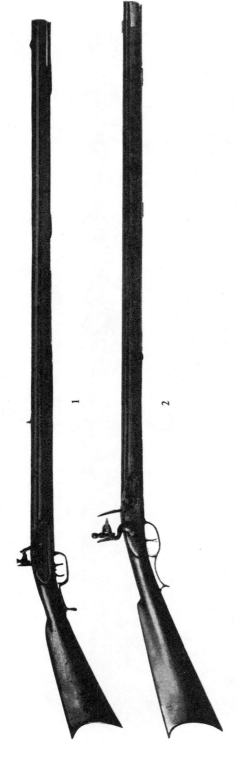

Two Excellent Examples
of Southern Kentuckys

No. 1. The Alexander Clege rifle used by him at Kings Mountain, October 7, 1780. Length of barrel 48 inches; calibre .50; weight 10 pounds. Now the property of William Critchfield, of Chattanooga, Tenn., who is a lineal descendant of its former owner. Note the hole in the stock for grease.

No. 2. Simon Kenton's rifle, one of the best specimens extant of the single-trigger southern-type weapon. This rifle was Kenton's mainstay during many years of frontier and wilderness life. Kenton, a Virginian, fled across the Kentucky frontier in 1770, erroneously believing he had killed a rival. Under the name of Simon Butler, assumed to escape recognition, he was almost constantly in conflicts with the Indians from that time until the treaty of Greenville was signed, and probably figured in more expeditions against the red men with more consequent narrow escapes than any man of his time.

In 1778, Kenton joined Alexander Montgomery and George Clark in a foray to obtain Indian horses. Having achieved their purpose, they were pursued by the Indians; Montgomery was killed and scalped, Clark escaped and Kenton was taken prisoner and forced to "run the gantlet." Surviving this ordeal, he was sentenced to death, and on his way to the designated place of execution he was taken to two Indian villages and compelled to run the gantlet with consequent severe beatings at each town. His life was saved only through the intervention of the notorious Simon Gerty.

But after living among these Indians for a time Kenton was again made prisoner in revenge for the Indian defeat at Wheeling and a second council again sentenced him to death. On this occasion the payment of a heavy ransom resulted in the Indians surrendering him to the British and he remained at Detroit as a prisoner of war until his escape a year later.

Kings Mountain Battlefield Where Col. Ferguson Fell

(Plate 74)

traditional history to give us facts of the tragedy of which these two rifle balls are the grim reminders.

The Kings Mountain bullets—twelve balls which were recovered by Walter M. Cline, of Tennessee, and which weigh from 180 to 300 grains—show conclusively the type of bullet used by the pioneers who figured in this memorable battle. Some idea of the killing power of these bullets can be gained from an excerpt from "The History of the British Army," by Hon. J. W. Fortescue.

The account says that Major Ferguson "on the 6th of October, chose a strong position on a hill known as Kings Mountain, and turned at bay.

"This hill was covered with tall forest, beneath which the ground was strewn with huge boulders, while on one side it was rendered absolutely inaccessible by a precipice; and Ferguson seems never to have dreamed that he could not hold it forever. On the following afternoon the advance party of the backwoodsmen arrived about a thousand strong and, having tied up their horses and divided themselves into three bodies, began to ascend the hill from three sides. Creeping up in silence, every man confident of his skill as a stalker and a marksman, the central division made its way up to the crest, where Ferguson met them with a volley and a charge with the bayonet.

"The backwoodsmen then fell back slowly, keeping their pursuers in check by a biting fire from behind the trees and boulders, until a storm of bullets in Ferguson's flank showed that a second division of his enemies was lying in wait for him. Turning at once upon them, Ferguson found that the third division of backwoodsmen, which had been hidden on the opposite flank, was firing steadily into his rear.

"Thus entrapped, the Militia found the odds too many against them. Still they fought hard until Ferguson was killed; and nearly four hundred of them had fallen killed and wounded before the remainder, rather more than seven hundred, laid down their arms.

"The whole loss of the backwoodsmen was eighty-eight killed and wounded, and the only marvel is that it should have been so great, for their exploit was as fine an example as can be found of the power of woodcraft, marksmanship, and sportsmanship in war. The victors celebrated their success by hanging a dozen of their prisoners before they dispersed, in revenge for the execution at Augusta of certain militiamen who had been taken in arms against the British after accepting service with them. The victims were of course Americans, for it was not Mother Country and Colonies, but two Colonial factions that fought so savagely in Carolina."

Recent experiments with a flint-lock rifle loaded with fifty-six grains of black powder and a ball weighing one hundred and fifty-nine grains gave a penetration of two and one-half inches into a backstop of very hard-seasoned chestnut planking at a distance of fifty feet from the muzzle. Examination of the ball, however, showed that it had not only been flattened badly but was actually torn to pieces, the fragments being driven deep into the pores of the wood in all directions, every evidence being that a bullet fired under such conditions would have great shocking power in animal tissue. A fifty-six-grain charge, giving an initial velocity of about 1600 feet, which is very high for an arm using black powder, showed a three-quarter-inch penetration in dry chestnut at three hundred yards, the ball being greatly flattened.

The velocities as shown in the reports reproduced in Plate No. 70 were recorded at a distance of 52 feet from the muzzles of the rifles, and therefore do not represent the actual initial velocity of the ball.

It is probable this would approximate 1600 feet and, while this is considered a high speed for this type of rifle, a still greater velocity could doubtless be obtained with a larger powder charge, which the barrels would safely fire. It is believed that the velocity could be brought up to nearly 2000 feet, but the charge used in the tests represented what would have been called "a full load" in pioneer days, giving the most accurate results to the experiments in accordance with the usages of the period of the guns.

The Flint-lock as a Practical Arm

CHAPTER THIRTEEN

TIME and again riflemen and collectors have asked whether the flint-lock rifle is a practical arm; how it compares with modern guns as a game-getter.

There is no dearth of evidence historical and contemporary to prove that the Kentucky, within the limits of its range, was entirely practical and worthy of the confidence reposed in it by the American pioneer.

While well-authenticated tradition is to be regarded as good corroborative testimony, the best evidence is found in actual experience.

In the winter of 1921, the Kauffman rifle shown in Plate No. 78, and known as Old Killdeer, was taken to a farm for a trial. There was no wild game in season, but the farmer gave permission to shoot his pigeons, the English starlings and the sparrows. The rifle was placed in the hands of a well-known, off-hand rifleman. A few shots fired at targets showed the gun to be accurate and reliable. During the day three shots were fired at pigeons roosting on the peak of a very high barn. One shot was a clean miss. The other two scored dead birds, both being shot through the neck. One was hit close to the head, the other at the junction of the neck with the body, probably two inches lower than the position of the first hit. In each case the rifleman called his shot in advance of picking up the dead birds, saying, "They are hit pretty high up as I aimed above the centre of the body." The distance was from 30 to 35 yards.

Attention was next given to the smaller birds, and during the day five shots were fired at starlings and sparrows. Three starlings and one sparrow were netted at a distance ranging from 15 to 40 yards, a total for the day of six dead birds in eight shots fired from a strictly offhand position. The performance was witnessed by four greatly interested spectators, who were at first very sceptical, but who at the conclusion of the firing exclaimed, "Hats off to the old rifle."

The following October the author took a good flint-lock rifle with him to Ontario and tried it out on wild ducks with these results:

A small lake just below the home of a friend was occasionally frequented by wild fowl. About 150 yards across this lake was a small island around which three ducks were swimming. The rifle was shot from a sitting position with slightly miscalculated allowance for the drop of the ball, which struck too high, resulting in a clean miss. The duck flew away badly scared. Later in the day more fowl appeared at the same spot, which proved a favorite feeding-place. This time the aim was a trifle lower and the ball passed almost squarely through the body.

With a third opportunity, which came about an hour or so later and under almost identical conditions, the duck was hit but escaped, the ball having disabled a wing.

The next day a rabbit pursued by a hound stopped long enough to lose an important part of his head at a distance of possibly 30 yards. This ended all shooting with a flint-lock for that trip, making a total of three hits in four shots.

A former owner of "Old Killdeer", a most reverend gentleman whose veracity is unquestioned, informed me that on a visit to a nearby farm he shot three large chicken hawks in three consecutive shots at a distance of about 125 yards. It was winter and the hawks had a habit of lighting on a dead tree about that distance from the barn. The clergyman was secreted behind good cover and fired from a prearranged rest, the distance requiring a high hold. On one occasion the wind was blowing very hard, his allowance for drift was too great, and the ball wounded the bird in the wing.

On several occasions the author has taken a flintlock on hunting trips but has never had the opportunity to try the guns on deer. In all firing, however, of either the flint rifle or shotgun during the past ten years, both have given entire satisfaction, the rifle with its long barrel being far less sensitive to faulty holding than the short-barrel rifles of the present day. This is noticeable when game often falls under a doubtful aim.

Undoubtedly there are many practical riflemen today who find keen enjoyment in the accuracy possibilities of the Kentucky rifle as a game-getter, if they could be located. One such—B. C. Broome, of Connecticut—in the December, 1923, number of *Outers' Recreation*, declared that a flint-lock rifle, vintage of 1820, is his favorite rifle.

" 'Old Hornet' and its pouch and horn mates," he said, "hang over my kitchen fireplace. Other guns are in my den but this one is always loaded, for here in the country are predatory hawks, foxes and woodchucks; and worst of all, ex-housecats gone wild. They all need to be stung and many are, for 'Old Hornet' may be an old insect but its sting is still going strong.

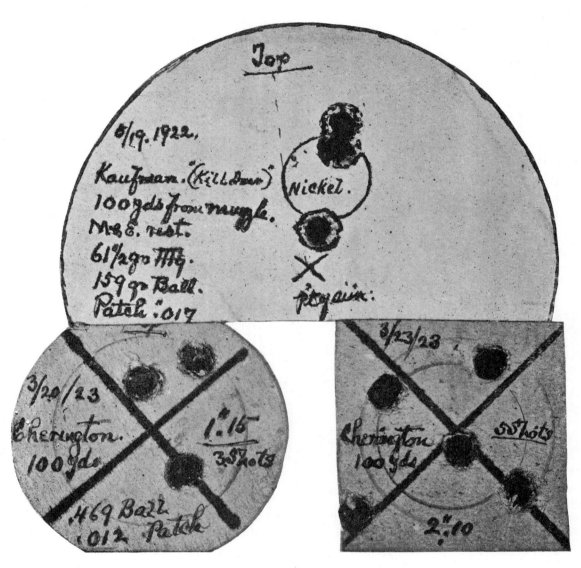

First Trial of "Old Killdeer"

Top: first target trial flint-lock rifle, "Old Killdeer;" self-explanatory.
Below: target trials with Cherrington flint-lock rifle; West Virginia, 1923; self-explanatory.

(Plate 75)

SECOND TRIAL OF "OLD KILLDEER"

Second target trial of flint-lock rifle, "Old Killdeer," at Essington Range. Five shots; 200 yards; muzzle and elbow rest; powder charge, 60 grs. FFFG; round ball weighing 159 grs.; drop of ball 39½ inches below aim.

(Plate 76)

'Old Hornet' will shoot with any gun I know of at 50 yards. At 75 yards it will keep up with many, but at 100 yards the light bullet is easily deflected by wind.''

Doubt has been cast by some writers upon the value of the early American rifle in battle, while others have made claims for its accuracy and deadly effect upon troops which have come down through the years as nothing short of miraculous. To fully demonstrate the possibilities of the weapons with which our ancestors so completely dominated the best troops of Europe, tests were arranged for, and, in company with Walter M. Cline, of Tennessee, were made with spiral-groove, straight-cut and smooth-bore rifles, the last named being a rifle, the accurate life of which was gone and which had been re-bored smooth. In each case the arm selected was in first-class condition and in all probability shot up to its original form.

The sizes of the several calibres ranged from .45 to .50. In each instance a greased patch was used for the ball, and the piece shot from muzzle rest. Distances were 100 yards, 200 yards, and 300 yards. A full charge of black powder was used, and round ball. The standard silhouette target represents the size of an average man.

Records were carefully kept of 10 shots with each type of rifle and were as follows:

At 100 yards, with spiral-groove rifle, number of hits, 10
   '' '' '' '' straight-cut '' '' '' '' 10
   '' '' '' '' smooth-bore '' '' '' '' 10
At 200 yards, with spiral-groove rifle, number of hits, 10
   '' '' '' '' straight-cut '' '' '' '' 5
   '' '' '' '' smooth-bore '' '' '' '' 4
At 300 yards, with spiral-groove rifle, number of hits, 5
   '' '' '' '' straight-cut '' '' '' '' 2
   '' '' '' '' smooth-bore '' '' '' '' 1

At any considerable distance beyond 300 yards the percentage of hits with any of these arms was small and in a great measure a matter of chance. The drop of the ball fired from a spiral-groove rifle of the above type at 200 yards is about 40 inches; at 300 yards approximately 6 feet. The straight-cut and the smooth-bore shoot a little flatter than the spiral-groove, which results in a few inches' less drop.

The penetration of bullets fired from any of these rifles at 300 yards, and even beyond that distance, was sufficient to kill, or put out of action, any one hit, and while both accuracy and trajectory beyond 200 yards are vastly inferior to those possessed by modern military arms, there can be no doubt, from the results obtained in the above tests, that the flintlock rifle was used with telling effect upon large bodies of troops in close formation.

The marksman of Revolutionary days, as well as the pioneer hunter, knew without question the effect of gravity upon rifle balls and constant experience had taught him the limits of accuracy. That the high officers of the Continental Army were convinced that the flint-lock was a practical battle arm is evidenced by the special rifles ordered by General Washington which were made in .70 caliber. They were heavy and strong in construction to fire safely a heavy charge of powder, and, as he wrote to his friend, would hit a sheet of 8 x 10 inch note paper at 80 rods three shots out of five.

And now, concerning the reliability of ignition, which as in all arms had much to do with the practical performances of the flint-lock.

If credence is placed in statements, so often quoted, concerning what may be appropriately called the freak actions of the old flint-lock rifle, a decision would be immediately reached that the guns of our ancestors were not only unreliable, but were mere apologies for weapons of either offense or defense. We are told that to fire one was a task; that it sputtered and threw fire into the face of the rifleman; and that the interval between the pan flash and the actual explosion was so great that the game would walk away unharmed. Other details are equally ridiculous and equally at variance with fact.

A flint-lock arm, if properly loaded and primed, is a most satisfactory weapon to handle. Like all other firearms it must be kept in order. In loading, the channel between the pan and the barrel must be kept clear, and the frizzen pick should be used after each shot. Just as the nipple of the percussion must be open, so must the channel of the flint-lock. Hang fires and misfires are unknown under these conditions, and having had a wide experience with both flint-lock and percussion, the author hesitates to give the claim for superiority to the latter system. Ignition by the percussion system was by no means infallible. Snaps and hang fires were quite common with some guns, which required considerable nursing, particularly in wet weather, and naturally both types were inferior to the breech-loader under such weather conditions.

With regard to the interval between the pan flash and the explosion, actual tests under exacting conditions have proved that it is so trifling as to be negligible; that there is no time to flinch and therefore no bad deliveries.

In a later chapter of the book, targets are shown which record the results of off-hand shooting. A glance at them should convince any rifleman that nothing whatever interfered with the holding of the marksman on these occasions. About the only advantage the percussion system had over the flint was that it was a trifle more economical, as it burned a little less

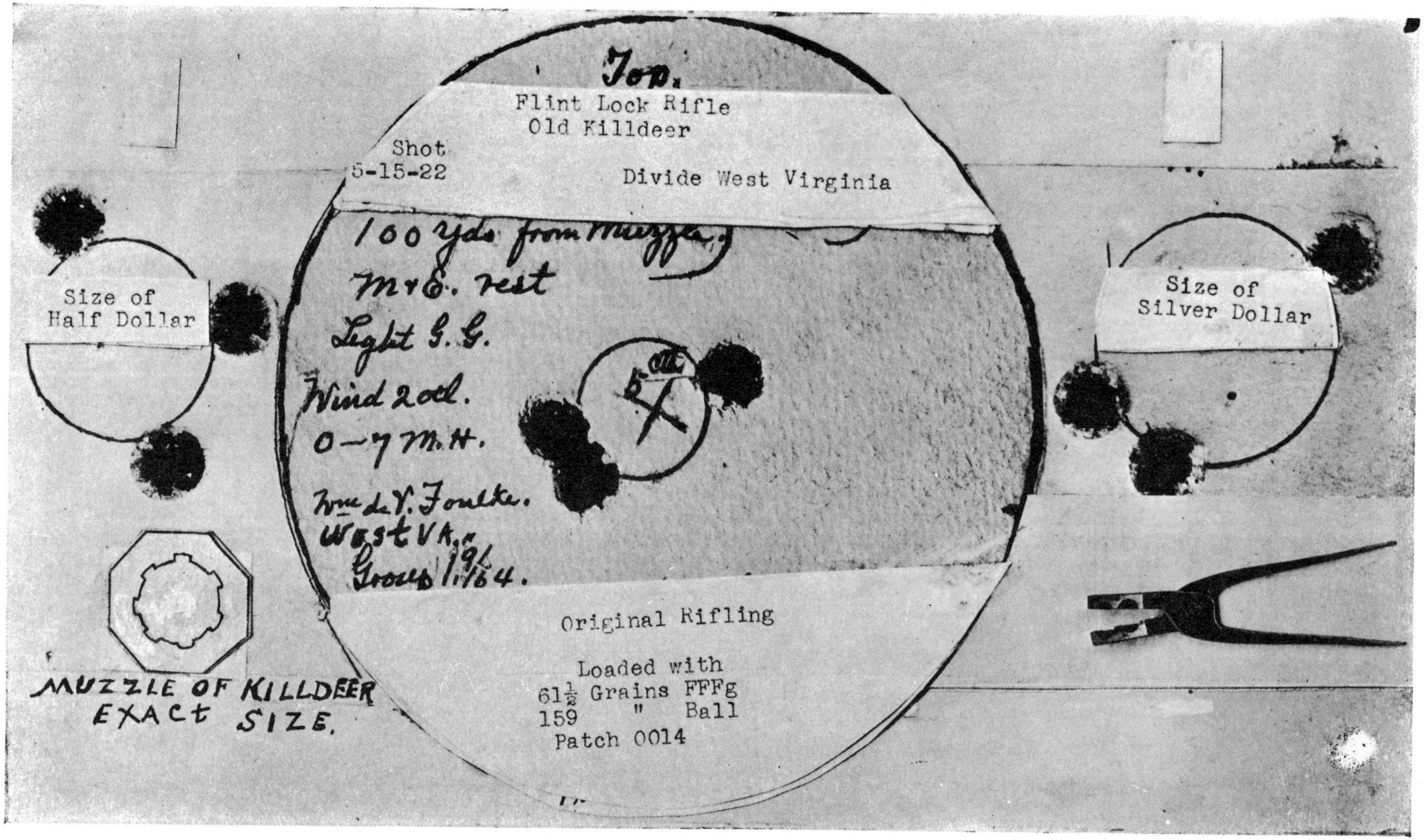

Top.

Flint Lock Rifle
Old Killdeer

Divide West Virginia

Shot.
5-15-22

160 yds from muzzle
M+O rest
Light S.S.
Wind 2 od.
0—7 m.H.
Fred Y. Foulke
West Va. 5.
Group 11/64.

Size of Silver Dollar

Size of Half Dollar

Original Rifling

Loaded with
61½ Grains FFFg
159 " Ball
Patch 0014

MUZZLE OF KILLDEER
EXACT SIZE.

MORE TARGETS MADE BY "OLD KILLDEER"

(Plate 77)

THE KAUFFMAN RIFLE—"OLD KILLDEER"

Apparently the work of Adam Smith, period of about 1760, evidenced by style of workmanship, etc.; length over all, 57 inches; full stocked with broad flamed curly maple, which has all the beauty of that in Stradivarius violins; the stock is embellished with low relief carving of artistic design, and fine execution; the coloring seems to have been done by the old soot and oil rubbing process; butt measures 13 inches from center of butt plate to trigger; drop of stock at heel 3¼ inches; at comb 1⅛ inches; barrel is 44 inches long; it is made of fine homogeneous charcoal iron, no flaws can be seen; as no weld seems in evidence, it was probably drilled from the bar; bore now is 0.4785; to bottom of groove 0.516; width of groove ⅛ inch; width of lands 0.019; depth of star 1/32 inch; pitch of rifling, 1 turn in 48 inches; rifling is right hand; number of grooves 7; number of balls to pound 43; rear sight; flat top open; front sight Barley corn of yellow brass; distance of rear sight from eye 19 inches; sight radius 28½ inches; the lock has a fly and temper screw to adjust trigger pull, and although it is single or plain trigger, the mainspring is the old hook type, there being no stirrup; weight of rifle 11¼ pounds; mountings are yellow brass; patch box opens on pressure of a dummy screw head, and it is hard to find how to open it; wire loops for a pick are set under the cheek piece of stock.

The great groove depth indicates this barrel was cut for use of buckskin patches. Linen was scarce and high priced then, while buckskin was to be had at cost of the powder and bullet, the latter being recoverd and generally used again.

(Plate 78)

TARGET RECORDS MADE WITH A LEMAN FLINT-LOCK
RIFLE

(Plate 79)

STRAIGHT CUT *vs.* SMOOTH BORE

Target record made with smooth bore rifle; 1922; distance 75 yards; muzzle rest; greased linen patch. (*Left.*)
Target record made with straight cut rifle; 1922; distance 75 yards; greased linen patch. Insert shows actual size of bore and rifling. (*Right.*)

(Plate 80)

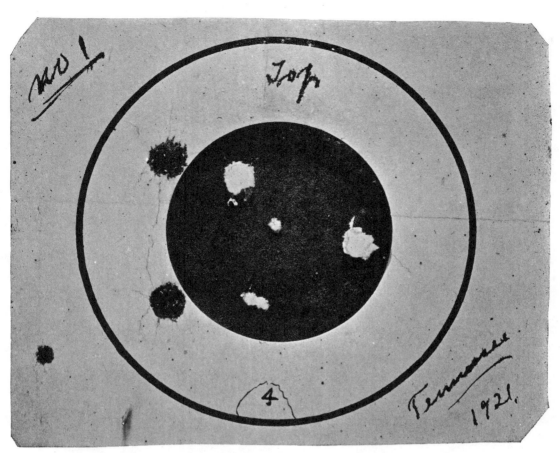

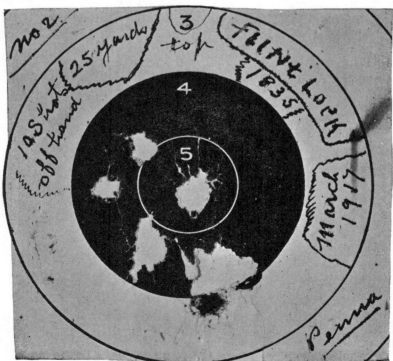

MODERN RIFLE *vs.* FLINT-LOCK

Target at top shows result of match between an up-to-date .22 calibre rifle
and an early flint-lock, muzzle rest; distance 100 yards. Points registered are
the same, as the .22 rifle fired one wild shot. Four bullets only were available
for the flint-lock, hence the unusual four-shot match. (Tennessee, 1921.)

Lower target shows result of ten shots fired off-hand at 25 yards, in March,
1917, in Pennsylvania, from a flint-lock made in 1835.

(Plate 81)

Engraved for BARNARD's New Complete & Authentic HISTORY of ENGLAND.

Portrait & Uniform of An
AMERICAN GENERAL.

A real representation of the Dress of An
AMERICAN RIFLE-MAN.

(Plate 82)

Representation of an American General and an American Rifleman from Barnard's "History of England." This shows one of the regular "Provincials" who were armed with muskets and who were joined by the backwoodsmen outfitted with Kentucky rifles.

powder, and the gun could be loaded a second or two quicker, but, all things considered, the advantages were comparatively few.

There was no danger of injury to the rifleman's face under ordinary conditions. If a very hard wind was blowing directly into the rifleman's face at the time of firing the piece, a slight heat wave from the flash pan was felt, too weak to cause injury or even discomfort.

The great majority of flint-lock guns now in existence are naturally in very bad condition and as a matter of course firing them can only give poor results and produce upon the mind of the experimenter a wrong impression.

The mainsprings are very apt to be weak and a weak spring will invariably produce a feeble spark. This, thrown into a pan of coarse-grained powder which never was intended for a primer, may cause slow ignition. This is in great contrast to the action of a stiff spring, which throws a shower of sparks into a pan of fine powder which gives practically instantaneous ignition. Still another feature adding difficulty to the proper discharge of the flint-lock is the condition of the flint itself. Such flints as are occasionally found in the old locks are as a rule worn out, or worn to such an extent that they will scarcely produce a spark, even if driven by a stiff spring. The flint will wear smooth and become unreliable after from 40 to 60 rounds have been fired, and while it may still produce sparks, it was never considered by the old hunters to be certain in action after such use and was replaced by a new one. It may be noted here that the flint was always clamped in the jaws of the hammer (or cock) between two pieces of thin leather.

The frizzen steel, against which the flint struck in producing the spark sometimes became badly worn and quite irregular. When this condition was noted, a new steel face was carefully fitted and sweated to the base.

These are the material points to be considered before passing judgment on the flint-lock rifle; and before criticizing the reliability of the lock, it might be worth while to question whether the men who carried these rifles would have been satisfied to entrust their lives to an arm which burned their faces with the flash from the pan, hung fire when split seconds meant starvation or missed fire altogether and handed them over to the torture stake.

In considering the practical aspect of the flint-lock it is well to remember that, being the product of careful and painstaking experiment under the actual conditions which were to surround its use rather than theoretical laboratory conditions, each ballistic feature of this weapon was tried and proved before adoption. W. J. Stillman, writing in *The Atlantic Monthly* in 1859—a period when it was still possible to get first-hand testimony on matters pertaining to the Kentucky rifle—said:

"The Kentucky rifle is to American mechanism what the chronometer is to English: a specialty in which rivalry by any other nation is out of the question."

Mr. Stillman also pointed out a most interesting feature of early American gunmaking—a definite relationship between weight of rifle and weight of projectile. This he declared to be about 500 to 1. While he did not find that any of the riflesmiths of the later flint-lock and early percussion days, when calibres had grown materially smaller, had reduced this principle to an exact mathematical formula, he did find a corresponding relation between weight of rifle and projectile, as witness these figures which he presented:

> For a 10-pound rifle, a 140-grain bullet.
> For a 11-pound rifle, a 154-grain bullet.
> For a 12-pound rifle, 1 168-grain bullet.
> For a 13-pound rifle, a 182-grain bullet.

This same relation, Mr. Stillman states, was to be found among the weapons used for target shooting by the most expert offhand marksmen of the late fifties.

The Rifle in the Revolution

CHAPTER FOURTEEN

OSSIBLY no better estimate of the practical value of the flint-lock rifle is obtainable than the very authentic data compiled by Horace Kephart concerning the rifle in the Revolutionary War. The essentials of Mr. Kephart's writings follow:

When the result of the battle of Bunker Hill became known in England, there was such an outburst of indignation that the British Army found itself sore pressed for explanations. General Gage wrote frankly to the Earl of Dartmouth that "the trials we have had show the rebels are not the despicable rabble too many have supposed them to be"; but this was not the kind of explanation that the public wanted. Surely there must be some better reason why a brigade of regulars, supported by ships and artillery, should lose a third of their number in dislodging an inferior force of Yankee farmers from breastworks that had been thrown up in a couple of hours.

It was under the stress of this demand that the London *Chronicle* gravely published the following item in its issue of September 14–16, 1775:

"It is said that the reason why the royal army killed so very few of the rebels, in proportion to the number His Majesty lost at the battle of Bunker Hill, was entirely owing to an unfortunate mistake in some who had the care of the artillery; in the hurry of their proceedings, they took with them, by mistake, a prodigious number of twelve-pound shot for their six-pound field pieces. Hence it naturally required a great while to ram down such disproportioned shot, nor did they, when discharged, fly with that velocity and true direction they would have done, had they been better suited to the size of the cannon."

I unearth this paragraph, first, because it is positively brilliant—worthy of a modern Sunday newspaper—and, secondly, because it is to this same *Chronicle* that we are indebted for the information that rifles were used at Bunker Hill. In the number for July 27–29, 1775, it stated:

"The Americans load their rifle-barrel guns with a ball slit almost in four quarters, which, when fired out of those guns, breaks in four pieces, and generally does great execution."

This is of a piece with the Tory merchant's story, written from Boston after the engagement:

"I cannot help mentioning one thing, which seems to show the hellish disposition of the accursed rebels: by parcels of ammunition which were left on the field, their balls were all found to be poisoned." ("American Archives," 4th series, II, 1079.)

In the *Chronicle* of August 1–3, and again September 9–12, there appeared items to the effect that the provincials used "rifles peculiarly adapted to take off the officers of a whole line as it marches to an attack," and that each rifleman was attended by two men to load for him, "and this is the real cause of so many of our brave officers falling, they being singled out by these murderers, as they must appear to be in the eyes of every thinking man."

Such is the origin of the oft-repeated story that Bunker Hill was fought with "the unerring American rifle."

On the contrary, Grimshaw says explicitly: "None of the provincials had rifles." ("History of the U. S.," 3d ed., 1822, p. 6.) Botta, an unprejudiced historian, remarks: "Their sharpshooters, for want of rifles, were obliged to use common firelocks; but as marksmen they had no equals." ("American War," tr. by Otis (1837), I, 204.) General Duane says: "In the War of the American Revolution, the use of riflemen was demonstrated, and soon improved upon by those European officers who had, by being allies or enemies of America in the contest, witnessed the effect of the desultory and direct fire with smooth barrels at Bunker Hill, with rifle barrels at Saratoga and in all the subsequent actions of the Revolutionary War." ("Hand Book for Riflemen," 3d ed., Phila., 1813, p. 3.)

In his description of the battle of Bunker Hill, written from Roxbury under date of August 15, 1775, and published in his "History of the American Revolution," I, 364, Dr. William Gordon says:

"The provincials have not a rifleman among them, not one being yet arrived from the southward; nor have they any rifle guns; they have only common muskets, nor are these in general furnished with bayonets; but then, they are almost all marksmen, being accustomed to sporting of one kind or other from their youth."

Nothing could be more explicit.

The introduction of the backwoodsman's rifle as a factor in winning our independence occurred thus:

On the 14th of June, 1775, the Continental Congress, facing actual war, issued its first call for troops. It is interesting to note the class of men to which America turned in her hour of extreme peril. Congress, having resolved itself into a committee of the whole, decided thus:

"Resolved, That six companies of expert riflemen be immediately raised in Pennsylvania, two in Maryland, and two in Virginia; that each Company consist of a Captain, three Lieutenants, four Sergeants, four Corporals, a Drummer or Trumpeter, and sixty-eight Privates.

That each Company, as soon as completed, march and join the Army near Boston, to be employed as Light-Infantry, under the command of the chief officer of that Army . . ."

Such was the beginning of the United States Army; for these were the first troops ever levied on this continent by authority of a central Government. On the following day George Washington was appointed commander-in-chief.

It may seem strange that the first men called into service should be those furthest from the scene and hardest to reach, the nomadic hunters on the frontier. When hostilities were so imminent (Gage was already penned up in Boston, and Bunker Hill was but three days off), why did Congress send hundreds of miles into the wilderness, when the seaboard towns were alive with men eager to enlist?

I think the action was due to a subtler policy than appears on the surface, and that it was suggested by the only man in Congress who knew the backwoodsmen like a brother; who had marched with them, camped with them, fought side by side with them—by Washington himself.

It was plain enough that a corps of these incomparable sharpshooters, hardy, indomitable, experienced in war, would be the right stuff to meet British regulars. But there was another and a deeper motive which impelled Congress at this critical hour to hazard the delay of sending for the mountaineers. It is disclosed in a letter which Washington addressed to the President of Congress a few weeks later. Speaking of the lack of clothing among the troops at Cambridge, he said: "I am of opinion that a number of hunting-shirts, not less than ten thousand, would in a great degree remove this difficulty, in the cheapest and quickest manner. I know nothing in a speculative view, more trivial, yet which, if put in practice, would have a happier tendency to unite the men, and abolish those provincial distinctions that lead to jealousy and dissatisfaction."

The colonies at this time were still separated by petty jealousies and local pride. Cavalier mocked at Puritan, and Knickerbocker mistrusted both. Would these discordant elements act together when the supreme hour arrived? Would Virginia strike hands with Massachusetts? Would Pennsylvania fraternize with Connecticut and Maryland? Granting that war was inevitable, it was above all else essential that this continental army should have a nucleus that was not provincial, but American.

Where, then, were these Americans to be found?

As a surveyor in the back country, as scout and diplomat on his long midwinter march through the wilderness to the French outpost in the Ohio country, and especially with his Virginians in Braddock's fatal expedition, Washington had formed the acquaintance of a set of men whose like was to be found nowhere on earth. These were the hunters, Indian fighters, pioneers of the Alleghenies.

Most of our colonists lived within shipping distance of tidewater, and had periodical communication with England. They depended on the mother country for a market, and for most of the luxuries, if not for some of the necessities, of life. Ties of kindred were kept alive by mails and newspapers, as well as by personal contact with representatives and visitors from abroad. They were a commercial people, with selfish interests staked upon peaceful trade with their brethren over sea. They were, then as now, dominated, or at least restrained, by capitalists and speculators, whose patriotism is but a feeble flame, quenched too often by sordid ambitions. War, to such people, meant a tugging at pursestrings and heartstrings. It was doubtful how they would bear the strain.

But far in the interior there dwelt or roamed a class of men who remembered no fatherland but the wilderness they trod. Their food was won with the rifle, and their shelter with the axe. Procuring everything they wanted from the forest with their own hands, they asked nothing of civilization, and were never in debt.

Here were Americans. Original in all things, they were not be be confounded with this or that province, or with any European race. Their freedom needed no proclamation; it showed in every movement and looked straight from their eyes.

We see, then, the significance of Washington's fondness for the hunting shirt. It was an emblem of liberty, which never in the history of man was worn by an enslaved people. It was distinctive. It meant: We are Americans.

And when Congress drew its first levies from the backwoods, it was not alone to secure the services of the finest marksmen living. Something more was sought. It was the moral effect, upon the camp at Cambridge, of

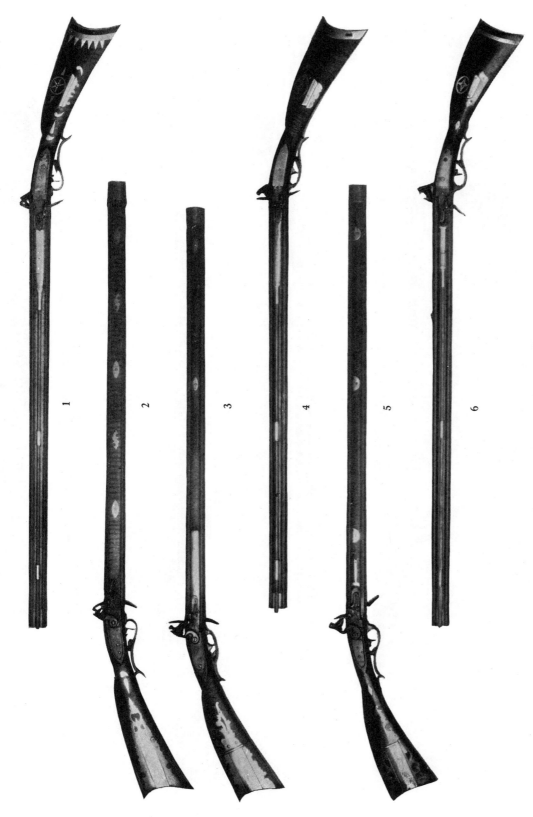

OFFERMAN COLLECTION

Nos. 1-2. Unidentified; superposed rifle; barrels break from trigger guard; highly decorated; weight 12 pounds; fine workmanship.
Nos. 3-4. Unidentified; 53½ inches over all; 38-inch barrel; superposed rifle of the single hammer type; one barrel rifled, the other smooth bore; a very fine specimen. Period of 1810-1830.
Nos. 5-6. Unidentified; same class as No. 1 and built on similar lines.

(Plate 83)

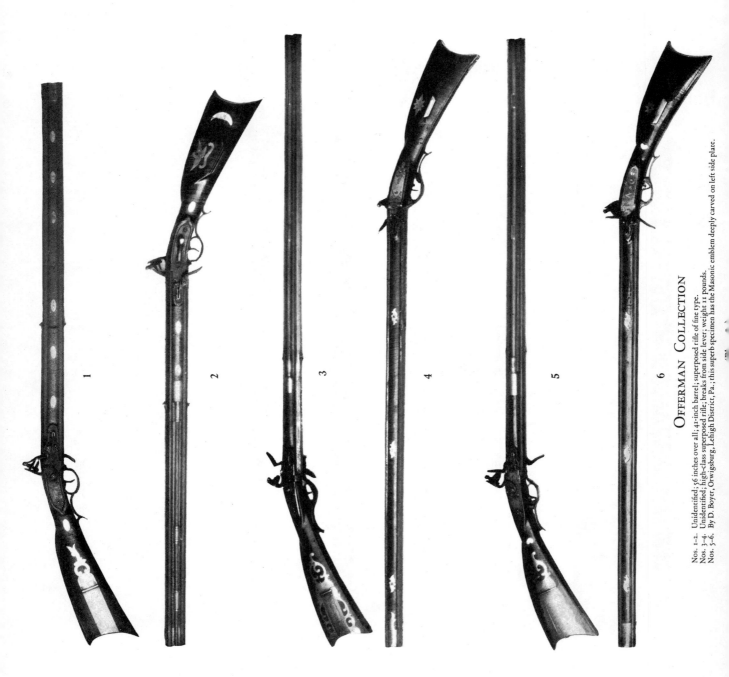

Offerman Collection

Nos. 1–2. Unidentified; 56 inches over all; 41-inch barrel; superposed rifle of fine type.
Nos. 3–4. Unidentified; high-class superposed rifle; breaks from side lever; weight 11 pounds.
Nos. 5–6. By D. Boyer, Orwigsburg, Lehigh District, Pa.; this superb specimen has the Masonic emblem deeply carved on left side plate.

independence typified by flesh and blood, clad in American garb, and wielding an American weapon.

On the 22d of June, Congress directed Pennsylvania to raise two more companies of riflemen, making a total of eight from that colony. Pennsylvania acted promptly. The commissions of the officers are dated June 25, which was Sunday. Within a few days the quota had been more than filled. On the 11th of July, Congress was informed that two companies had been raised in Lancaster County instead of one, and accordingly the nine companies from Pennsylvania were formed into a battalion under Colonel William Thompson, of Carlisle, and were mustered into the Continental service. The men were enlisted as follows: two companies from Cumberland County under Captains Chambers and Hendricks, two from Lancaster under Ross and Smith, and one each from York under Doudel, from Northumberland under Loudon, from Bedford under Cluggage, from Berks under Nagel, and from Northampton under Miller. Of course, the limits of these counties were more extensive then than now, taking in nearly all of Western Pennsylvania. Imperfect rolls of the officers and privates are published in Pennsylvania Archives, 2d series, Vol. X.

The Southern Colonies responded with equal zeal. The two Maryland Companies were commanded by Michael Cresap, a famous frontiersman, and Thomas Price. One of the Virginia Companies was led by the lion-hearted Morgan, who became one of Washington's favorite generals.

Cresap made a phenomenal march over difficult roads, leaving Frederick, Md., July 18 and arriving August 9, having covered 550 miles in twenty-two days. But this performance was in turn eclipsed by Morgan, who had raised ninety-six woodsmen in ten days and marched them 600 miles from Winchester to Cambridge in twenty-one days, without losing a man.

Custis says ("Recollections of Washington," 270):

"When Morgan cried, with his martial inspiration, 'Come, boys, who's for the camp before Cambridge?' the mountaineers turned out to a man. Short was their 'note of preparation.' The blanket buckled to their backs, their baggage; a supply of food in their pouches, scanty as an aborigine would take for a long march, their commissariat; they grasped their rifles and strode away to the North, a band of young giants, for the combats of liberty."

Speaking of commissariat, Bancroft states that the mountain men subsisted on parched corn and such game as they could shoot. This parched corn, pulverized, was the same "cold flour" of the Mexicans, or *pinole* of Mr. Van Dyke's entertaining essay on Desertcraft, which the Indians taught our backwoodsmen to carry as the lightest of all nutriment. Early in the eighteenth century it is described as "rockahominy" by Colonel

Byrd in his journal—dated 1728-29—of the survey of the boundary line between Virginia and Carolina.

The costume of the mountaineers is described by Colonel Trumbull, who painted a well-known portrait of Morgan:

"The dress of the Virginia riflemen who came to Cambridge in 1775 (among whom was Morgan) was an elegant loose dress reaching to the middle of the thigh, ornamented with fringes in various parts, and meeting the pantaloons of the same material and color, fringed and ornamented in a corresponding style.   The officers wore the usual crimson sash over this and around the waist; the straps, belts, etc., were black, forming, in my opinion, a very picturesque and elegant, as well as useful, dress. It cost a trifle; the soldier could wash it at any brook he passed; and however worn and ragged and dirty his other clothing might be, when this was thrown over it he was in elegant uniform." (Peterson's National Portrait Gallery, 1852, Vol. II.)

It should be remembered that this was in August. The hunting shirt for summer wear was made of linen, instead of buckskin, which would have been intolerably hot.

Judge Henry, who accompanied the rifle corps, thus describes the outfit of those companies which marched to Quebec under Arnold in the autumn:

"Each man of the three companies (two Pennsylvania and one Virginia) bore a rifle-barreled gun, a tomahawk, or small axe, and a long knife, usually called a 'scalping-knife,' which served for all purposes in the woods. His under dress, by no means in a military style, was covered by a deep ash-colored hunting-shirt, leggins and mockasins, if the latter could be procured. It was the silly fashion of those times for riflemen to ape the manners of savages."

The figures hitherto given of the distances which the riflemen marched refer only to the trips from their respective rendezvous; but, as a matter of fact, some of them had already traveled many leagues through the wilderness to join their commands. For example, Cresap's Company was enlisted at Frederick, Md., but the men had been summoned from far and wide, as appears from the following "extract of a letter to a gentleman in Philadelphia, dated Fredericktown, Md., August 1, 1775," which I copy from Force's American Archives, 4th series, Vol. III, col. 2.

". . . I have had the happiness of seeing Captain Michael Cresap marching at the head of a formidable company of upwards of one hundred and thirty men, from the mountains and backwoods, painted like Indians, armed with tomahawks and rifles, dressed in hunting shirts and moccasins, and though some of them had traveled near eight hundred miles, from the

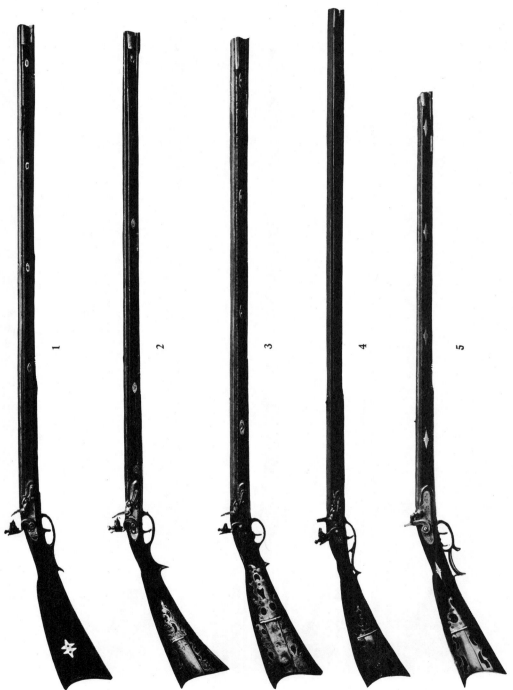

Van Rensselaer Collection

No. 1. By Philip Hep, Jr.; 58 inches over all; 42½-inch barrel; smooth bore; calibre 45.
No. 2. By F. Kantz; 58 inches over all; 43-inch barrel; calibre 44; a beautiful specimen.
No. 3. Unidentified; 57½ inches over all; 43-inch full octagon barrel; calibre 45; fine work.
No. 4. By Miller; 61 inches overall; 46-inch full octagon barrel; calibre 50.
No. 5. Unidentified; 53 inches over all; 38-inch barrel; altered from flint lock to percussion; very fine specimen.

(Plate 85)

Van Rensselaer Collection

No. 1.   By Tryon, Phila.; 56 inches over all; 41½-inch full octagon barrel; calibre 28; a turkey or squirrel rifle.
No. 2.   Unidentified; lock marked "H. Elwell, Warranted;" 53 inches over all; 37½-inch barrel; smooth bore; calibre 44.
No. 3.   By C. Bird & Co., Phila.; 57 inches over all; 41¾-inch barrel; smooth bore; calibre 45.
No. 4.   By W. Adams; 58 inches over all; 43-inch barrel, which is round with flat rib; calibre 55; lock marked W. Ketland & Co.; fine workmanship.
No. 5.   Unidentified; 57½ inches over all; 42-inch barrel, which is one inch in diameter, rifled; calibre 44.

(Plate 86)

Sherwood Collection

Five of these rifles are unidentified. No. 2 is by Jacob Christ. All were originally flint-locks. This plate will give some idea of the widespread practice of altering to percussion.

(Plate 87)

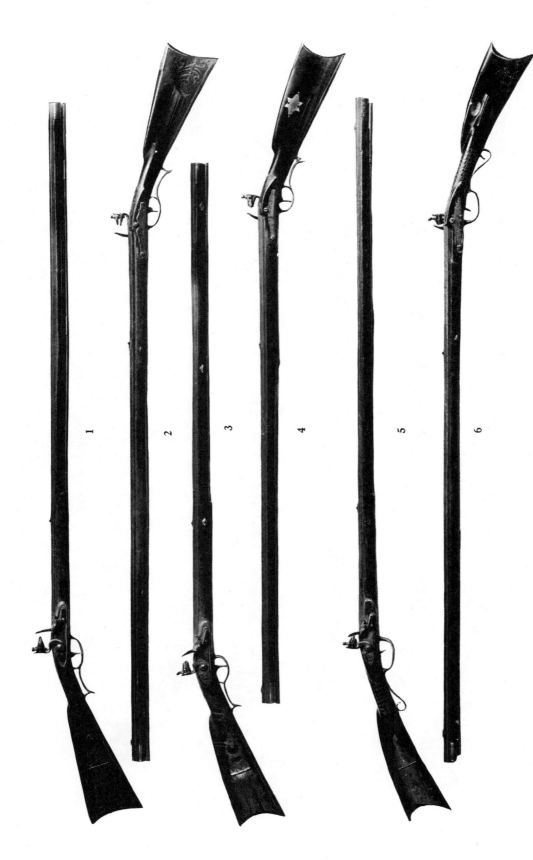

PRICE COLLECTION

Nos. 1-2. By Agy; 62 inches over all; 47-inch full octagon barrel; calibre 45; neatly made; early period.
Nos. 3-4. Unidentified; 57 inches over all; 42-inch full octagon barrel; calibre 45; fine work.
Nos. 5-6. Unidentified (except by mark "H. H."); 61 inches over all; 46-inch barrel; octagon trigger guard (not original); came from Minnesota and is of very high and unusual workmanship. A puzzle to all who have seen it.

(Plate 88)

banks of the Ohio, they seemed to walk light and easy, and not with less spirit than at the first hour of their march. Health and vigour, after what they had undergone, declared them to be intimate with hardship, and familiar with danger . . .

"Yesterday the company were supplied with a small quantity of powder from the magazine, which wanted airing, and was not in good order for rifles; in the evening, however, they were drawn out to show the gentlemen of the Town their dexterity at shooting. A clapboard, with a mark the size of a dollar, was put up; they began to fire offhand, and the bystanders were surprised, few shots being made that were not close to or in the paper. When they had shot for a time in this way, some lay on their backs, some on their breast or side, others ran twenty or thirty steps, and firing, appeared to be equally certain of the mark. With this performance the company were more than satisfied, when a young man took up the board in his hand, not by the end, but by the side, and holding it up, his brother walked to the distance, and very coolly shot into the white; laying down his rifle, he took the board, and holding it as it was held before, the second brother shot as the former had done. By this exercise I was more astonished than pleased. But will you believe me when I tell you, that one of the men took the board, and placing it between his legs, stood with his back to the tree while another drove the center. What would a regular army of considerable strength in the forests of America do with one thousand of these men, who want nothing to preserve their health and courage but water from the spring, with a little parched corn, with what they can easily procure in hunting; and who, wrapped in their blankets, in the damp of night, would choose the shade of a tree for their covering, and the earth for their bed?"

When this company arrived at Lancaster, Pa., they gave a similar exhibition. An eye-witness described the performance in the *Pennsylvania Packet* of August 28, and I transcribe his remarks verbatim from that paper, both because they give additional details, and because this allows us to balance two independent testimonies against each other:

"Philadelphia, August 23. Extract of a letter from Lancaster, August 7:

"On Friday evening last arrived here, on their way to the American Camp, Captain Cresap's (sic) Company of Riflemen, consisting of 130 active, brave young fellows; many of whom had been the late expedition, under Lord Dunmore, against the Indians. They bear in their bodies visible marks of their prowess, and show scars and wounds, which would do honour to Homer's Iliad, etc. They shew you, to use the poet's words—

'Where the goar'd bull bled at every vein.'

" 'One of these warriors, in particular, shows the cicatrices of four bullet holes through his body. These men have been bred in the woods to hardships and danger from their infancy. They appear as if they were entirely unacquainted with, and had never felt, the passion of fear. With their rifles in their hands they assume a kind of omnipotence over their enemies. You will not much wonder at this when I mention a fact, which can be fully attested by several of the reputable inhabitants of this place, who were eye-witnesses of it. Two brothers in the company took a piece of board, five inches broad, and seven inches long, with a bit of white paper, about the size of a dollar, nailed in the center, and while one of them supported this board perpendicularly between his knees, the other, at the distance of upwards of sixty yards, and without any kind of rest, shot eight bullets successively through the board, and spared a brother's thighs! Another of the company held a barrel stave perpendicularly in his hand, with one edge close to his side, while one of his comrades, at the same distance, and in the manner before mentioned, shot several bullets through it, without any apprehensions of danger on either side. The spectators, appearing to be amazed at these feats, were told that there were upwards of fifty persons in the company who could do the same thing; that there was not one who could not plug 19 bullets out of 20 (as they termed it) within an inch of the head of a ten-penny nail; in short, to evince the confidence they possessed in their dexterity at these kinds of arms, some of them proposed to stand with apples on their heads, while others at the same distance undertook to shoot them off; but the people, who saw the other experiments, declined to be witnesses of this. At night a great fire was kindled round a pole planted in the courthouse square, where the company with the Captain at their head, all naked to the waist and painted like savages (except the Captain, who was in an Indian Shirt), indulged a vast concourse of the inhabitants with a perfect exhibition of a war dance, and all the manoevures of Indians holding council, going to war, circumventing their enemies, by defiles, ambuscades, attacking, scalping, etc. It is said by those who are judges, that no representation could possibly come nearer the original. The Captain's agility and expertness, in particular, in these exhibitions, astonished every beholder. This morning they will set out on their march to Cambridge.' " (Dunlap's *Pennsylvania Packet* or *The General Advertiser*, Monday, August 28, 1775. No. 201. Postscript, *i. e.*, extra folio).

This peculiar method of target shooting was a common diversion of the frontiersmen. In 1796 General Victor Collot, who was making a careful survey of the political, commercial, and military state of the West under orders from the French Government, witnessed a similar frolic in Kentucky.

SNYDER COLLECTION

No. 1. By I. Gorg; 59½ inches over all; 44½-inch full octagon barrel; full maple stock; brass mountings and silver inlay; brass patch-box. There were apparently two riflesmiths of the same name, one as late as 1818.

No. 2. Unidentified; 57 inches over all; 42-inch full octagon barrel; full curly maple stock; brass mountings, brass patch-box; a very handsome piece.

No. 3. By J. J. Henry; 57½ inches over all; 42½-inch full octagon barrel; full curly maple stock; brass patch-box; a very plain but beautiful rifle.

No. 4. By Peter Augstead; 58 inches over all; 43-inch full octagon barrel; full curly maple stock; brass patch-box; exquisite workmanship.

No. 5. By T. Grubb, Philadelphia, Pa.; 55 inches over all; 40-inch full octagon barrel; full curly maple stock; brass mountings and silver inlay; brass patch-box; beautifully made.

No. 6. By T. Grubb, Philadelphia, Pa.; pair of duelling pistols; very ornamental and made with the utmost care.

(Plate 89)

Laidacker Collection of Superposed Rifles, All by Different Makers. Thirty-eight Specimens Shown

(Plate 90)

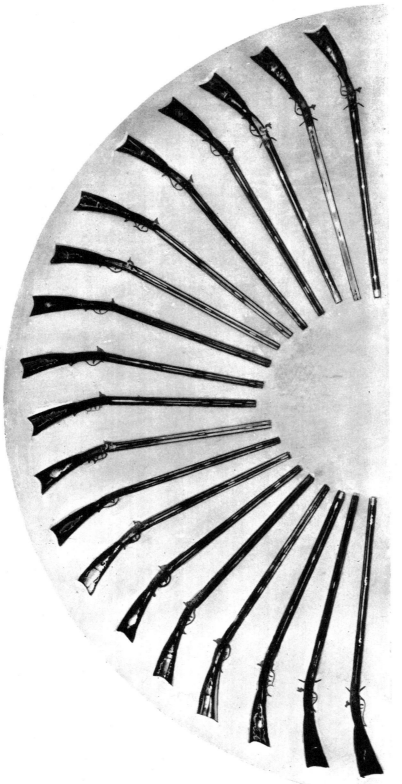

ANOTHER GROUP OF THE LAIDACKER SUPERPOSED RIFLES

(Plate 91)

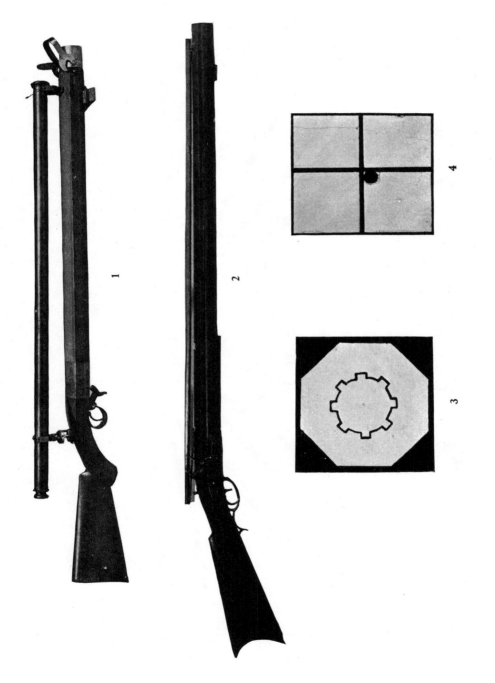

Two Match Rifles

No. 1. Under hammer percussion, telescope sight rifle, made and used by Warner, of Warner-Perry Match fame. The rifle is now owned by Capt. W. deV. Foulke and is shown for the purpose of comparison with—

No. 2. A splendid example of the early Pennsylvania Flint-lock Match Rifle. This gun weighs 19¼ pounds, was made by I. Moll period of about 1810. The gun is fitted with a so-called telescope which is a half-inch brass tube containing aperture and pin-head. The loading rod is shown underneath. The rifle is in beautiful shooting condition.

No. 3. Pennsylvania shooting match target.

No. 4. Exact size bore of the flint-lock match rifle.

(Plate 92)

He describes it in his book, which is by far the best description of the Ohio and Mississippi Valleys at that time, but is, unfortunately, extremely rare:

"The inhabitants of Red Bank are only hunters, or what are called foresters. They cultivate no ground, but subsist on the produce of their hunting and fishing, and are almost naked. The following trait may serve to give an idea of their character. At our arrival we found a number of these hunters who had assembled to regale themselves on the banks of the river with the spoils of their chace on the preceding day, when they had killed a very fine buffalo. They had drunk plentifully of whiskey, and though the greater number were intoxicated, they were amusing themselves in firing with carabines against a piece of plank tied to a tree, which is called shooting at a mark. The board, probably ill-fastened, fell at each shot; one of the party at length losing patience, took it up, and placing it between his legs, called out to his companions, 'Now, fire away!' which they did immediately, and always with the same address; whilst he who held the board exclaimed at each shot, 'It is in!' This amusement, which lasted two hours without any accident taking place, may appear incredible to those who are not acquainted with the singular skill of these men; but it is sufficient to observe that they will aim at the head of a squirrel or a turkey and very rarely miss. The seeming intrepidity of the man who held the board becomes, therefore, only an ordinary circumstance." (A Journey in North America, I., 172–73, Harvard College copy.)

Collot wrote his narrative in French, and it was translated by an Englishman, which accounts for some verbal errors. "Foresters" above should be woodmen, and "carabines" should be rifles, as the French for rifle is carbine.

As the riflemen moved swiftly toward Cambridge, there was rejoicing all along the line of march. The brothers Bradford, printers of Philadelphia, wrote to a London publisher:

"This province has raised 1000 riflemen, the worst of whom will put a ball into a man's head at the distance of 150 or 200 yards, therefore advise your officers who shall hereafter come out to America to settle their affairs in England before their departure." (London *Chronicle*, August 17–19, 1775, p. 174.)

England was warned from many sources. A minister of the Church of England sent the following letter to the Earl of Dartmouth:

"Maryland, December 20, 1775 . . .Rifles, infinitely better than those imported, are daily made in many places in Pennsylvania, and all the gunsmiths everywhere constantly employed. In this country, my lord, the boys, as soon as they can discharge a gun, frequently exercise themselves therewith, some a-fowling and others a-hunting. The great quantities of game, the many kinds and the great privileges of killing, making the Americans the best marksmen in the world, and thousands support their families principally by the same, particularly riflemen on the frontiers, whose objects are deer and turkeys. In marching through woods, one thousand of these riflemen would cut to pieces ten thousand of your best troops." (Niles, "Principles and Acts of the Revolution," '76 ed., 265–6.)

When the riflemen arrived at Cambridge they excited a sensation throughout the camp. Dr. James Thatcher, surgeon's mate in the hospital at Cambridge, kept a careful diary of events that came under his notice, from which I extract this description:

"August . . .Several companies of riflemen, amounting, it is said, to more than 1400 men, have arrived here from Philadelphia and Maryland, a distance of from 500 to 700 miles. They are remarkably stout and hardy men; many of them exceeding 6 feet in height. They are dressed in white frocks, or rifle shirts, and round hats. These men are remarkable for the accuracy of their aim; striking a mark with great certainty at 200 yards distance. At a review, a company of them, while on a quick advance, fired their balls into objects of 7 inches diameter, at the distance of 250 yards. They are now stationed on our lines, and their shot have frequently proved fatal to British officers and soldiers who expose themselves to view, even at more than double the distance of common musket shot." ("Military Journal during the American Revolutionary War," 2d ed., 1827, pp. 33–4.)

The *Pennsylvania Gazette* of August 5, 1775, says of the corps: "A party of these men at a late review on a quick advance, placed their balls in poles of 7 inches diameter, fixed for that purpose, at the distance of 250 yards." This statement was copied into the London *Chronicle*, August 3–5, and into Almon's *Remembrancer* for 1775, 4th ed.

The riflemen were scattered about in small parties to pick off British officers during the rather dull weeks that followed. That they succeeded is abundantly testified. The *Pennsylvania Gazette* of August 16 reported: "We are also told that the riflemen had in one day killed ten of a reconnoitering party; and it is added likewise, that they have killed three Field officers. A centry was killed at 250 yards distance."

Dunlap's *Pennsylvania Packet* of August 14 says:

"The express, who was sent by the Congress, is returned here from the Eastward, and says he left the Camp last Saturday; that the riflemen picked off ten men in one day, three of whom were Field-officers, that were reconnoitering; one of them was killed at the distance of 250 yards, when only half his head was seen."

These items were promptly republished in the London papers, and excited wrath. In the British camp the riflemen were called "shirt-tail

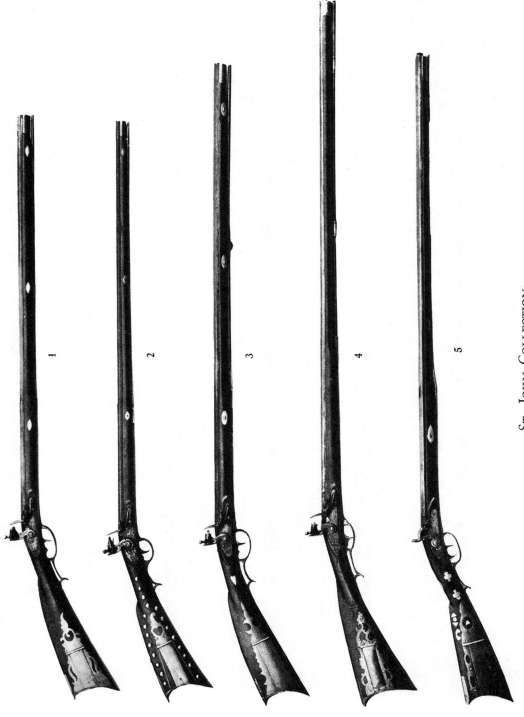

St. John Collection

No. 1. Unidentified; 51 inches over all; 36-inch barrel; about 44 calibre; full maple stock; 8 silver inlays; perfect condition.

No. 2. Unidentified; 51½ inches over all; 36½-inch barrel; full maple stock; 9 brass inlays and 53 brass-headed tacks; an unusually light rifle.

No. 3. Unidentified; 56 inches over all; 41-inch barrel; full maple stock; 11 white metal inlays; full brass mountings, including entire cone, cheekpiece and forestock underneath; in perfect order.

No. 4. By P. Berry; 60 inches over all; 43½-inch barrel; 45 calibre; very deep grooves; full curly maple stock of the finest quality ornamented with carving.

No. 5. By Peter White; 57 inches over all; 42-inch barrel; 40 calibre; altered from flint-lock to percussion; curly maple stock; 30 silver and 6 brass inlays. This rifle was obtained from a man who scouted with Buffalo Bill.

(Plate 93)

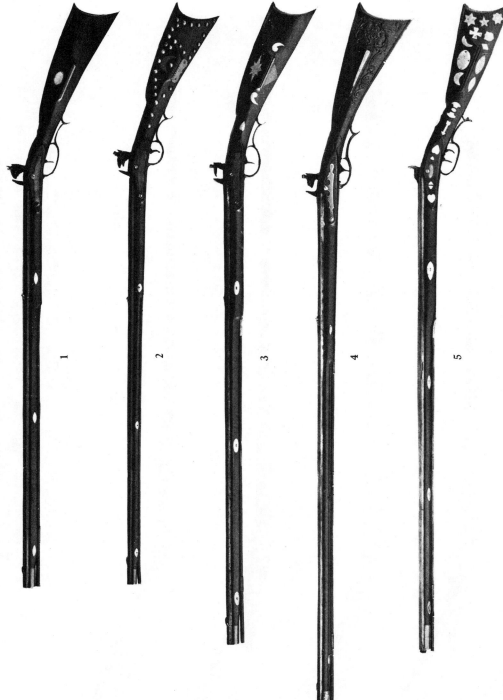

1

2

3

4

5

St. John Collection
Reverse of rifles shown on preceding page.

(Plate 94)

men, with their cursed twisted guns, the most fatal widow-and-orphan-makers in the world." (Drake's "Old Landmarks of Middlesex," 88.)

In the *Pennsylvania Gazette* of August 21 is the following item from Newport: "A gentleman from the American camp says—Last Wednesday, some riflemen, on Charlestown side, shot an officer of note in the ministerial service, supposed to be Major Small, or Bruce, and killed three men on board a ship at Charlestown ferry, at the distance of full half a mile."

This shows that there was a good deal of ammunition wasted in reckless firing, for the round bullet of half ounce or thereabouts will not carry half that distance with precision, though General Lee probably overdid the matter when he issued to Colonel Thompson the following order: "It is a certain truth, that the enemy entertain a most fortunate apprehension of American riflemen. It is equally certain, that nothing can contribute to diminish this apprehension so infallibly as a frequent ineffectual fire. It is with some concern, therefore, that I am informed that your men have been suffered to fire at a most preposterous distance. Upon this principle I must entreat and insist that you consider it as a standing order, that not a man under your command is to fire at a greater distance than an hundred and fifty yards, at the utmost; in short, that they never fire without almost a moral certainty of hitting their object." ("Correspondence of the Revolution," ed. Sparks, II, 501–2.)

The value of large calibres was soon learned, and in May of the following year we find Lee writing to Washington: "I have formed two companies of grenadiers to each regiment, and with spears of 13 feet long. Their rifles (for they are all riflemen) slung over their shoulders, their appearance is formidable, and the men are conciliated to the weapon. I am likewise furnishing myself with four-ounced rifle-amusettes, which will carry an infernal distance; the two-ounced hit a half sheet of paper 500 yards distant." (Same, I., 202.)

When Gates was opposing Burgoyne, Washington sent Morgan's sharpshooters to assist him, and the victory of Stillwater was due to them, General Frazer being picked off by one of the "Tomahawks." Immediately after the battle, Washington wrote Gates, asking for the return of the riflemen if he could possibly spare them; to which Gates replied: "In this situation Your Excellency would not wish me to part with the corps the army of General Burgoyne are most afraid of." (Custis, "Washington," 268.)

The fame of the backwoods riflemen had not a little to do with the purchase of the Hessian mercenaries by Great Britain. On the principle of fighting fire with fire, it was sought to procure from Germany the only other riflemen who were thought fit to cope with our frontiersmen. It was expressly stipulated in the bargains with German princes that as many as possible of the troops should be "chasseurs," or sharpshooters.

No discussion of the flint-lock in war would be complete without some of the salient facts attending the repulse of the British at New Orleans in which the deciding factor was admittedly the marksmanship of Carroll's Tennesseeans, Adair's veterans of the old Kentucky Rifle Brigade, Hinds' Mississippi Rifles and Jugeat's Choctaws.

These backwoodsmen, especially Adair's men, who had fought through the Northwest Campaign and many of whom had been at Tippecanoe, together with 1300 other Kentuckians, were armed with the American frontier weapon—the Kentucky Rifle. In addition, such a reliable source as Buell's "History of Andrew Jackson" states that some militia contingents were equipped with weapons made by the best American gunsmiths from Lancaster, Pa., to Camden, S. C., which came about in this wise:

Upon the declaration of war, the government at Washington wisely curtailed the trading of weapons to Indians, and this tied up some 400 first-class weapons which were part of trading stocks. These were purchased for about $15 each and "the voice of every rifle in the 400 was afterward heard at Talladega, Tohopeka and New Orleans." (See Buell's "History of Andrew Jackson," Scribners, 1873, pg. 259.)

The work which the Kentucky Rifles did from the cypress-log and molasses hogshead redoubts is too well established to call for detailed comment; but of the fight itself, it may be mentioned that in the first engagement the British forces numbered 8390 men against 2287 Americans, and by January 8, when the principal engagement took place, the arrival of Adair's Kentuckians and other backwoodsmen brought the American total to 3918 against Great Britain's force of 10,084.

Among the American reinforcements were Carroll's 800 Tennesseeans. Most of these men, Buell records, were armed with the rifles they had used in the Creek campaign. Others were outfitted from 120 new Lancaster-made rifles impressed from a trader's boat which the detachment met on its flat-boat journey down the Ohio to the Mississippi.

Against the inconsequential American losses among Jackson's forces of 8 killed and 13 wounded in the deciding engagement, the British Army returns give the English loss at 381 killed on the field; 487 died of wounds; 1251 wounded and permanently disabled and 1217 wounded and temporarily disabled, a total of 3336.

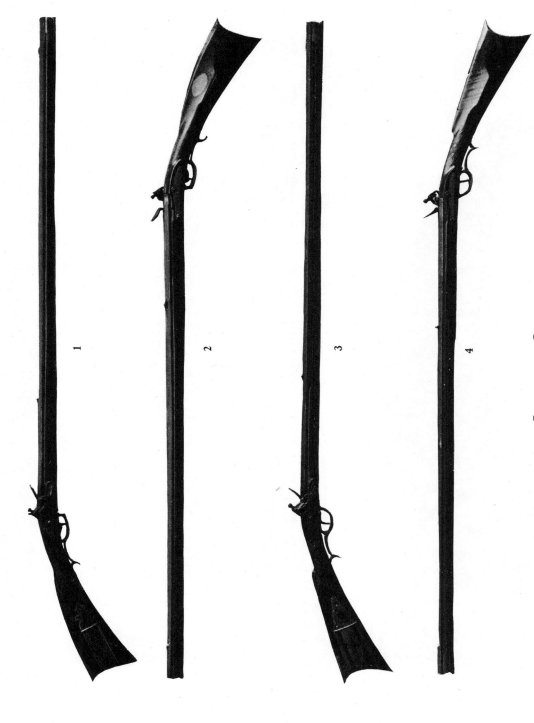

LOCKWOOD COLLECTION

Nos. 1-2. Unidentified; 57 inches over all; 42-inch full octagon barrel; 48 balls to the pound; full maple stock; brass-mounted and brass inlay; brass patch-box.

Nos. 3-4. Unidentified; 55½ inches over all; 40½-inch full octagon barrel; 60 balls to the pound; full maple stock; checkered grip; brass mountings; brass patch-box; weight 9 pounds.

(Plate 95)

Two Fine Powder Horns

Above: Powder Horn made by Nathaniel Bosworth to commemorate his escape from a British prison ship. Now the property of Mrs. A. G. Clyne, Arkansas, a descendant of Bosworth.

Below: Powder Horn from Berks County, Pennsylvania; east slope of Blue Ridge. Shows plan of early block house, or fort. Opposite side pictures sentries guarding approach. Dillin collection.

(Plate 96)

Powder Horns and Game Bags

CHAPTER FIFTEEN

O F secondary interest only to the rifle itself, in the estimation of many collectors, are the powder horns and game bags which were important items in the frontiersman's equipment.

A horn seems to have been the chosen container for powder from the very birth of firearms through the first third of the Nineteenth Century, when the copper or brass flask of commercial manufacture made its appearance in America. A powder horn from central Europe, dated 1595, which the author examined, seemed genuine. The earliest dated American horn which has been brought to the author's notice is marked 1745. It is highly engraved, very interesting as a relic, and apparently bonafide.

Powder horns, from an American standpoint, were divided into two classes, home-made and those to be purchased at the general stores. In early days the former were more abundant, in fact the great majority of horns were made by the hunters who used them, but in the later days of the flintlock period the reverse was the case.

These horns, as a rule, came from domestic cattle; occasionally from the buffalo. The horn of a mature steer was most sought for, it being long, graceful and light in color. When a steer horn was not available, well-shaped horns from the cow or bull were substituted. Priming horns, which were small, were taken from any young cattle.

The very large horns, so often seen, were taken from the work ox and generally carried by those who used a musket or shotgun, as these arms required a greater supply of powder than the rifle.

The average length of powder horns was about 11 inches and their capacity was from one-half to three-quarters of a pound of powder. The small horn was filled with a very fine-grain powder to be used for priming exclusively, and was carried generally in the pocket or hunting bag. This fine powder gave a quicker and more certain ignition.

Powder horns were decorated by both hunters and soldiers with scenes, characters and letters, two very artistic examples being shown on Plate No. 96.

Decorated horns today bring a high price but care should be exercised in the purchase of them as, because they are so highly prized, counterfeits are numerous and are far more easily produced than spurious rifles.

The powder horn was in general use until the end of the flintlock days or perhaps a little later. It was superseded by the metal flask with its measuring feature, which came in with the percussion period and passed with it.

The manufacture of powder horns during the flintlock period was quite an industry and somewhere in Philadelphia there was a shop with a large output.

It is very easy to distinguish between the horn made by the hunter and one made commercially, the latter showing the mark of the turning lathe, while the former was polished by hand.

The first of the two decorated horns shown in Plate No. 96 is the property of Mrs. Lucy Bosworth Clyne, wife of Dr. A. G. Clyne of Paragould, Arkansas, and tells the story of Nathaniel Bosworth and two other Continental soldiers who were captured by the British and sent to a prison ship which lay off shore from Guildford, Massachusetts, in 1779. One cold March night, the three prisoners agreed to escape, if possible, and at the first opportunity slid down into the cold waters and struck for shore. Desperate as the venture was, it was successful, and the powder horn, which he later made, vividly reflects the memory of the exploit which gave him his liberty.

The hunting bag to which the horn was so often attached was often made of dressed buckskin. Sometimes the hair was left on; sometimes it was removed by the dressing process. In the late flintlock period a large percentage of these hunting bags were made of tanned calfskin. The hunting bag of both the early and late periods almost invariably was divided into two and three parts. In these were carried patches and patch material, flints, unspun flax for swabbing the bore, a bullet pouch, and a few light tools. Some hunters did not use the patch box in the stock for ready-made patches, preferring to carry them in the pouch. When this was the case the patch box was invariably filled with hard grease and a fresh lubrication was given to the patches as they were used. In a careful examination of many old hunting bags we find an abundance of proof for these assertions.

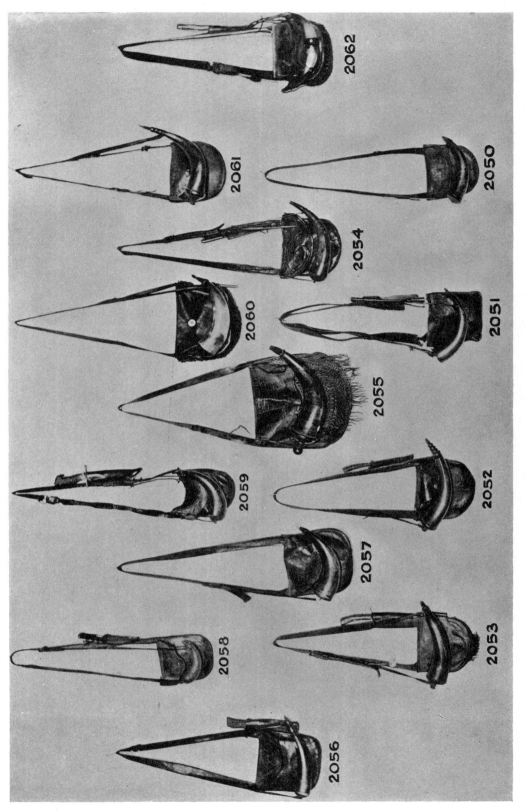

PENNSYLVANIA HUNTING OUTFITS

Hunting bags and powder horns from the mountain districts of Pennsylvania. From the Laidacker collection.

(Plate 97)

SOUTHWESTERN POWDER HORNS

Specimens of powder horns from the Southwest, shown in the collection of Dr. A. G. Clyne, Arkansas.

(Plate 98)

SOUTHWESTERN HUNTING BAGS

Fine specimens of hunting bags, from the Southwest, shown in the collection of Dr. A. G. Clyne, Arkansas.

(Plate 99)

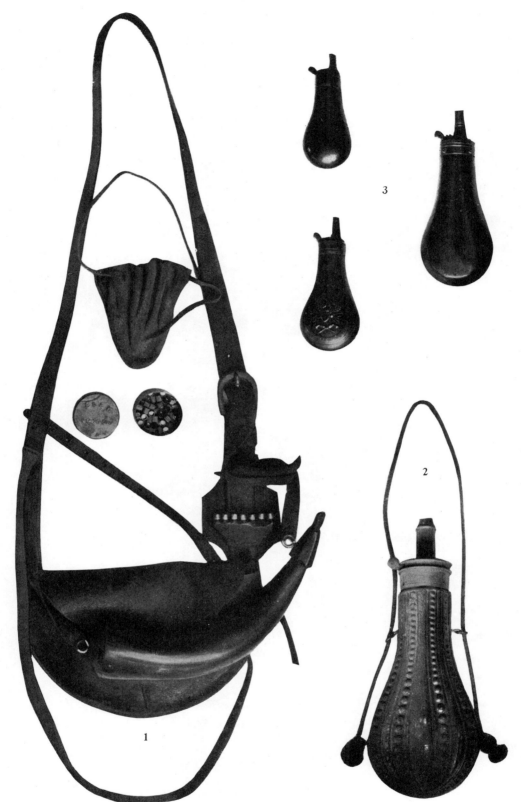

Types of Accoutrement

At the time when flint-lock arms were giving way to percussion rifles and shotguns, many hunters still preferred the powder horn to the metal flasks which came into vogue with the percussion locks. In this photograph are shown an old-time horn and bag, which has been equipped with an ingenious device for carrying caps. When the author found this bag, there was discovered within it a box of Ely's London Waterproof Caps and a well-made and preserved deerskin tobacco pouch. The equipment was secured in the Blue Ridge district of Pennsylvania.

The four powder flasks represent comparative sizes of metal flasks, which supplanted the powder horn. They were as a rule made of brass, and occasionally of copper. The sizes run from one pound capacity down to two ounces. Even smaller flasks were made, but rarely.

(Plate 100)

The Rifle and the Redskin

CHAPTER SIXTEEN

No history of the early American rifle would be complete without mention of the Indian and his firearms which, during Colonial days, were true Kentuckys and which even for a century and more thereafter continued to all intents and purposes to perpetuate the distinguishing features of the weapon of the white pioneer.

In undertaking a warfare of extermination such as the Redskins waged upon the settlers in the early eighteenth century, it was but to be expected that the Indian would at every opportunity seize upon the weapons which outranged so greatly the bow and arrow. Among the Indian raiders who in 1755 and 1756 harried the settlers of what are now the Pennsylvania counties of Lancaster, Cumberland and Northampton, whose incursions during the French and Indian War caused a chain of blockhouse forts to rise along the borders of Dauphin, Lebanon and Berks counties, the long guns of the white man were at a premium. And from those days, and the dark times of Pontiac's conspiracy in 1763, down through the years until the Redskin was driven to his last strongholds in the Far West, following the vanishing bison trail, the rifle and the Redskin were inseparable.

It was generally known that the Iroquois raiders were armed with rifles as early as 1750. But it remained for a fragment of manuscript in the St. Louis Mercantile Library—part of the Journal of Col. Auguste Chouteau, founder of St. Louis—to establish the fact that thirty years earlier, in 1736, the Chickasaws were not only armed with rifles but were generally good shots.

In the beginning the Redskin's rifle was a close parallel of the white man's long-barreled weapon, especially since in most instances it was in fact the weapon of some slain and scalped settler, and in others was obtained from that picturesque frontier character, the Indian trader. Later the Indian rifle was to assume individual distinguishing features which, however, unmistakably preserved the earmarks of its lineage.

The Indian trader, who was responsible for much of the contact between the pioneer and the red tribes in the early days, appeared soon after the settlements were established.

From the moment the White Man landed on the shores of the American continent, the natives were interested in his wares. They were not slow to recognize the vastly superior ingenuity of their Paleface visitors from beyond the mysterious seas, and it is needless to say that about every product displayed of the White Man's craft was viewed with an intense admiration, and it is not improbable that but for this fact, coupled with the Red Man's appreciation of comparative values, the conquest of the Western Hemisphere might have been delayed for a century or more.

But the comparison between implements made of stone and those of iron and steel was well calculated to melt away any prejudice held by the Red Warrior against the visitors from another world, and if his opposition to the invasions by these strangers was not held in restraint by a display of beads, cutlery and gaudy fabrics, there is little doubt but that the climax was reached when he sipped of the mysterious "Fire Water" and witnessed the terrible havoc wrought by powder and ball when a charge was fired from an old Fuzee musket, for it is a matter of history that the Indian would barter his last garment for a drink of common rum, and a matter of record that the great Munsey Chief, Shickillamey, gave the Isle of Wait for a rifled gun.

When the White Trader invaded the Red Man's domain, he exacted a mighty profit in an exchange for his wares. A gun is said to have been paid for with a stack of furs, high as the gun was long, and as beaver were the chief furs of export from the early Colonials, an idea can readily be obtained as to the price exacted from the Indian, as northern beaver skins in Colonial days sold for about six shillings each, and such guns as traders carried were, as a matter of reason, the poorest to be had, worth perhaps twenty shillings. Thus, when the Indian piled his beaver skins by the side of a 60-inch weapon, he paid for it at the rate of about twelve hundred shillings, for, from actual measurements, we find that a pile of beaver skins 60 inches high, when laid flat and carefully stretched, will contain a little above two hundred pelts. This is when opened, stretched and dried for export. If dressed, and perhaps this was exacted in the deal, the number of skins would be still greater.

INDIAN RIFLES

Typical examples of the Indian rifles made by the Pennsylvania gunsmiths on government contract. Note how these weapons follow the contours of the late flint-lock Kentucky rifles of which they are the direct descendants. Most of these rifles were made by Leman.

(Plate 101)

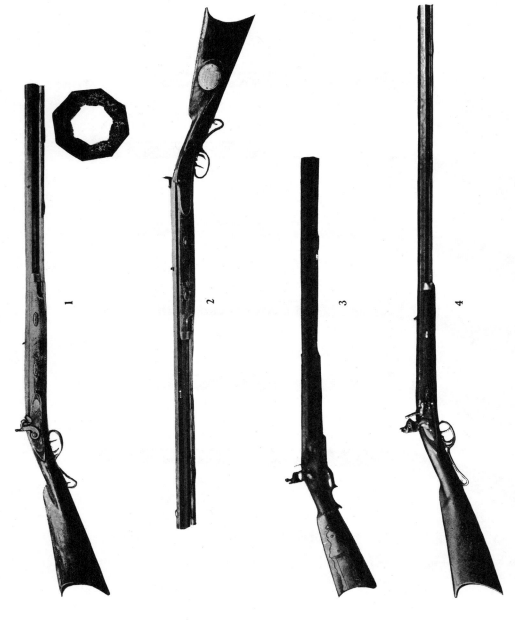

RIFLES OF KNOWN LINEAGE

Nos. 1-2. Hawken rifle owned by Kit Carson now in Montezuma Lodge, Taos, New Mexico. Cut of muzzle about ¾ size is shown. This was the Early Plains rifle.

No. 3. Flint-lock gun which tradition says was given by Kit Carson to a Taos Indian in 1848. It is now the property of Bertram C. Broome, of Connecticut. The rifle weighs 12 pounds, has a 35-inch octagonal barrel with 55 calibre bore. The barrel, once about 40 inches long, is cut off. Around the wrist of the gun is shrunk and sewed with a sinew a broad, thick band of buffalo rawhide. On the barrel is engraved B. D. Gill and a small oval stamp showing a cross, arrow and tomahawk.

No. 4. The first Remington rifle.

(Plate 102)

A trader of the early period, as a rule, traveled by canoe or packhorse, and of necessity carried light wares only. He in reality traded largely by what today we would call sample. He penetrated to the remotest Indian villages and actually took orders; he exacted that the Indian deliver his wares to a certain point and at a specified time. It may have been to the border of the settlement or to a convenient point by a river or lake, where accessibility by boat was possible.

Following these primitive methods of the trader came the Trading Post, often located on the border of the great wilderness, sometimes by the river for easy transportation. At these Posts a limited stock of such wares as the Red Man craved were carried—guns, flints, powder and lead, knives, beads, cheap jewelry, fabrics of many colors and, if allowed by the Provincial Government, Fire Water. The Indian gave in exchange for these wares of the White Man his catch of furs—in fact furs constituted the chief article he had to offer.

In these bartering trips, the Indian traveled, in many instances, great distances and many days were necessary for his return. He carried his offerings, and in view of their bulk and weight, his task was a laborious one. If his exchanges were in beaver pelts, they would average about one and one-half pounds each—other skins in proportion. Thus, if he purchased a gun five feet long and paid for it with raw beaver, he would have to carry about three hundred pounds, but it is needless to say that he was not alone on these bartering trips, but on the contrary, was accompanied by many tribesmen with their squaws as burden-bearers.

Now, while the profits exacted by the trader were doubtless large, it must be remembered that such trips as were made by these hardy adventurers were laborious and fraught with many dangers, and it is also a safe venture to say that he made the best of his opportunities.

As time passed, the Indian rifles underwent many changes. These largely kept pace with the differences apparent in the White Man's weapons, but continuing in form to pattern after the original type. As the Indians disappeared from the East, and the trader came in contact with the mounted plains savage, perhaps the greatest change of all took place—the shortening of the erstwhile long barrels for handier use from the saddle, and the full-length stocks gave way to half stocks with ribs underneath the barrel.

Although many percussion rifles found their way into Indian hands, the flintlock remained a favorite with the Red Man, since its use obviated the necessity of the third percussion component, fulminate caps.

The plains Indian obtained these later weapons through two sources—the Indian traders who were still active, and from the United States Government, which furnished rifles to many of the tribes for meat-getting purposes, and as part of that system of paternalism which developed the degenerate "blanket Indian."

What is now spoken of by collectors as "Indian Rifles" were these later arms furnished the Indians by the Government. This arm was as a rule of rather large caliber and came at about the end of the flint-lock period.

The contract Indian rifle was supplied both in flint and percussion ignition, was of medium length, strong and well built, though very plainly finished, since this weapon was produced by the Pennsylvania gunmakers at a cost of about $12.

Records indicate that these rifles were far from being the pot-metal product which is naturally associated with firearms produced for use by savages. Before the arm was accepted, it was subjected to a very severe test. In some instances, taking in account the possible vagaries of the savage mind, as much as three regular loads of powder and two balls were required before acceptance.

Taking as representative of this type of gun the specimens in one collection—about twenty, most of which were captured from or surrendered by hostile Sioux and Cheyenne warriors during the Indian troubles of the seventies—examples are found by Leman, Golcher, Henry and "G. O. and Co." of Cincinnati, with the Lemans, however, in the majority. This particular group of rifles show these calibers: .50, .52, .54, .58 and .68. All are of the percussion type, generally with single triggers but in a few instances equipped with sett triggers.

It is recorded that in the year 1816 the Astoria Fur Company of Oregon sent a representative to the Henry Rifle Works at Boulton, Pa., and contracted for a number of special guns which conformed rather closely to the Indian rifle though a little lighter in weight. One of these arms is still in the possession of the Henry family.

The Indian rifle is usually very readily distinguished by the almost invariable propensity which the Red Man possessed for ornamenting his weapons. The Indian rifle may have been plain when it left the forges of the Lancaster makers but its warrior owner lost no time in relieving its severe exterior with intricate patterns made with brass tacks, while a split stock or fore-end was customarily repaired with wrappings of raw buckskin.

OFFERMAN COLLECTION

No. 1. By A. B. Smith, Pa.; 60½ inches over all; 45-inch full octagon barrel; 2 grooves; 52 balls to the pound; set trigger; full cherry stock; weight 10¼ pounds; exceptionally fine piece.

No. 2. Unidentified; 59 inches over all; 44-inch full octagon barrel; 40 balls to the pound; a rare piece of early date. A duplicate of this rifle is known.

No. 3. By J. J. Henry & Son, Boulton, Pa.; 56 inches over all; 41-inch full octagon barrel; a beautiful arm.

No. 4. By D. Glasbremer; 55½ inches over all; 40-inch full octagon barrel; weight 9½ pounds; fine workmanship.

No. 5. By D. K.; 54 inches over all; 38½-inch full octagon barrel; stock handsomely decorated with ivory, silver and brass; upper stock in two parts, the only example of its kind known to the author; weight 7½ pounds; a very beautiful rifle.

(Plate 103)

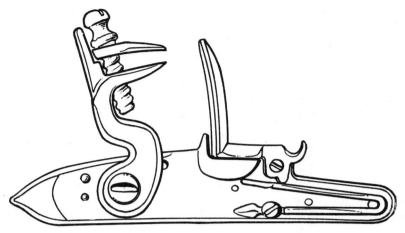

No. 1. The very early type of Pre-Revolutionary lock with goose-neck hammer.

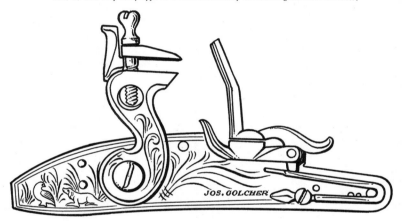

No. 2. The latter form of lock with engraved plate and improved hammer.

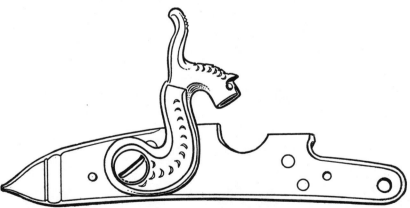

No. 3. An early lock altered to percussion, a fate which befell many fine weapons.

(Plate 104)

Identification of Kentucky Rifles

CHAPTER SEVENTEEN

o intimately is the Kentucky rifle interwoven with the formative era of early America, that the efforts of firearm collectors to preserve extant specimens should be appreciated and encouraged. Every example of early Americana which can be perpetuated for the benefit of posterity adds to our permanency as a nation.

And so one of the most important and difficult problems which confronts the antiquarian is that involved in determining the identity of the gunsmith and the place of manufacture of early American rifles. Each of these features is of paramount importance and substantially adds to the sentimental, as well as the intrinsic, value of an exhibit.

In almost every other field which has attracted the collector there have been available authentic records which, when carefully searched, would yield the desired key. But diligent investigation has revealed no such data in connection with Kentucky rifles. Contemporary firearm anthology, save in a general way, is either silent or indefinite. What little has been known has never before been collated and exists largely as unwritten information acquired by collectors themselves through the course of years of dragging from oblivion the fine specimens of Kentucky Rifles which exist today.

The matter of identification is further complicated by the fact that a majority of the riflesmiths of the flint-lock period neglected to mark their product. The remainder—about forty-two per cent—struck their names or initials deep into the barrel, often using a hard steel die, more frequently on top, but sometimes on the side or even underneath. Yet the presence of a name on the barrel, as will develop later, does not in every instance warrant the assumption that the original artisan who bored and rifled the iron bar is indicated.

Every collector will now and again encounter a specimen the origin of which will be unmistakable, provided the antiquarian is familiar with his subject. But for every clear-cut case there will be several obscure cases and these must be considered from many angles.

The prime requisite to the intelligent attribution of makers to rifles is a thorough familiarity with Kentucky rifles through actual handling and, whenever possible, exhaustive examination of the dismounted components, supplemented by whatever printed data may be available. The conclusions of others, however, are not necessarily to be regarded as incontrovertible unless they are supported by the examination of many examples. Therefore the collector of early American rifles should overlook no opportunity to examine a specimen whether it be good or poor, in prime original condition or restored; it is only thus that he can learn what to accept and—what is quite as important—in which circumstances to recognize danger signals.

Before any rifle may positively be attributed to any maker or any locality, approved as an original or rejected as a forgery—spurious specimens frequently being encountered especially since the search for Americana has revived old interest and kindled new enthusiasm for the Kentucky Rifle—the exhibit should conform to certain general specifications alike as to period and locality.

Early flint-locks were produced in both the North and the South, the latter, however, of less frequent occurrence and easily distinguishable from the Pennsylvania product.

The southern type of early American rifle, while following the general lines of those of the northern smiths, was given scant ornamentation and was rather plainly finished. Many were made entirely without the patch box; in some examples, I have seen a hole bored in the right side of the stock and filled with hard grease. Occasionally Southern rifles with applewood stocks are encountered, and generally the calibers are a little larger than in the Pennsylvania product. About the same percentage of southern rifles as among the northern type were equipped with sett triggers.

The northern, or Pennsylvania, type which is more familiar to collectors is usually to be instantly recognized by its barred or curly maple stock, finely tooled patchbox and fittings and other features with which the collector becomes familiar through personal contact with specimens.

In fixing the period, the architectural forms evidenced in the specimen under consideration are of the greatest importance.

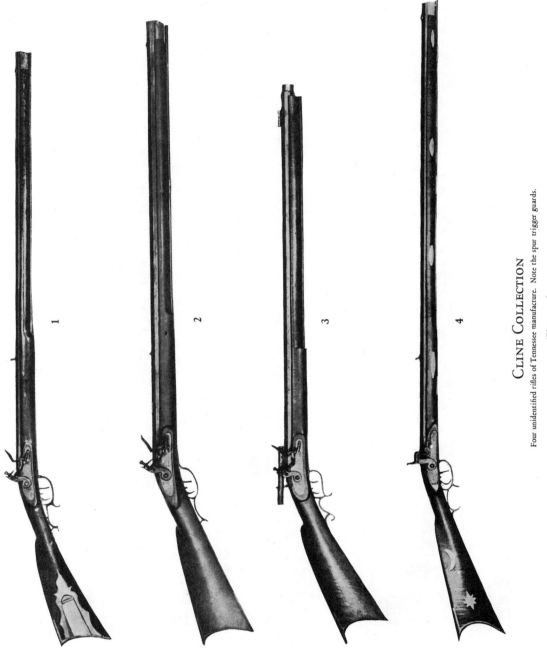

CLINE COLLECTION

Four unidentified rifles of Tennessee manufacture. Note the spur trigger guards.

(Plate 105)

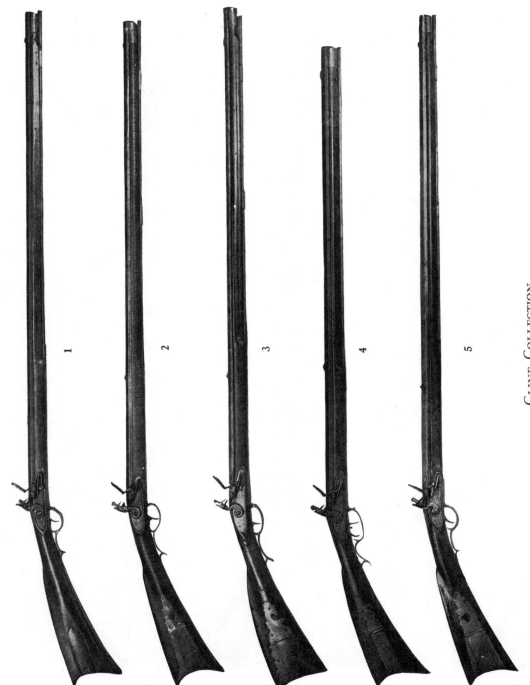

CLINE COLLECTION

Five unidentified rifles of Tennessee manufacture.

(Plate 106)

CLINE COLLECTION

No. 1. Unidentified; 57 inches over all; 42-inch full octagon barrel; full maple stock, hand-carved; brass-mounted; brass patch-box; beautiful workmanship.

No. 2. Unidentified; 56 inches over all; 41-inch full octagon barrel; full maple stock; brass-mounted and brass ornament; brass patch-box; well made.

No. 3. By Isaac Berlin, Easton, Pa.; 61 inches over all; 46-inch octagon barrel; maple stock; hand-carved; brass-mounted; brass patch-box; fine workmanship.

No. 4. By N. Beyers; 59 inches over all; 44-inch octagon barrel; maple stock, hand-carved; brass-mounted; brass patch-box; a well-made piece.

No. 5. By Simon Miller, Hamburg, Pa.; 58 inches over all; 43-inch octagon barrel; maple stock, hand-carved; brass-mounted; brass patch-box; a fine specimen.

(Plate 107)

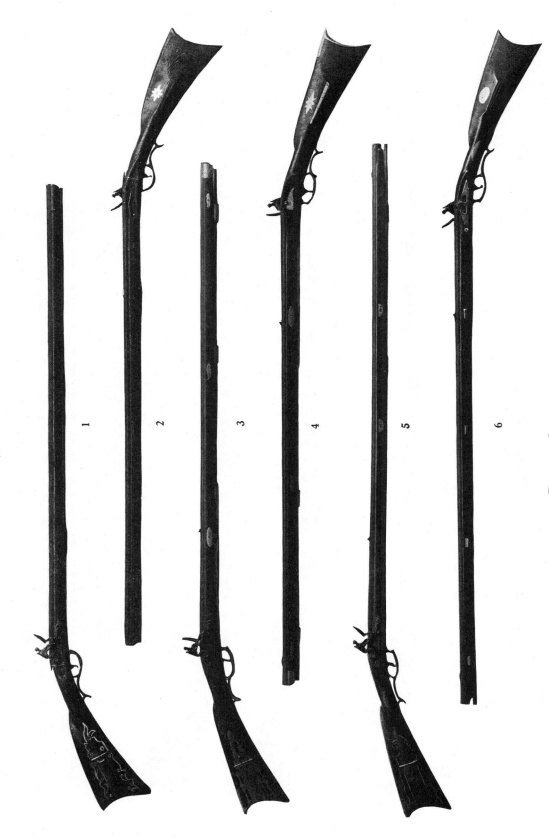

DILLIN COLLECTION

Nos. 1–2. By H. Mauger; 61 inches over all; 46-inch full octagon barrel; 42 balls to the pound; full maple stock, hand-carved; brass patch-box; splendid work.

Nos. 3–4. By H. Ehrms; 56½ inches over all; 41½-inch full octagon barrel; 52 balls to the pound; full maple stock; all mountings silver; weight 9 pounds; splendid work.

Nos. 5–6. By John Derre, Pa., 1831; 57½ inches over all; 42½-inch half octagon barrel; 42 balls to the pound; full maple stock; brass-mounted; brass patch-box; weight 7½ pounds. (Derre was an extensive maker.)

(Plate 108)

The earliest American rifles were as a rule of medium length, say an average of about 42-inch barrels, the calibers were comparatively small, seldom above a .45 and many as small as .40—a radical departure from the ways of the Continent. A large percentage of the barrels were only one-third octagon. A distinguishing feature of the early rifle was its small wrist (grip) and high, sharp comb. The butts showed but a trace of the "crescent" so pronounced in the later guns. The stocks almost invariably showed scroll work and often carving that stood in relief as a rule. Both were beautifully done. There was no checkering on the wrist of the early rifle. The locks were also a distinguishing feature, always plain and in all probability made by the smith himself; the hammer was always of the goose-neck type and very graceful. The only trace of ornamentation on the early lock was one or two straight, narrow grooves cut across the lock-plate back of hammer, being done sometimes with a file, sometimes with a tool while the plate was hot. I have never seen an early lock-plate that was engraved.

The early rifle had invariably a flat, wide trigger, very often straight. It was woefully lacking in grace and beauty, and suffers by comparison with other features. The patchbox of the early rifle, like the later ones, was made of brass. As a rule, they were narrower than the later ones, often scrolled and engraved. A striking feature of the early patchbox was that it was often fastened to stock with metal pins, instead of screws. On some of the early ones stocks were finished with varnish of exceptional quality—an oil varnish put on quite thin, on a stock that had been darkened and polished.

The early rifle had few ornaments, and they were as a rule in brass, not often more than three pieces. The star that seems to have been born with the rifle, as in the later gun, was set on the cheek piece. The sights were the regulation open type, used throughout the entire flint-lock period. Early rifles were not supplied with sett triggers. Highly ornamented rifles were rare before 1770. The early riflemaker used curly maple to the exclusion of all other woods, and took pride in selecting the best curl. The barrels were fastened to stock with iron pins, four in number.

From about 1790 some change in the style of the American rifle is noted. Occasionally we find the wrist checkered and made thicker, the stock not so deep, the comb is reduced, the crescent butt is more pronounced, ornaments increase, imported locks are much in evidence. These are chased and very neat. Many barrels run to extreme lengths. Some rifles are quite heavy, weighing as much as 11 to 12 pounds. Of hunting type, barrels are mostly octagon. Straight cuts are less frequent. The scroll and carved work is rarely seen. Sett triggers are numerous. Many highly ornamented silver-mounted guns are seen. Once in a while we see one stocked with cherry, but curly maple remains the standard wood. Many barrels are also fastened to stock with the flat keypins instead of the round ones.

From 1820 to 1840 we again note a still greater reduction in the calibers, running down to the .33 caliber Turkey Rifle. Late rifles also were often varnished with a splendid oil varnish.

Very late rifles were reduced in length of barrel during all periods. They were stocked full to the end. All used hickory rods and the early guns were often supplied with rods striped with a reddish brown color.

In connection with the identification of rifles through barrel marks, it is important to bear in mind that among the early riflemakers of the South, including Virginia, Kentucky and North Carolina, there were gunsmiths who did not forge out their barrel blanks, but purchased them in bulk from some factory like that of Eliphalet Remington. These barrels were ordered in some instances completely rifled, when the gunsmith lacked rifling facilities; in other cases simply bored to caliber, to be sold as so-called "smooth-bores" or rifled by the smith. These barrels were then fitted to hand-made stocks with American factory or English locks, and the barrel in many instances marked with the name of the assembling smith. As an example of this practice, I recall a rifle the barrel of which was plainly marked on top "R. A. Ayres," who I was reliably informed was located in Alexandria, Va. The barrel underneath bore the die mark of Remington.

Whenever marks appear on the barrel of a flintlock, these supply a most fruitful field for identification. Either full names or initials may appear. Such marking was more frequently practiced in the late period than in the early days, and in the later period it was also a custom of the riflesmith to etch his name on the barrel with acid. This was done by covering the barrel with wax, then marking the desired letters through the wax, pouring acid in the lettering and so discoloring the iron. This method was not permanent and at this late day has almost entirely disappeared. A few traces of this process have come to the attention of the author.

When a name is cut on the top of the barrel it is probable that such name is that of the maker, but in instances of names cut on the side or underneath the barrel, they must be carefully considered, as such marks were often put there by the smith who later repaired the arm. By close scrutiny it is often possible to determine between the maker and the repairer. If the barrel shows an entire originality, no tampering, and the letters cut or stamped thereon show much rust and age in general harmony with the rest of the iron work, it is fairly safe to consider mark the name of the maker; but if on the other hand the barrel shows that it has been repaired, with distinct marks of the hammer and anvil, then the letters are doubtless the work of the repair smith.

Dillin Collection

Nos. 1-2. Unidentified; 59 inches over all; 44-inch full octagon barrel; 60 balls to the pound; full maple stock; brass-mounted; brass patch-box; weight 8 pounds; well made.

Nos. 3-4. Unidentified; 59 inches over all; 44-inch full octagon barrel; 60 balls to the pound; full maple stock; brass-mounted; brass patch-box; globe and peep sights; weight 9½ pounds; fine workmanship.

(Plate 109)

DILLIN COLLECTION

Nos. 1-2. By Henry Gibbs, Lancaster, Pa.; 55½ inches over all; 40½-inch full octagon barrel; 45 calibre, straight cut; full maple stock; brass-mounted; brass patch-box; weight 7½ pounds; fine workmanship.

Nos. 3-4. By J. M. Aldenderfer, Pa.; 59½ inches over all; 44½-inch half octagon barrel; 48 balls to the pound; full maple stock; brass-mounted; brass patch-box; silver inlays; weight 9¼ pounds; date 1818.

Nos. 5-6. By Cramer, Pa.; 56 inches over all; 41-inch full octagon barrel; 52 balls to the pound; full maple stock; brass-mounted; brass patch-box; silver inlays; weight 8¾ pounds.

(Plate 110)

It is well to bear in mind that about eighty per cent of the rifles made in the flint-lock period have a metal ornament neatly fitted in the upper small of the stock, sometimes called the wrist of the rifle. This ornament is, as a rule, of silver; very often carries the engraved initials of either the maker or the man for whom it was made; and it sometimes happens that it isn't possible to determine which of the two it represents. Recently the author came across a rifle with the name "I. Shob" cut in the barrel. On the silver plate were cut the initials "I. S.", strongly suggesting that in this instance the maker had put both his name and his initials on one of his rifles. Two other rifles by the same maker, however, bear different letters on the plate, one being marked "M. W." and the other "P. J." suggesting that the smith was not bound by any fixed rule, but probably engraved the initials of the purchaser on the plate, if so ordered, and, when no specifications were given, used the letters of his own name.

On numerous occasions two or more initials have been found cut on the barrel or plate of a rifle. They were meaningless, and unimportant in determining whether they stood for the maker or owner, until another rifle by the same smith turned up carrying the same initials, when it was safe to say that they were those of the smith. N. Byers always cut his name on the barrel in deep script and his initials "N. B." on the plate.

Few riflemakers finished their barrels plain. There was almost invariably shallow scrolling on the breech end of the barrel; sometimes on the muzzle end and occasionally by the rear sight. It was often in the form of a wreath and cut with a fine-pointed tool. Many traces of this work are still visible though badly worn by constant handling. It is almost certain that in many instances names and dates were engraved on the gun in this way, but have been wholly obliterated by time and wear.

The lock of the rifle is a very poor guide to identification. In the early riflemaking days the greater percentage of rifle locks were made by the smiths themselves, or by a local lockmaker. They were very plain and the plates rarely bore either name or engravings. Later the reverse was true, for a very large number of American riflesmiths were using locks of foreign manufacture. These came largely from England, were as a rule strong and artistic and all bore the name of the makers. The invasion of these foreign locks seems to have stimulated an interest in domestic manufacture, for early in the nineteenth century a number of gunlock factories were in operation in Eastern Pennsylvania. Conspicuous among these were the Golchers, of which family there were at least five members. Later one of them, Joseph, emigrated to California and opened a shop there.

The Golchers, like many other lockmakers, stamped their names upon their product and this practice has caused an almost endless confusion in the identification of the flint-lock rifle, as the maker of the lock is very often credited with the manufacture of the rifle itself. This is especially true when the name of the maker is not found on the barrel.

It is safe to say that the name on a rifle-lock rarely indicates who made the rifle. The exceptions are so few as to be notable.

At least two of the Golcher family, James and John, were riflesmiths, but their names and those of others of the same family are found on a great number of locks of old rifles known to be the work of many makers. This may account for the numerous so-called Golcher rifles. James Golcher branded his name on both his barrels and locks. The author has knowledge of only one of his guns. John Golcher doubtless made many rifles, but there is no credible evidence that others of that family were extensive makers. Drepperd, of Lancaster, stamped his locks and barrels but, as already stated, few makers did so and a name on a lock is of little or no value as a means of identification.

When the pertinent marks of a rifle under examination have been discovered, recourse should be had to an authentic checklist of flint-lock rifle makers, and the finding of the name or initials on the list should settle the question of identity unless there are apparent anachronisms such as inconsistencies between the date when the riflesmith worked (if shown on the checklist) and the period into which the weapon falls by reason of its architecture.

Marks upon barrel or stockplate being absent, the best that can then be expected in the matter of identification is the general place of manufacture and the probable identity of the smith.

Kentucky rifles of the better types evidence a high degree of individuality, not only in the shaping of the stock but even to a greater extent in their patchboxes, trigger-guards and decorative brasses. Although I know of no exhaustive study of these components, with a view to listing the characteristics which by their similarity would point to a common origin either in design or technique, much undoubtedly could be learned from this source—at least to the extent of a probable common origin in two rifles—exhibiting closely parallel designs or detail of construction.

The list of early riflemakers which follows represents the research of years. It has been carefully assembled, revised many times, and is considered reliable. It is not perfect, for the compilation of a complete list at this late date would be out of the question. Valuable information was found in a study of the early county records of Pennsylvania and many names are those found cut on the barrels of the rifles by the maker. Another source of information was opened by talks with old Pennsylvania hunters who knew where the early rifle shops were located, men who were familiar with the

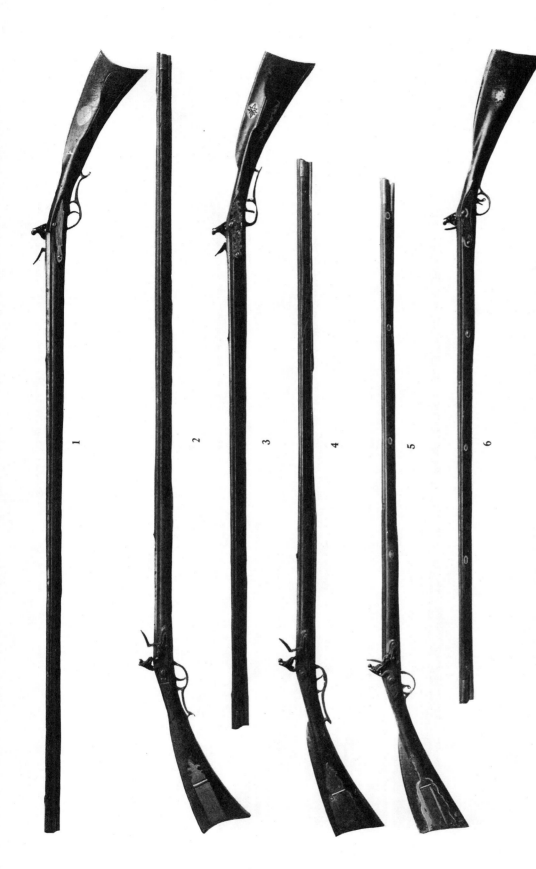

DILLIN COLLECTION

Nos. 1–2. Unidentified; 67 inches over all; 52-inch half octagon barrel; full maple stock on which is carved an Indian; brass patch-box, the author has seen three rifles almost identical with this one. All show very early workmanship evidently by Pennsylvania riflesmiths;

Nos. 3–4. By Matthias Roesser, Lancaster Pa.; dated 1746; 59 inches over all; 44-inch half octagon barrel; originally about 42 calibre, small wrist type; weight 8 pounds; bust of Indian engraved on upper butt plate; very handsome piece.

Nos. 5–6. By Reading; an original smooth bore and called a smooth bore rifle; rare; two others by same maker are known.

(Plate III)

DILLIN COLLECTION

No. 1. By John Krider, Philadelphia, Pa.; 51 inches over all; 36-inch full octagon barrel; percussion lock; half walnut stock; brass patch-box; a rifle of the early percussion era, showing great beauty of workmanship.

No. 2. By Andrew Wurfflein, Philadelphia, Pa.; 51 inches over all; 36-inch full octagon barrel; percussion lock; half walnut stock; brass patch-box; one of the most beautiful rifles in existence. Andrew Wurfflein was the father of the late William Wurfflein who was famed for his breech-loading target rifles and pistols. His factory was located on North Second street, Philadelphia, Pa.

No. 3. Showing inlays and decorations on under side of stock of rifle illustrated in No. 2.

No. 4. By John Smith; 49 inches over all; 34-inch half octagon barrel; percussion lock; peep sight; half walnut stock; silver cap box engraved "Jay Cooke—1869." This rifle was the property of the great financier.

Nos. 5, 6. By J. Granstatt; 65 inches over all; 46-inch full octagon barrel; 60 balls to the pound; full maple stock; brass-mounted; brass patch-box, fitted with sunshade for match shooting; fine work. *(Frank Butler Collection.)*

(Plate 112)

names of the smiths who had made their grandfathers' rifles. No names which appear on the locks alone are included in the list, for, as before stated, such marks, with few exceptions, identify the lockmaker only.

In a final revision a number of names have been eliminated because of a conviction that they represented makers of muskets or gun parts.

It will be noted that in some instances special stress is placed on the meritorious work of certain smiths while no credit for skill is given to others. It is only fair to say that these notes are not intended as a comparison of the handiwork of the smiths listed. Such criticism would be unjust. Some makers were known far and wide for their beautiful work and in other instances the rifle under inspection was particularly fine and the impression was strong that the maker was an exceptional artisan. There were smiths who made two grades of rifles, and having seen only an indifferent specimen, it would be unfair to put such a smith on record as a producer of only poor rifles.

On the whole, the great majority of the early riflesmiths were splendid workmen, skilled in handling both metal and wood, and the arms they produced show both character and beauty.

The collector of early American rifles is concerned mainly with flint-lock makers before 1840 and the list of riflesmiths which covers this period includes:

A A
An early maker who used only his initials. Period 1760. Seems to have specialized on straight cuts.

ADAM, DANIEL
Location unknown.

ADAMS, W.
Location unknown.

AGER, A.
Rumley, Ohio. Later maker. Probably made only a few flintlocks.

AGY
Pennsylvania. Period 1780.

ALDENDERFER
Pennsylvania. Early maker. A rifle by this smith, dated 1763, is known.

ALDENDERFER, M.
Lancaster, Pa. Was working in 1817. His rifles were highly decorated.

ALLBRIGHT, HENRY
Pennsylvania. Before and after 1744. Employed at Durham Iron Works. Made rifles and some very fine pistols. A skilled workman.

ALLBRIGHT, J.
Manheim, Pa.

ALLEN, SILAS
Shrewsbury, Mass. A workman of great merit.

ALLISON, T.
Pennsylvania.

ANGSTADT, PETER
Pennsylvania. Early period. Fine smith.

ARMSTRONG, JOHN
Maryland.

BACKHOUSE, RICHARD
Easton, Pa. An early maker.

BAER, J.
Lancaster, Pa. Famed for straight cut rifles.

BAKER, JOHN
Lancaster, Pa. An early maker.

BARLOW, J.
Moscow, Ind. 1840. Made a few flint-lock rifles.

BARNHARDT, W.
Pennsylvania. A workman of splendid ability making very highly decorated rifles. About 1780.

BARTLETT
Lancaster, Pa. Early maker. Excellent work.

BAUER, GEORGE
Lancaster, Pa. An early maker.

BAUER, J.
Location unknown.

BEAN, BAXTER
East Tennessee.

BEAN, JAMES
East Tennessee.

BECK, C.
Pennsylvania. An early maker. Made two grades of rifles but turned out many fine arms of a heavy hunting type.

BECK, ISAAC
Mifflinburg, Union County, Pa. About 1835.

BECK, J.
Location unknown.

BECK, J. P.
Union County, Pa.

BELL, CONDER
Location unknown.

BELLIS
Lancaster, Pa. Early maker. A straight cut by this smith is known. It shows great age.

BENFER, AMOS
Snyder County, Pa. A late maker.

BENFER, ARNIG
Beaverstown, Snyder County, Pa.

BERLIN, ABRAHAM
Eastern Pennsylvania.

BERLIN, ISAAC
Pennsylvania. A fine workman.

BERRY, A. P.
Location unknown. A fine workman.

BERSTROW, H. T.
Buffalo, N. Y. 1835. A squirrel rifle made by this smith has been used by the author.

BERY, R. B.
Location unknown. A very good workman.

BEST, M.
Pennsylvania. One superposed rifle by this smith is known. A late maker.

BLOODGOOD
North Carolina.

BOONE, E.
Oley Valley, Pa. Was making rifles there in 1818. Second cousin to Daniel Boone.

BOONE, SAMUEL
Came to Berks County, Pa., from North Carolina in 1768 and learned rifle-making. A nephew of Daniel Boone.

BOONE, SQUIRE
Rowan County, North Carolina. Made rifles before 1800. Brother of Daniel Boone.

BOSSWORTH
Lancaster, Pa. Early maker.

BOYER, D.
Orwigsburg, Pa. Son of M. Boyer. An extensive maker of superposed and heavy match rifles.

BOYER, M.
Lehigh District, Pa. An early maker.

BOYER, N.
Lehigh District, Pa.

BREY, ELIDS
Location unknown. Made side hammer percussion rifles and is believed to have made flint-locks. A splendid workman.

BRONG, J.
Lancaster, Pa.

BRONG, PETER
Located at 700 North Queen Street, Lancaster, Pa., in 1800.

BROWN, F. B.
Lancaster, Pa.

BULOW, CHARLES
Lancaster, Pa. Was operating in 1797.

BURD, C.
Philadelphia, Pa. Made very handsome rifles and pistols.

BURNETT, F. L.
Location unknown.

BUSCH
Lancaster, Pa. An early maker.

BUTLER, JOHN
Lancaster, Pa.

BYERS, N.
Pennsylvania. Made a great many rifles without patch boxes. The author has seen seven of his rifles, apparently about the period 1780 to 1800. His scroll work was exceptionally fine.

CARLISLE, H.
Pennsylvania. A fine workman.

CAUP, LEVI
West Buffalo, Snyder County, Pa. A late maker.

CHARLOTTESVILLE RIFLE WORKS
Charlottesville, North Carolina. 1740.

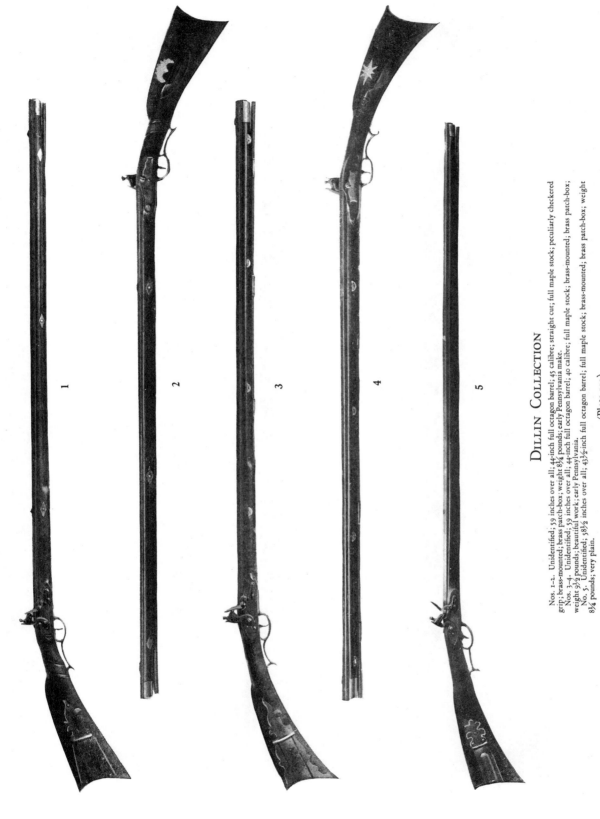

DILLIN COLLECTION

Nos. 1–2. Unidentified; 59 inches over all; 44-inch full octagon barrel; 45 calibre; straight cut; full maple stock; peculiarly checkered grip; brass-mounted; brass patch-box; weight 8¼ pounds; early Pennsylvania make.

Nos. 3–4. Unidentified; 59 inches over all; 44-inch full octagon barrel; 40 calibre; full maple stock; brass-mounted; brass patch-box; weight 9½ pounds; beautiful work; early Pennsylvania.

No. 5. Unidentified; 58½ inches over all; 43½-inch full octagon barrel; full maple stock; brass-mounted; brass patch-box; weight 8¼ pounds; very plain.

(Plate 113)

DILLIN COLLECTION

Nos. 1–2. Unidentified; 54 inches over all; 39-inch full octagon barrel; 40 calibre; full maple stock; brass-mounted; brass patch-box; weight 6½ pounds; poor work.

Nos. 3–4. By S. Pannabecker; 55½ inches over all; 40½-inch full octagon barrel; full curly maple stock; brass-mounted; brass patch-box; an early rifle of fine workmanship; weight 10¾ pounds.

Nos. 5–6. Unidentified; 58½ inches over all; 43½-inch full octagon barrel; full curly maple stock; hand-carved; brass-mounted; brass patch-box; fitted with original sunshade; weight 11 pounds; fine work.

(Plate 114)

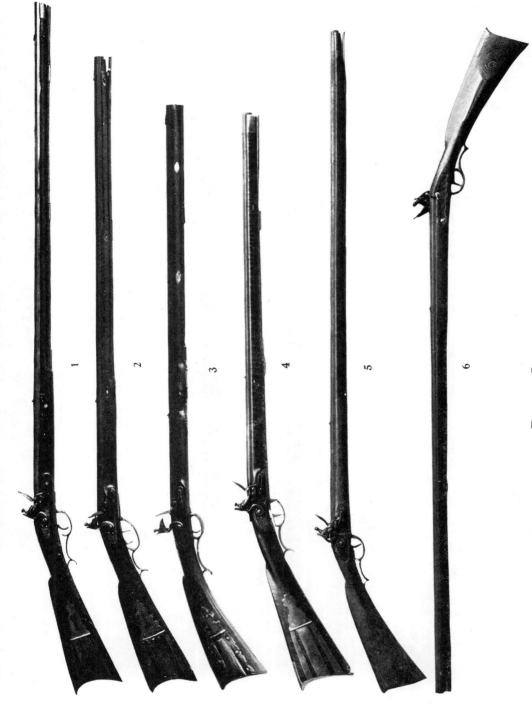

DILLIN COLLECTION

No. 1. Unidentified; 59 inches over all; 44-inch full octagon barrel; 60 balls to the pound; full maple stock; brass patch-box; weight 9 pounds; workmanship fair.

No. 2. By H. S. Graff; 53 inches over all; 38-inch full octagon barrel; 70 balls to the pound; full maple stock; basket weave checkered grip; weight 7¾ pounds. This rifle was used in California until late in the percussion period.

No. 3. Unidentified; 51 inches over all; 36-inch full octagon barrel; 60 balls to the pound; full maple stock; Indian carved on upper stock; brass patch-box; an early Pennsylvania rifle; weight 8½ pounds.

No. 4. Unidentified; 50 inches over all; 35-inch full octagon barrel; full maple stock; brass patch-box; weight 7¾ pounds; fine workmanship.

Nos. 5-6. By E. Boone, Oley Valley, Pa.; dated 1817; 57 inches over all; 42-inch half octagon barrel; 60 balls to the pound; no patch-box; very plain workmanship. (E. Boone was a cousin of the famous Daniel Boone.)

(Plate 115)

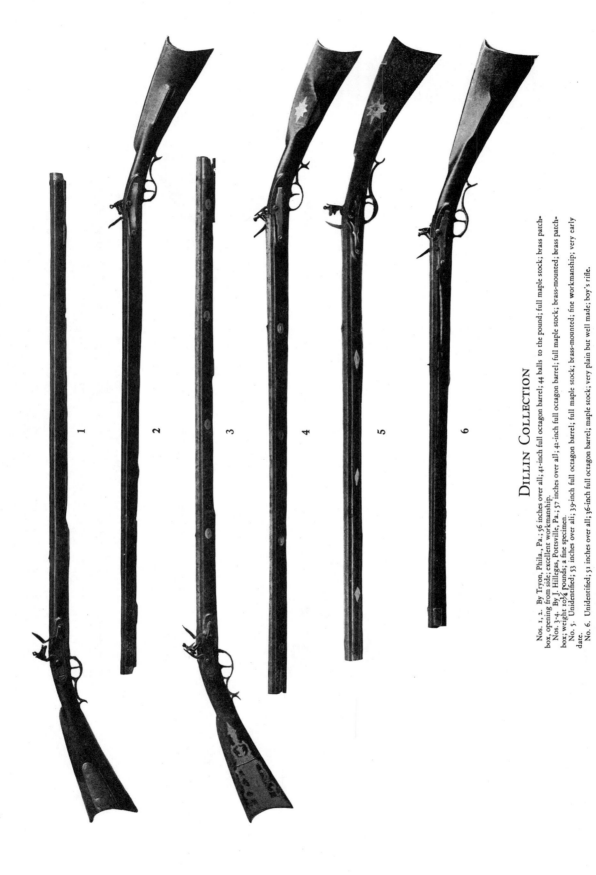

DILLIN COLLECTION

Nos. 1, 2. By Tryon, Phila., Pa.; 56 inches over all; 41-inch full octagon barrel; 44 balls to the pound; full maple stock; brass patch-box, opening from side; excellent workmanship.

Nos. 3-4. By J. Hillegas, Pottsville, Pa.; 57 inches over all; 42-inch full octagon barrel; full maple stock; brass-mounted; brass patch-box; weight 10¼ pounds; a fine specimen.

No. 5. Unidentified; 53 inches over all; 39-inch full octagon barrel; full maple stock; brass-mounted; fine workmanship; very early date.

No. 6. Unidentified; 51 inches over all; 36-inch full octagon barrel; maple stock; very plain but well made; boy's rifle.

(Plate 116)

CHERRINGTON, SR.
Pennsylvania. Father of Thomas P. Cherrington.

CHERRINGTON, THOMAS P.
Cattawissa, Pa. Son of above. A very celebrated and scientific workman. Was associated with the late George Schalk, of Pottsville, Pa. During the Civil War both Cherrington and Schalk were employed by the Government.

CHNADER, J.
Pennsylvania. His rifles show excellent workmanship though very plain.

CHRISKY, L.
Philadelphia, Pa.

CHRIST, D.
Lancaster, Pa. Excellent work.

CHRIST, JACOB
Location unknown.

CLAUSE, NATHAN
An early Pennsylvania smith. A splendid superposed rifle of his make is known. A workman of exceptional merit.

CLEWFLIN, W.
Location unknown. Excellent workmanship.

CLINE, C.
Pennsylvania. An early maker of many rifles.

COLDERWOOD
Philadelphia, Pa.

COOLEY, D.
Location unknown.

COONS, E.
Philadelphia, Pa. Beautiful work. Later members of his family made shotguns.

COPE, JACOB
Location unknown.

COWELL, EBENEZER
Allentown, Pa.

COWELL, P.
Pennsylvania.

CRAMER
Pennsylvania.

CRANDALL, M. F.
Conanda, N. Y. A late maker.

CRYTH, JOHN
Lancaster, Pa.

DAUB, J.
Berks County, Pa. An early workman. His patch boxes open horizontally.

DECHARD, JACOB
Lancaster, Pa. Also spelled Dechart and Dickart. Period before and after 1753. There seems to be a confusion over this name, but in all probability it represents one maker.

DEEDS, W.
Pennsylvania. A heavy barrel smooth bore by this maker is known.

DeHUFF, HENRY
Lancaster, Pa. Was operating in 1802.

DeREINER
Lancaster, Pa.

DERINGER, HENRY
Easton, Pa. His rifles were long and very neat. The famous Deringer pistol was made by his son.

DERR, JOHN
Oley Valley, Berks County, Pa. A late maker of numerous fine rifles. He also made pistols.

DETERER, ADAM
Lancaster, Pa.

DIETS
Pennsylvania

DISBOCH
Pennsylvania. One beautiful specimen of his work is known.

DOOLEY
Location unknown, but two of his rifles are known to author.

DOPLER, ROBERT
Wheeling, West Virginia. A late maker.

DORN, OR LORN
Location unknown.

DOUGLASS, JOHN
Huntingdon, Pa. Was making rifles in 1830.

DOYLE, JOHN
Lancaster, Pa. About 1784. Made a plain, neat rifle.

DREPPERD, HENRY
Lancaster, Pa. An early maker and one of the few riflesmiths who put their names on lock plates. He was known as the smith whose name could be spelled from either end.

DRIPPARD
Pennsylvania. Probably same as Drepperd.

DRISBACH, G.
Location unknown.

DULL, OR DOLL, JACOB
Lancaster, Pa. 1802.

DUNKLE, G.
Location unknown.

EBERLY
Lancaster, Pa.

ECKLES, H.
Pennsylvania. About 1820.

EHLERS
Location unknown. One fine specimen
of his rifle is known to the author.

EHRMON, H.
Pennsylvania. Made fine, highly decorated rifles.

EICHOLTZ AND BRO.
Lancaster, Pa. Late flint-lock period,
continuing in business until about
1888.

ERNST
Maryland.

FARNOT, FRANK
Pennsylvania. Was making rifles in 1780.

FARNOT, JACOB
Pennsylvania.

FEDER, G.
Location unknown. Two straight cuts
by this maker are known to the author.

FEHR, J.
Nazareth, Pa. A rifle dated 1835 by this
smith is known.

FERREE, JACOB
Lancaster, Pa. 1785. With his son Joel
moved to a point 24 miles north of Pittsburgh on the Monongahela River.

FERREE, JOEL
Leacock Township, Lancaster County,
Pa. Was located along Pequa Creek.
Before and after 1750. One rifle is known.

FOLLECHT
Pennsylvania. An early maker.

FONDERGRIFT
Pennsylvania.

FONDERSMITH & SON, JOHN
Lancaster, Pa. In 1749 they were located
at Strassburg, Pa. Name also appears in
1802.

FORD, J.
Virginia.

FORDNEY, C.
Maryland.

FORDNEY, I.
Location unknown.

FORDNEY, MELCHIOR
Lancaster, Pa. Extensive maker.

FOULK, ADAM
Allentown, Pa. Probably Easton, Pa.,
about 1770.

FRANCK
Lancaster, Pa. Early maker.

FRENCH, T.
Canton, Mass. An excellent workman.

FROCK
Location unknown. Made fine, highly
decorated rifles.

GABLE & SON, HENRY
Williamsport, Pa. Late makers.

GASPARD
Lancaster, Pa. An early maker.

GEORG, JACOB
Pennsylvania. Was making rifles in 1817.
Three of his rifles are known to the
author.

GIBBS, H.
Lancaster, Pa. 1824. Made very plain
rifles.

GINGERICH, HENRY
Lancaster, Pa.

GLASSBREMER, G.
Pennsylvania. A rifle marked No. 207
and made by this smith is known.

GOLCHER, GEORGE
Location unknown. Possibly made locks
only.

GOLCHER, JAMES
Philadelphia, Pa. Also a locksmith. A
descendant was making shotguns in
Philadelphia in 1877.

GOLCHER, JOHN
Easton, Pa. An extensive maker. His old
rifle shop stood until 1920.

GOLCHER, JOSEPH
Philadelphia, Pa. Later operated on the
Pacific Coast. Perhaps a lock maker only.

GOLCHER, MANUEL
Philadelphia, Pa. 1824. Made guns. Not
certain he made rifles.

GONTEC, PETER
Lancaster, Pa. 1780. May be the same as
Peter Gonter.

GONTER, PETER, SR.
Lancaster, Pa. An early maker.

GONTER, PETER, JR.
Lancaster, Pa., North Queen Street.
Died in 1818. Is also spelled Gonder and
possibly Gontee. Name seems confused.

DILLIN COLLECTION

Nos. 1-2. By Leaman, Lancaster, Pa.; 51 inches over all; 36-inch full octagon barrel; 60 balls to the pound; sett trigger; German silver mountings; small patch-box; full curly maple stock; checkered grip; weight 11 pounds; probably made about 1845, as patch-box reflects influence of percussion era and is only one known to the author. Known as the Captain Erb rifle.

Nos. 3-4. By Robert Woods; 57½ inches over all; 41½-inch full octagon barrel; 41 balls to the pound, full maple stock; brass mounted; brass patch-box; weight 8¾ pounds. A very beautiful rifle.

Nos. 5-6. Unidentified; 56 inches over all; 41-inch full octagon barrel; 40 balls to the pound; full maple stock. checkered grip; brass-mounted; brass patch-box; sett trigger.

(Plate 117)

Dillin Collection

Nos. 1-2. Unidentified; 57 inches over all; 42-inch full octagon barrel; 36 balls to the pound; full maple stock, hand carved; basket checkered grip; brass-mounted; brass patch-box; weight 7½ pounds; a most beautiful rifle.

Nos. 3-4. By P. Gonter, Lancaster, Pa.; 59 inches over all; 44-inch full octagon barrel; full maple stock; brass-mounted; brass patch-box; weight 11 pounds; plain workmanship; very early date.

Nos. 5-6. By William Pannabecker, Lancaster County, Pa.; 58 inches over all; 43-inch full octagon barrel; 48 balls to the pound; full maple stock; hand-carved; brass patch-box; globe and peep sights; weight 13 pounds; very good work.

(Plate 118)

GOODLING, P.
Location unknown.

GORSAGE, THOMAS
Mt. Pleasant, Ohio. A late maker.

GRAEFF, JOHN
Lancaster, Pa. 1798. A fine workman.

GRAEFF, WILLIAM
Lancaster, Pa. Before and after 1751.

GRAHAM, J.
Location unknown.

GRANDSTATT, J.
Location unknown. A workman of great merit, producing highly decorated rifles.

GRESHEIM
Lancaster, Pa. An early maker.

GRIMES
Pennsylvania. Possibly made only barrels.

GROFF, H. S.
Location unknown. One of his rifles is still in use.

GRUBB, T.
Philadelphia, Pa. A high-class workman. About 1820.

GUEST, J.
Pennsylvania. A superposed rifle and a pistol by this maker are known.

GUGER, J. P.
Pennsylvania. A late maker.

GUMPH, A.
Location unknown.

GUMPH, CHRISTOPHER
Lancaster, Pa. Produced some very long rifles. Made a flint-lock rifle as late as 1888.

GUMPH, JAMES
Lancaster, Pa., died about 1887.

HALK, I.
Location unknown.

HAEFFER, J.
Berks County, Pa. Two specimens of his work are known. Fine workmanship.

HAEFFER, P. B.
Location unknown.

HAGI, J.
Pennsylvania. The author knows of one fine specimen of his work.   Early.

HAINES, ISAAC
Pennsylvania. Very early maker. Probably before 1730. His rifle strongly suggests English ideas.

HALDEMAN, F.
Heidelberg Township, Berks County, Pa.

HALL, CHARLES
Lancaster, Pa. Died about 1887.

HALL, JOHN
Yarmouth, Maine. 1811. Maker of the famous Hall Breech-loading Flint-lock Rifle.

HARPER'S FERRY RIFLE WORKS
Harper's Ferry, Virginia.

HARRIS, JASON L.
Pennsylvania.

HARTER
Lock Haven, Pa. Late maker.

HAWK, NICHOLAS
Monroe County, Pa. A late maker of exceptionally beautiful rifles, two of which are known to the author.

HAWKEN, JACOB
Louisville, Ky., about 1822. Maker of the famous Hawken rifle of the Far West.

HAWKINS
Pennsylvania. An early maker.

HENCH
Pottsville, Pa. Made beautiful rifles.

HENRY, WILLIAM, 1ST
Lancaster, Pa. Born in Chester County, Pa., 1729; died 1786. Apprenticed to M. Roesser, 1750; later started in business for himself with one Joseph Simons, the firm being known as Simons & Henry. Partnership dissolved 1759.

HENRY, WILLIAM, 2ND
Known as William Henry, Jr.; son of William Henry of Lancaster; started in business in 1778, Nazareth, Northampton County, Pa., about 70 miles northeast from Lancaster. In 1800 he operated a forge at Jacobsburg, same neighborhood. In 1812-13 he built the Henry Rifle Works at Boulton, located three miles northeast of Nazareth.

HENRY, WILLIAM, 3RD.
Son of William Henry, Jr.; in 1810 went to Philadelphia and located at 3rd and Noble Streets, where in partnership with his brother John Joseph, they manufactured gun parts. In 1822 he sold his interest to John Joseph Henry, who continued the business until November of the same year, employing forty or fifty men.

HENRY, JOHN JOSEPH
Proprietor of the Boulton Gun Works from November 22, 1822, until his death December 2nd, 1836. He contracted with the United States Government to furnish 10,000 muskets, but through a political connivance at Washington, lost his contract, which was completed by a man named Wickham.

HENRY, JAMES
Son of John Joseph Henry; born in Philadelphia, 1809. Became proprietor of the Boulton Gun Works on death of his father. Later took his son Granville Henry as a partner, who continued the business of rifle and gun making until sometime in the '80s when the business was discontinued.

HENRY, JOHN
Lancaster, Pa. In 1762, a deed conveyed to John Henry and Peter Lane a property in the Borough of Lancaster. Some time later he started a gun works, and everything seems to indicate that he was an extensive maker of rifles. He died intestate early in the '70s and his wife Eliza carried on the business for many years on East King Street, near the square. It is not known what relationship, if any, existed between John Henry and the famous William Henry, Sr.

HENRY, ABRAHAM
Lancaster, Pa. In 1798, with John Graeff, contracted to make 2,000 rifles for the Commonwealth. An Abraham Henry was in the family of William Henry, of Lancaster, but proof of his being a son is lacking.

HEP, PHILIP, JR.
Location unknown. A workman of merit.

HESS, J.
Location unknown.

HILLEGAS, H.
Location unknown.

HILLEGAS, J.
Pottsville, Pa. An extensive maker. Period 1820.

HERTHE, AUGUST.
Pennsylvania.

HOAKE, J.
Location unknown.

HOLBURN, CASPAR L.
Location unknown.

HORN, CONRAD
Hazleton, Pa. Specialized on superposed rifles. Was a fine workman.

HORN, STEPHEN
Lancaster, Pa.

HORN, WILLIAM
Hazleton, Pa. Brother of Conrad Horn.

HUMBLE, MICHAEL
Louisville, Kentucky.

HUNTINGDON, V.
Allensville, Pa. One beautiful specimen of this maker's work is known.

HUTCHINSON, R. J.
Williamsport, Pa.

HUTZ
Lancaster, Pa. Was there in 1803.

ISCH, CHRISTIAN
Lancaster, Pa.

JAMES, M.
Pennsylvania. A rifle by this maker has a wind gauge feature in the muzzle. An expert workman.

JONES, CHARLES
Lancaster, Pa.

JONES, ROBERT
Lancaster, Pa.

JOSAN
Pennsylvania. An early maker. One very fine specimen of his work is known to the author.

KANTZ, F.
Location unknown. A workman of great merit.

KAUP, LEVI
Union County, Pa. A late maker.

KEFFER, JACOB
Lancaster, Pa. There in 1802.

KELLER, I.
Cumberland Valley, Pa.

KELLY, SAMUEL.
Location unknown.

KEMMERER
Location unknown. Made very highly decorated rifles.

KENNEDY, E. M.
Location unknown.

KEY, R.
Central Pennsylvania.

KILE, NATHAN
Raccoon Creek, Jackson County, Ohio. 1817. A workman of merit.

WOODMANSEE COLLECTION

No. 1. By P. J. Brong; lock by Ketland & Co.; 62½ inches over all; 47-inch octagon barrel; calibre about 48; full curly maple stock; brass-mounted and with 10 silver inlays.

No. 2. By J. Clark; lock by Ketland & Co.; 60 inches over all; 44-inch octagon barrel; 40 calibre; full curly maple stock, brass-mounted and with 12 silver inlays.

No. 3. By W. Barnhart; 60 inches over all; 44-inch octagon barrel; 38 calibre; engraved flint-lock; full curly maple stock, brass-mounted and with 47 silver inlays; maker's name inlaid with silver on barrel, which carries 5 other silver inlays.

No. 4. Unidentified; 59½ inches over all; 44-inch octagon barrel; 30 calibre; engraved flint-lock by J. J. Henry; full curly maple stock with basket weave checked grip and 10 silver inlays.

No. 5. By M. Fordney; 59 inches over all; 44-inch octagon barrel; about 30 calibre; engraved flint-lock; full curly maple stock, brass-mounted; silver-studded checked grip; 10 silver inlays and 2 of brass.

(Plate 119)

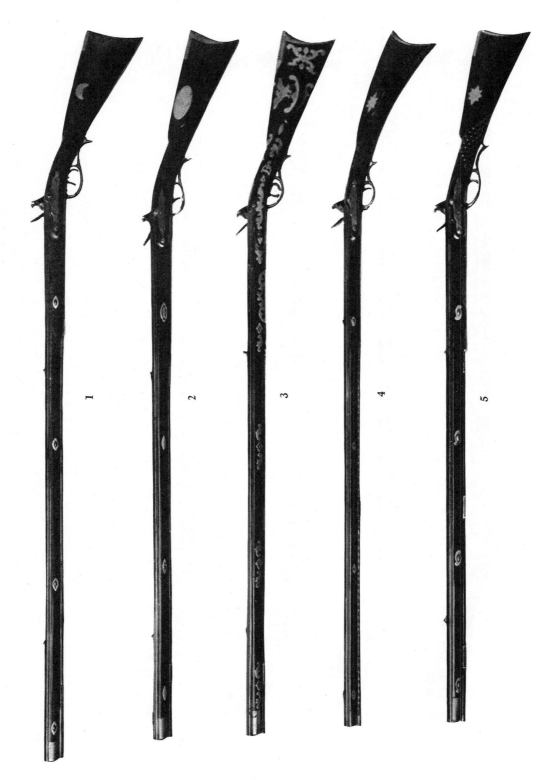

KISER, A.
Location unknown. Made highly decorated rifles.

KITCHEN, WHEELER
Broadway, Luzerne County, Pa.

KLEIST, DANIEL
Lehigh District, Pa. Seems to have made many rifles about 1810.

KLINE, C.
Pennsylvania. Three of his rifles are known to the author.

KOCHLER, P.
Lewisburg, Pa. Late maker, fine worker.

KOESLER
Location unknown.

KOONS, FRANK
Berks County, Pa. A smith of rare ability who made highly decorated rifles.

KORNMAN, A. D.
Central Pennsylvania. Made both swivel and single-barrel rifles.

KRIDER, JOHN
Philadelphia, Pa. 1826. Was an extensive maker. The old shop still stands at corner of 2nd and Walnut Streets and is operated by L. K. Siner.

KUNZ
Philadelphia, Pa.

LAGUNBRA
Pennsylvania.

LAYENDECKER
Allentown, Pa.

LECHILER
Location unknown.

LEFEVRE, PHILIP
Beaver Valley, Lancaster County, Pa. 1731-1756. Records show him to have been a gunmaker and it seems probable that he made rifles.

LEMAN, HENRY E.
Lancaster, Pa. Began manufacturing 1832. Died 1887. Extensive maker. Sent many rifles over the Pittsburgh Wagon Trail to the frontier.

LEMAN, PETER
Lancaster, Pa. An early maker.

LENNARD
Location unknown. An early maker.

LITTLE, D.
Bellefonte, Pa. A late maker.

LLOYD, WILLIAM
Snyder County, Pa. A late maker.

LODER
Location unknown. Early.

LONG, JAMES
Beaver Springs, Snyder County, Pa.

LORNEY, M.
Boalsburg, Pa.

LUDDINGTON
Pennsylvania.

LUDWIG, PAUL
Pennsylvania. Before 1831.

MANGE, H.
Location unknown. One of his guns known is of very superior workmanship.

MARKER, DANIEL
Pennsylvania. Highly decorated rifles. He also had a son in business whose rifles were of a very high character.

MARSHALL, JOB
Fairmount Township, Luzerne County, Pa.

MARTIN, M.
Location unknown. A fine workman.

MARTIN, T.
Location unknown.

MAUGER, H.
Location unknown. A maker of rare merit, about 1780.

MAUSE, F. E.
Mausedale, Montour County, Pa. A late maker.

MAYESCH
Lancaster, Pa. An early maker.

MELCHIOR, M.
Location unknown.

MESSERSMITH, JOHN
Lancaster, Pa. Was working in 1777.

MEYLAN, MARTIN
Lancaster Pa. 1719. Is known to have operated a barrel-boring mill and probably made rifles also.

MILES, THOMAS
Location uncertain, thought to have been Philadelphia. A late maker.

MILLER, I.
Location unknown. An excellent workman.

MILLER, JOHN
Lancaster, Pa.

MILLER, MATHIAS
Easton, Pa.

MILLER, SIMON
Hamburg, Pa. One of Pennsylvania's best riflesmiths.

MILLS, BENJAMIN
Harrodsburg, Ky.

MOLL, I.
Location unknown.

MOLL, JOHN
Hellertown, Pa. An early maker and a fine workman.

MOLL, J. & W. H.
Hellertown, Pa.

MOLL, PETER & DAVID
Allentown, Pa. Made high-class rifles and also pistols.

MORRISON
Milton, Pa. A late maker. May have made percussion only but is thought to have made a few flintlocks.

MOWER, P.
Columbia County, Pa. A late maker.

MUSSER, H.
Mulheim, Pa.

MYER, HENRY
Lancaster, Pa.

W. G. M.
This smith used only his initials. Several of his rifles are known. He was a splendid workman and colored his rifles almost black.

McK. & BRO.
Baltimore, Md.

NEWHARDT, JACOB
Allentown, Pa. Before 1800.

NEWHARDT, PETER
Whitehall, Pa. Before 1800.

OBERHOLTZER
Lancaster, Pa.

OGDEN, OR ODGEN
Omega, New York.

PALM, JACOB
Pennsylvania; New York. Period 1768. Made match rifles; also the regulation hunting rifles; numbered his rifles; author has seen one No. 4 and another No. 109.

PALM, JOHN
Lancaster, Pa.

PANNABECKER, JEFFERSON
Hopeland, Lancaster County, Pa. 1800. Riflemaker and commercial barrel maker.

PANNABECKER, JOHN
Near Adamstown, Lancaster County, Pa. Brother of Jefferson. Made rifles and shotguns for forty years. Early percussion period. Still resides at same place and is the last of the gunsmiths bearing the name. A skilled artisan.

PANNABECKER, JESSE
Near Adamstown, Lancaster, Pa. The author has seen a two groove barrel by this man. He was a fine workman.

PANNABECKER, S.
Muddy Run, Lancaster County, Pa. About 1780.

PANNABECKER, WILLIAM, SR.
Mohntown, Berks County, Pa. 1800. Made rifles complete; also made and sold locks and rifle barrels; and barrels for shotguns.

PANNABECKER, WILLIAM, JR.
Mohntown, Berks County, Pa. Born 1818. Succeeded his father in business. Went to Trenton, N. J., in 1860 and took charge of a factory doing Government work. Returned to Mohntown in 1865 and carried on business until his death in 1880.

PARRISH, W. A.
Pennsylvania. Very early maker.

PAUL, ANDREW
Pennsylvania. A turkey rifle by this maker is known; is highly decorated and dated 1831. It weighs six pounds.

PERKINS, J.
Philadelphia, Pa.

PHILPY, J.
Location unknown. One of his rifles known to the author shows peculiar but exceedingly fine workmanship.

PICKLE, HENRY
Lancaster, Pa. There in 1802.

PULING, J.
Location unknown.

RATHFONG, GEORGE
Lancaster, Pa. Was making rifles in 1774. A nine-grooved rifle by this maker is known to the author.

REASOR, DAVID
Lancaster, Pa. Records show him to have been a gunsmith in 1749.

REDFAN
Lancaster, Pa. Possibly same as Rathfong.

REED, JOSEPH
Lancaster, Pa. An early maker.

REID. TEMPLETON
Milledgeville, Georgia. Was there in 1824.

RINER, MICHAEL
Lancaster, Pa.

REMMERER, DAVID
Location unknown.

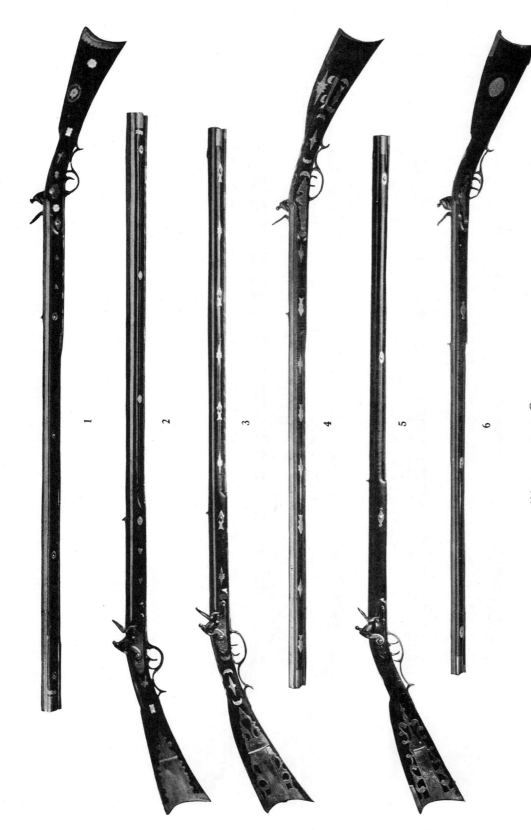

WOODMANSEE COLLECTION

Nos. 1–2. By Peter Moll; 59½ inches over all; 44-inch barrel; 48 calibre; name and marks on barrel in gold inlay "Peter Moll, Heller-town; Warranted; May the 26, 1826, No. 40;" engraved flint-lock by Tayler; full curly maple stock; brass-mounted; with 21 silver inlays; 10 of ivory, and 10 of brass.

Nos. 3–4. By J. D.; 59 inches over all; 43-inch octagon barrel; 38 calibre; engraved flint-lock by C. Bird & Co., Phila.; full curly maple stock; brass-mounted; with raised carving, 45 silver inlays and 2 of brass.

Nos. 5–6. Unidentified; 58 inches overall; 42-inch octagon barrel; 30 calibre; full curly maple stock; brass-mounted; with 9 silver inlays.

(Plate 121)

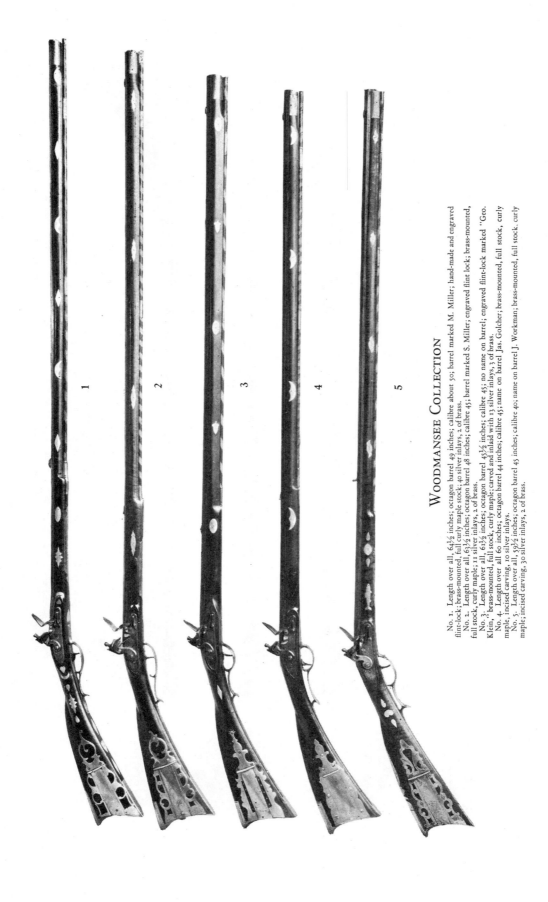

WOODMANSEE COLLECTION

No. 1. Length over all, 64½ inches; octagon barrel 49 inches; calibre about 50; barrel marked M. Miller; hand-made and engraved flint-lock; brass-mounted, full curly maple stock; 40 silver inlays, 2 of brass.

No. 2. Length over all, 63½ inches; octagon barrel 48 inches; calibre 45; barrel marked S. Miller; engraved flint lock; brass-mounted, full stock, curly maple; 11 silver inlays, 2 of brass.

No. 3. Length over all, 61½ inches; octagon barrel 45½ inches; calibre 45; no name on barrel; engraved flint-lock marked "Geo. Klein," brass-mounted, full stock, curly maple; carved and inlaid with 13 silver inlays, 3 of brass.

No. 4. Length over all 60 inches; octagon barrel 44 inches; calibre 45; name on barrel Jas. Golcher; brass-mounted, full stock, curly maple, incised carving, 10 silver inlays.

No. 5. Length over all, 59½ inches; octagon barrel 45 inches; calibre 40; name on barrel J. Workman; brass-mounted, full stock, curly maple; incised carving, 30 silver inlays, 2 of brass.

(Plate 122)

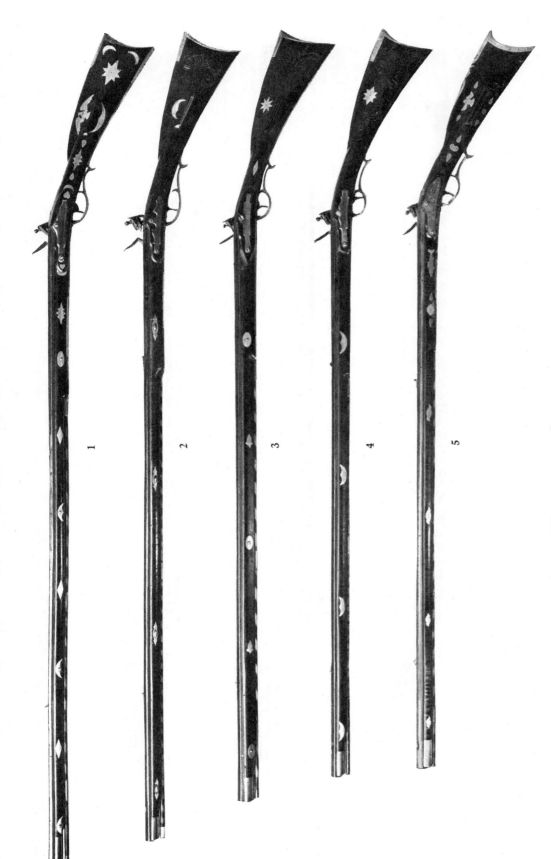

1

2

3

4

5

WOODMANSEE COLLECTION
Reverse of rifles shown on preceding page.

(Plate 123)

Huston Collection

No. 1. Unidentified; 36-inch octagon barrel; 52 balls to the pound; 21 silver inlays; splendid work; weight 7 pounds.
No. 2. By J. Hoak, Pa.; 45½-inch octagon barrel; 56 balls to the pound; bone ornaments; weight 10¾ pounds.
No. 3. By J. Roop, Pa.; 42-inch octagon barrel; 62 balls to the pound; fine checking on patch-box; 9 silver ornaments and 2 silver fishes inlaid.
No. 4. Unidentified; very early Pennsylvania rifle; good work; two known specimens exist.

(Plate 124)

RESOR, J.
Location unknown. An early maker. One specimen of his work is known to the author.

REYNOLDS
Lancaster, Pa.

RIDDLE
Lancaster, Pa. An early maker.

RIGERT, OR REIGART, PETER
Lancaster, Pa. An early maker.

RIGHTER, J. G.
Cadiz, Ohio. A late maker. Possibly made a few flintlocks.

ROBINSON
Philadelphia, Pa.

ROBERTSON
Philadelphia, Pa. Both Robertson and Robinson were working at the same period.

ROESSER, MATTHEW, OR MATHIAS
Lancaster, Pa. Before and after 1744. His rifles are very beautiful in outline and finish.

ROESSER, PETER
Lancaster, Pa. Before and after 1780.

ROOP, JOHN
Allentown, Pa. Lehigh District. Before and after 1775. An extensive maker who often decorated his rifles with the Masonic emblem.

ROTH, HENRY
Wilkes-Barre, Pa. A late maker.

RUPPERT, WILLIAM
Lancaster, Pa. Period of 1777.

RUSILY, JACOB
Lancaster, Pa.

RYNES, MICHAEL
His shop was on Pequa Creek, Lancaster County during the Revolution. The ruins of his shop are still visible.

ST. CLAIR, S. H.
Pennsylvania. An early maker and a very fine workman.

SCHO'B, I.
Pennsylvania. One of the finest riflesmiths in the State. Period 1780 to 1815. Five of his rifles are known to the author, all very beautiful specimens, but were a mystery until recently, when the name was found on the barrel. Other specimens examined had his initials on the silver plate only.

SCHORER, ANDREW
Bethlehem Township, Pa.

SCHRIDT, JOHN
Reading, Pa. Before and after 1758.

SCHULER, JOHN
Liverpool, Perry County, Pa.

SCHULL, M.
Location unknown.

SELL, FREDERICK
Maryland.

SENSENY, J.
Pennsylvania. With this maker J. H. Johnson, of Pittsburgh, Pa., learned his trade.

SHAFER, JOSEPH.
Location unknown.

SHEESLEY, GEORGE
Hartley Township, Union County, Pa. A late maker.

SHEETS, M.
Virginia.

SHELL, JOHN
Leslie County, Kentucky. Died in 1922 at an extreme age. In 1920 he told Walter M. Cline that, as a young man, he made rifles.

SHELL, M.
Pennsylvania. An early maker.

SHELL, SAMUEL
Kentucky.

SHULTZ, H.
Pennsylvania.

SLOCUMB, SAMUEL D.
New Orleans, La.

SMITH, ANTHONY
Bethlehem Township, Pa.

SMITH, J. F.
Huntingdon, Pa. A fine workman of the late flintlock period.

SMITH, JOHNSON
Easton, Pa.

SMITH, STOEFFEL
Pennsylvania. Before and after 1794. Put his name in silver inlay on barrels. His work was plain but very good.

SNEIDER, ANTHONY
Lancaster, Pa.

SNEIDER, T.
Location unknown.

SNYDER, IRA.
Woodward, Pa. A late maker.

SNYDER—JOHN, HENRY, GEORGE and ADAM, representing several generations. Providence Township, Lancaster County, Pa. This family gave Pennsylvania her first Governor.

SPANG & WALLACE
Philadelphia, Pa.

SPANGLER, S.
Pennsylvania.

SPECHT, ELEY
Beavertown, Snyder County, Pa.

SPITZER & SON
Newmarket, Virginia.

STAHL, C.
Pennsylvania. One rifle by this maker is 81 inches long; small in caliber and with seven grooves.

STARR
Lancaster, Pa. An early maker.

STENZEL, OR STENGEL
Lancaster, Pa. An early maker.

STINGER, THOMAS
Antony Township, Lycoming County, Pa., also Jersey Shore, Pa. Before and after 1840.

SUNDERLAND
Boulton, Bethlehem District, Pa. Also Sunderland & Blair.

SWITZER, DANIEL, & CO.
Lancaster County, road to Millersville, Pa.

TAYLOR, GEORGE
Easton, Pa. Employed at Durham Iron Works.

TEAFF, NIMROD
Steubenville, Ohio, Served in the U. S. Army in the Mexican War.

TROUT, JOHN
Williamsport, Pa. A late maker.

TRYON, GEORGE W.
Philadelphia, Pa. Established 1811. Made a great many rifles of excellent quality. The firm is still in business under the name of E. K. Tryon & Co., handling guns and sporting goods.

TYLER, JOHN
Easton and Allentown, Pa.

UPDEGRAPH, JACOB
Schuylkill County, Pa.

VANDERSLICE, T.
Pennsylvania.

VELEE
Philadelphia, Pa. Was working, in 1826, at 2nd and Walnut Streets.

VOLVERT, OR VOLKERT
Lancaster, Pa. An early maker.

VONDERSMITH
Lancaster, Pa. An early maker.

WAGONHORST
Location unknown. A late maker.

WEAVER, CRYPRET
Pennsylvania. Before and after 1818.

WELSHENS, J.
Location unknown. Made a neat rifle.

WETZEL, J.
Pennsylvania. A very early maker and a fine workman.

WHITE, PETER
Location unknown. Highly decorated rifles.

WHITESIDES, JOHN M.
Tennessee.

WITHERS, MICHAEL
Lancaster, Pa. Was there in 1778.

WOLFHEIMER, PHILIP
Location unknown. An early maker.

WORL, H.
Pennsylvania. An early maker of fine superposed rifles.

WORKMEN, J.
Pennsylvania.

WORLY, J.
Location unknown. A fine workman.

WOODS, ROBERT
Pennsylvania. A workman of rare merit. Period of about 1800.

WURFFLEIN, ANDREW
Philadelphia, Pa. A late flintlock maker and a workman of great merit. Father of the late William Wurfflein, inventor of the celebrated Wurfflein rifles and pistols.

WURFFLEIN, J., & PESSOTA
Philadelphia, Pa.

YOCHUM, D.
Pennsylvania. A rifle by this maker is known to the author. It is of the heavy hunting type and shows exceptionally beautiful handiwork.

YOMENS
Charlotte, North Carolina.

YOST
Maryland.

YOUMANS
Lancaster, Pa. An early maker. Members of this family migrated to North Carolina and became famed as riflesmiths in that State.

YOUNG, D.
Middleburg, Snyder County, Pa.

YOUNG, HENRY
Easton, Pa. An extensive maker.

YOUNG, JOHN
Lehigh District, Pa. The Youngs were skilled workmen. Received a contract for 1,000 rifles from the Government in 1776 in association with Johnson Smith; and in April, 1776, with A. Foilke, contracted for 130 rifles for the Virginia Colony.

YOUNG, JOSEPH
Haynes Run, West Virginia.

ZIMMERMAN
Pennsylvania.

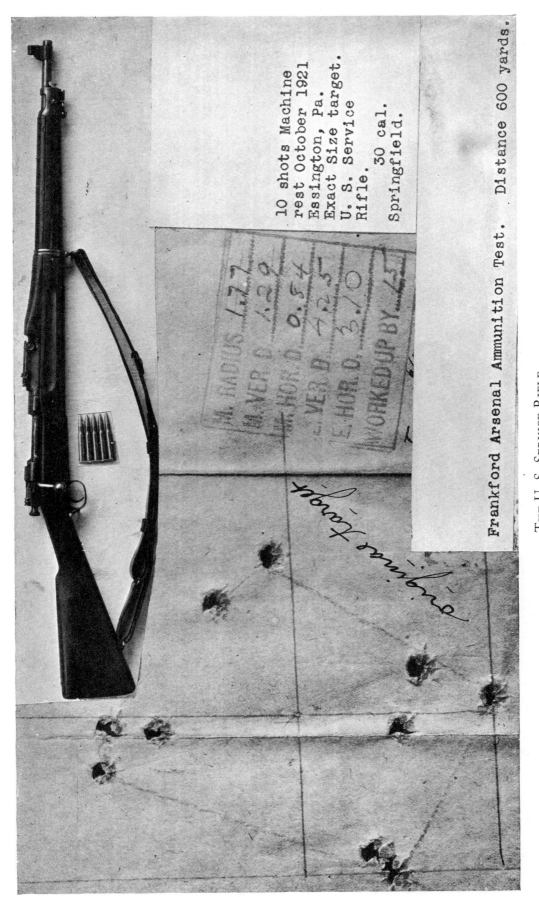

10 shots Machine
rest October 1921
Essington, Pa.
Exact Size target.
U. S. Service
Rifle.
30 cal.
Springfield.

M. RADIUS 1.7.7.
M. VER D. 1.39.
M. HOR D. 0.54
VER B. 72.5
E. HOR D. 3.10
WORKED UP BY

Frankford Arsenal Ammunition Test.   Distance 600 yards.

THE U. S. SERVICE RIFLE

Every up-to-date rifleman in the United States believes this rifle to be the best ever produced.

(Plate 125)

ADVERTISING POSTER ABOUT 1845–1850

Spurious Kentuckys and Forgeries

Chapter Eighteen

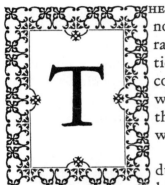

HE value of any collection of Kentucky rifles depends not upon how many examples it may contain but rather upon the rarity, original condition and authenticity of the specimens. There are many firearm collections containing literally hundreds of pieces which are virtually valueless. On the other hand, there are collections comprising a scant dozen pieces which are practically priceless.

Every collector at some time or other will acquire dubious examples or out-and-out forgeries. At times his enthusiasm will be to blame; at others an honest mistake of judgment in connection with a skillfully prepared camouflage. He who has never singed his fingers has not the true antiquarian urge.

How few of these experiences the collector suffers depends solely upon the degree of discrimination he has acquired and upon how well he has trained his perceptions to sound a warning even in moments of keenest enthusiasm.

True Kentucky flint-locks in original condition are sufficiently scarce and command a sufficiently substantial price in the antique market not only to bring to the dealer and collector a great number of questionable examples, but also to make the forging of specimens financially worth while to an occasional unprincipled but clever artisan.

Many of the spurious flint-lock rifles and pistols which have appeared during the past ten or fifteen years are so well executed that even seasoned collectors cannot always trust their first impressions, but must carefully consider any example offered in the light of the traditional best types of Kentucky rifles in the various periods.

Among European and Oriental weapons the uninitiated purchaser is frequently victimized with flint-lock rifles and pistols, armor, swords and shields which are being constantly manufactured from new material and given the semblance of age. These are 100 per cent counterfeit. But such an out-and-out counterfeit American flint-lock rifle is, in reality, a rarity; I doubt if it actually exists.

But there are two dangerous types frequently met which to all intents and purposes—and especially from the viewpoint of the discriminating collector—must be considered spurious. The first is what can appropriately be termed an "assembled rifle." The second is the early percussion that has been, for purposes of commercial deception, converted into a flint-lock.

When considering the question of spurious flint-locks in detail, it is essential to keep in mind the earmarks of the desirable specimen, which may be termed "a thoroughbred." The true American flint-lock rifle is invariably stocked to the muzzle end and nearly always found in curly maple wood. This especially applies to the early ones, some exceptions being noted among those found in the South. The patchbox and other necessary trimmings are in about 98 cases out of 100 made of brass, a few of the very late ones being supplied with German silver. The patchbox is long and as a rule hinged at the upper end, but in a small percentage of instances on the side. The short, round box of percussion days is in reality for caps and very rarely supplied to an original flint-lock. I have never seen but two so equipped, one of these being the late Leman displayed elsewhere in this work. Early flint-locks were equipped with the gooseneck hammer, but after about 1800 the musket type was extensively used. Open hunting sights were used with few or no changes from the beginning of the flint-lock period until the end of the percussion.

The assembled rifle is a subject which must be approached with an open mind and each case must be decided on its merits. It would be as obviously wrong to discard an example as worthless because the hammer, frizzen and pan were replacements, although kept in period, as it would be to accept a specimen made out of a lock, stock, barrel and fittings of widely different period and origin. Common sense and an appreciation of the fitness of things must throw the scales for or against any offering which has the character of an assembled piece.

As an example of how the unmistakably worthless, assembled rifle is made, we will assume that an unscrupulous artisan obtains a genuinely old stock and barrel from which several essential parts are missing. He hunts around until he finds an old lock. It may be too large or too small; it is seldom exact size. If too large, he cuts the lock bed in the stock until it will receive the lock. If too small, he may fill the space between the wood and the lock bed with some material as nearly invisible as possible, but in each instance doing his utmost to secure some semblance of a fit. It may be that the original lock plate is still on the gun, but the hammer and frizzen are gone; also the frizzen spring. Such being the case he is apt to find one of the cast-iron hammers and frizzens which have recently made their appearance in no small numbers. These he fits to his gun and they look neat and passable.

Now the rifle looks quite presentable, but he notes that it has no patch box, so he goes and gets one from an old discarded stock, fits it to his own gun, which seems to add a great deal of importance to this new-old arm. He then supplies a silver mounting to the wrist or cheek piece. This done, the rifle rubbed up and oiled, he has an exhibit which is cleverly enough camouflaged to deceive the collector who has not handled and examined many specimens. This rifle may not be exactly a spurious article, but one of a very dubious value as a specimen, and lacking in real interest.

Now for the other spurious type which is undeniably a counterfeit and is more dangerous; more to be despised. It is an original early percussion which has been converted into a flint-lock. Stocked to the muzzle as were these early percussions, they become dangerous counterfeits.

The conversion of this arm to flint is comparatively easy of accomplishment, especially when the basis for the fraud is that type of early percussion rifle upon which the nipple connected with the barrel by means of a drum, as described elsewhere in this work. The presence of this drum, which is screwed at a right angle into the barrel approximately at the point where, on a flint lock, the channel from the powder pan is located, together with the half-circle depression which forms its bed in the lock plate, greatly facilitates the alteration, as the necessary groundwork for the change is ready at hand.

The first step in changing from percussion to flint, with such a rifle, is to remove the percussion hammer and unscrew the drum. This leaves in the side of the barrel a round opening, larger than the channel requirement from the flash pan to the powder charge in the barrel, therefore it is necessary to plug up this hole. This is done by fitting a tight iron plug, threaded to conform to the thread already used by the drum, in the wall of the barrel. The plug, tightly screwed in, is then filed down flush with the outside of the barrel. This completed, a drill of proper size is centered in the plug and bored through, making an opening to the powder charge in the barrel. This is called the flash hole, and this completes the barrel work.

The lock is next to be considered, as it is desired to have the arm look as nearly original as possible. Therefore, the lock plate will be retained if possible. If it can be had, an old lock is secured and dismantled, and the parts fitted to the percussion plate. Great care is taken to get at least a reasonable degree of harmony in the appearance of the parts, for a total lack of harmony would at first glance seriously reflect on its genuineness.

The next step taken is the fitting of the flash pan, which should be in perfect alignment with the flash hole, center to center, then brazed or soldered to the lock plate; as the frizzen steel is attached to the pan the perfect alignment of steel to hammer is assured, provided the hammer is the right size, a feature for serious consideration when frizzen and pan are properly aligned and made fast.

The frizzen spring is the next to be considered. Two small holes are bored in the lock plate at the proper places to accommodate the pin and screw which hold the spring to the plate. This is an easy task. The next move is the fitting of the hammer, which simply means the substituting of the flint article for the percussion, the size being the main feature for consideration.

This altered rifle when carefully done is apt to be exceedingly interesting and collectors must weigh its points very carefully before accepting it as a genuine flintlock.

If the basis for the fake should be one of the later types of percussion lock, the problem is more difficult but not unsolvable. In these later rifles, the barrels were set about half an inch too far forward to permit the lock to properly connect with a faked vent. Therefore, in such cases the alterations to the lock are proceeded with in ways similar to those employed in altering the drum type of percussion while more refitting is necessitated in connection with the barrel. Two ways of refitting the barrel are followed, after the percussion vent has been filled.

The hit-or-miss method, and consequently that most easily detected, is to set the barrel back in the stock the required distance, cutting away the wood of the stock where required, plugging the old tang-screw holes and boring new ones.

The more painstaking method is to unscrew the breech plug, cut the barrel to the proper length, and reseat the plug. Such an alteration when skillfully done and carefully aged is very difficult for the novice to detect.

To infallibly detect the spurious in flint-lock rifles calls for a sixth sense, which can come only from long experience, but if the amateur collector will intelligently observe a few simple, fundamental rules he should be able to distinguish the spurious from the genuine in all except very obscure instances where the faking has been done by a master hand; therefore the following advice is offered.

The genuine early flint-lock must be a full-stocked gun. It should show a great deal of honest wear and some abuse. Take the lock off and see if the woodwork shows fresh cutting. See if it has been smudged with some substance to prematurely age a cutting. (It is easily detected.) Note the frizzen steel. See that the flint strikes fire. If it does not, when properly aligned, it is most likely a cast-iron affair and worthless; they will not strike fire. Both hammer and frizzen must show honest wear and age, the powder pan and flash hole should be in central alignment, lock plate should fit up close to barrel, pan cover should sit square over pan and not lose the powder. The flash hole may or may not have been bushed. If so, the bushing plug should not be more than twice the diameter of the hole, or say about $\frac{3}{16}$ of an inch. The butt plate should not show much of the crescent form, as this came late. Open the patchbox and see if it shows fresh cutting; if so, like the lock it strongly suggests tampering in the case of a conversion from percussion to flint. Observe the following: The pan will show new work at the fitting. The bushing at the flash hole is from $\frac{1}{4}$ to $\frac{5}{16}$ of an inch in diameter. It is not much corroded. Note the condition of hammer and frizzen, same as described in case of the made-over gun. The woodwork looks modern and firm. The stock is apt to be narrow, rather flattish, and decidedly a crescent-shaped butt. The hammer is sometimes set away from the lock plate to align it properly with the frizzen steel. The small box in stock must be carefully examined and, as already stated, is seldom found on an original flint-lock. If the long patch-box, note as described in the previous discussion of how fakes are made over. The "percussion flint-lock" is often seen with German silver mountings.

Spurious flint-lock pistols are very numerous and the collector must beware. They are mostly of foreign make and often show splendid workmanship. They are true flint-locks as a matter of course, but spurious because they are represented to be the work of early makers. Wealthy American tourists seem to delight in the acquisition of these bogus arms. These counterfeits are easily detected. They are new in appearance, solid, apt to show a little artificial coloring, or even some abuse. A great many of them are made in Belgium. Take the lock off and you find new wood.

Fakes among antique firearms are not always the result of a desire to intentionally deceive for money. Among experienced collectors there are known to exist several out-and-out fakes which were conceived as practical jokes and were allowed to persist, passing from one unsuspecting purchaser to another until now no one wishes to divulge the secret.

Such counterfeits are, of course, very dangerous, since they have invariably been fabricated by men who knew to the finest detail the model they were copying and whose task was simplified by the fact that only some slight differences existed between the rare subject of the fake and a more frequently encountered model. In connection with fakes of this nature—the production of which can scarcely be commended even though the whole matter be regarded as a joke by the perpetrator—several instances come to mind.

There are in existence today several "Walker Colts" which have been made from dragoon models with the square back trigger guard, by removing the original lever rammer and substituting a reproduction of the Walker rammer. Also numerous Army model pistols have been faked from time to time by the use of musket locks bearing rare dates and these have in some instances puzzled even experienced collectors.

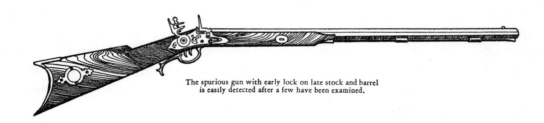

The spurious gun with early lock on late stock and barrel
is easily detected after a few have been examined.

Reconditioning Flint-locks

CHAPTER NINETEEN

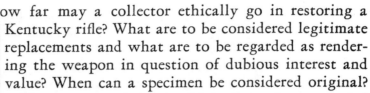

ow far may a collector ethically go in restoring a Kentucky rifle? What are to be considered legitimate replacements and what are to be regarded as rendering the weapon in question of dubious interest and value? When can a specimen be considered original?

These are questions which have long puzzled antiquarians, whether they have been collectors of period furniture, paintings, textiles or in any of the other and varied fields. They have at times even become the subject of legal argument in the course of lawsuits. Opinions concerning these matters among those dealing in or collecting antiques range from the manifestly absurd, which encourages the unethical restorer to build an "original antique bed" around a single original post and headboard, to the other extreme wherein for instance a connoisseur will reject an otherwise original chest of drawers because one foot is new.

But as applied to firearms, the line of demarkation between legitimate restoration and faking would seem to be less complicated and more clearly drawn.

That the desirable and valuable exhibit—the one in the possession of which the collector will find the greatest satisfaction—is the flint-lock of early date and original condition should be the paramount standard of every collection. But good original examples of Kentucky rifles in shooting condition are so seldom encountered as to be relatively rare; specimens of this character are, of course, the ones to be sought for and obtained whenever possible. However, the ravages of time on firearms of the past are many. Some of the old Kentuckys with unusually heavy barrels will break their stocks through the wrist unless they are consistently handled and used with the greatest of care. Frizzen springs and frizzens as well as flash pans are knocked off and lost. Hammers crack through where the graceful goose-neck turns. And more than frequently the collector finds magnificent examples of early flint-locks which temporarily, at least, have been seriously marred by alteration into percussion locks.

Should the collector, discovering inherently fine examples in such condition, pass them by or, acquiring them, feel a hesitancy in restoring them and regarding them as fit for inclusion in his collection as originals? There would seem to be no good ground for such a course, *provided that the restoration is accomplished by honest replacement with old parts, wherever available, and that the period of the piece is faithfully retained.*

In instances where the collector is desirous of putting the piece into shooting condition, as many of them do today, it may also be considered permissible to remedy such small defects as missing frizzens, springs and even pans by the fitting of new parts, if the parts are honestly hand-made and not mere cast-iron junk.

In the case of flint-locks which have been altered to percussion lock, the advisability of restoring the piece depends entirely upon how good the exhibit was originally. If by its form it is shown to have been an average mediocre piece of late vintage, it is not of sufficient importance to warrant the thought, time, and money which must be expended to accomplish restoration. But if a collector is fortunate enough to acquire an early stock, barrel and lock in good original condition, save for such alterations as were involved in fitting it for percussion ignition, and which gives plain evidence by period earmarks that it was formerly of the highly desirable type, reconditioning is justified, although a slight question arises as to whether it could ever be regarded as a first-quality piece. Such a gun can legitimately be restored by any skilled gunsmith, who can weld the vent in the barrel and bore a new touch hole, adding a hammer, frizzen and pan of the proper period—preferably old parts obtained from an old damaged rifle. In old rifles which have been changed to percussion the original lock, other indications failing, can always be identified by the holes where the pins which attached the pan and frizzen were located.

Aside from supplying missing small parts, there is considerable that can be done to a Kentucky rifle which comes from an attic or a cellar to the collector "in the rough"—to employ a term current among antiquarians. This broadly embraces a cleaning-up process, which may be limited to the removal of exterior rust and dirt, or which may extend to putting the weapon in first-class condition inside and out.

Even the most superficial reconditioning, however, should be undertaken only with a thorough understanding of what will enhance the interest of the piece and what will seriously mar it. Perhaps the safest standard to set is to endeavor to restore the exhibit to the condition in which it saw actual use—as it was when it was being used by its original owner. This means that the exterior metal parts must be cleansed of rust, the bore polished, the lock mechanism cleaned and oiled, the brass work cleared of verdigris and the stock well rubbed. It however emphatically *does not* mean that any of the many indicia of age—either from wear or the abuse which is always expected to have followed use under frontier conditions—should be obliterated, unless the woodwork of the stock is so badly chipped as to be unsightly and detract from the appearance of the exhibit.

To other than very superficially recondition a flintlock, the weapon must be disassembled. The barrel is removed by carefully driving back the pins which secure it to the stock through the fore-end, and by taking out the tang screws. The lock is detached by removing the "bridle screws" on the opposite side of the piece. There is no necessity, nor any reason ordinarily, for disturbing any of the brass ornamentation, unless the discoloration is very stubborn. Even then, perhaps, it is better to clean it as thoroughly as possible in the stock, taking care not to bring the cleaning agent used in contact with the wood, and be content with the results.

Fine old bronzes, through much handling and the oxidization from air, acquire a dark surface finish known as "patina". This is one of the best indications of age. Similarly, through the same agencies, fine woods, when use is combined with age, take on a dark, glossy patina. The stocks of old Kentucky rifles, when of maple or other hard wood, on which the old varnish remains, should for this reason never be scraped and refinished. To do so would largely destroy the deep yellow and rich brown tiger-markings which were so highly prized by the early gunmaker, and which the processes of aging have intensified.

Very little cleaning is needed on the average rifle stock. Usually a thorough rubbing with a linseed-oiled rag is sufficient to remove any surface accumulation of dirt. The stock may then be polished by waxing. If the dirt proves stubborn and the accumulation is heavy enough to conceal the grain, steel wool—*provided it is of the finest and most uniform grade*—may be used without harm. The rubbing should be done slowly and carefully, with frequent inspections. The safest plan is to do as little cleaning on the stock as possible.

Cleaning the barrel includes the removal not only of exterior rust spots but rust and dirt from the bore, if the old weapon is to be gotten into prime shooting condition.

Unless deeply pitted, barrel rust can frequently be removed by oiling and scraping with a piece of soft strip brass, similar to printers' brass rule. If care is taken, this will not scratch the barrel surface nor brighten it, a condition which should be avoided. If this is not effective, then some good abrasive grease may be needed but, before any is put on the barrel, it should be tried out on another piece of metal and the results from rubbing it noted.

In cleaning the inside of the barrel, the bore should be thoroughly coated with a good rust-solvent and permitted to stand until the dirt is softened. Then the breech plug may be removed and the bore swabbed out. This treatment failing to remove all the bore fouling, fine, uniform steel wool may again be resorted to, soaked with oil and used as a plug on the end of a ramrod. Even when used with great care, as is necessary, this usually proves efficacious.

Hints which are of great assistance to the collector desirous of reconditioning or repairing his exhibits are frequently to be found in old volumes devoted either to firearms or sport.

Colonel Hawker's "Instructions to Young Sportsmen" contains many such hints, among them instructions for setting flints and for dissecting and reassembling early type locks. Of the setting of flints—which every collector will do—he says: "The flint should be put in with the flat side upward. Screw them in between a piece of leather, as lead strains the cock, and cloth is dangerous from being liable to catch fire." Colonel Hawker also warns against the practice of keeping flint-locks at half cock since this tends to weaken them. A piece of tow should be put in the pan to prevent damp.

The Passing of the Kentucky Rifle

CHAPTER TWENTY

HEN the Rev. Alexander John Forsyth in 1807 per-fected the percussion ignition system, the death knell of the Kentucky rifle was sounded. Through the following two decades flint-lock rifles were still to be produced, in reduced caliber, and otherwise distinct from the early pioneer type. In fact, as late as the Mexican War, United States Army officers refused to consider arming General Scott's forces with percus-sion weapons.

Yet during the transitional period a majority of the old-timers lost their identity through conversion to the fulminate system, one of Forsyth's earliest patents having established the practicability of such an alteration.

Percussion locks were used on shotguns in America soon after their invention, but the older riflemen were prone for a time to regard the inno-vation with suspicion, arguing that the force of the cock striking the barrel would tend to depress the piece and cause the ball to strike low. This attitude, however, was of brief duration and soon gunsmiths were engaged in the alteration of flint-locks or in the manufacture of the improved type of lock.

The conversion of a flint gun to the percussion principle was a rather simple process. About the first steps taken in the adoption of this new feature were to dismantle the lock, the frizzen steel was taken off, together with its spring, the two screw holes plugged neatly with iron pins. This done, the smith then proceeded to remove the powder pan from the lock plate. If this pan was seated in the plate with either solder or brass it was a question of melting out, but before this was done the springs and other lock fixtures were removed to protect them from the destructive heat incident to the melting process.

As a rule the powder pan was seated to the lock plate in semicircular form and was sunk to a depth varying from three-eighths to five-eighths of an inch, these measurements being applicable to rifle and shotgun locks only. Occasionally, a powder pan was seated to the lock plate in octagon form, the fitting being beautifully done. And again we occasionally find one that is fastened to the lock plate by two screws. The final lock change was the hammer. This important feature was a radical departure and called for an entirely new addition, as no part of the flint hammer could be applied to the percussion principle. Sometimes a block of iron was clamped in the hammer in lieu of the flint and used, in the vernacular, to "bust the cap." Thus, in either case, a new hammer that was woefully lacking in both grace and beauty.

The lock now having been changed, the next move was the preparation of the barrel for the new requirement, and the first move by the smith in this direction was the enlargement of the channel known as the touch hole. This was plugged, centered, and bored, the hole being about three-eighths of an inch in diameter and extending through the barrel into the very extreme bottom of the bore, barely missing the end of the breech plug. In fact, the breech plug was often cut away at the near side to insure a fire contact at the lowest point of the powder charge. When the hole was bored and neatly finished it was then threaded preparatory to the fitting of what was called the drum, a feature which I shall now describe.

This drum was made by turning a piece of wrought iron in bolt form about one-half inch in diameter by one and one-quarter inches long. A hole was then bored in one end that extended about two-thirds of the entire length of the drum. This drum was then put on a lathe and turned down for a distance to correspond with the thickness of the barrel into which it must eventually go, and was also turned to correspond with the threaded hole through the barrel, as already described. When this was done the reduced end of the drum was threaded and fitted to the barrel in the neatest possible manner. It was screwed up tight against the barrel. The barrel was then put in its position on the stock. The lock also was screwed to its position. Then followed the final fitting of drum to the half-circle channel in the lock plate, this being done with a round file. Occasionally a smith would bore entirely through and then thread the outer end and fit therein a tight screw plug. This was done for the purpose of cleaning out the channel should it foul up, simply unscrewing the plug and pushing a wire through and into the barrel.

The next and final move of the smith was the fitting of the cap nipple to the drum. To do this the newly installed percussion hammer that was nicely fitted to the lock was let down until the nose rested on the drum. The center of the hammer was then determined, and its point of contact carefully marked on the drum. When this point was accurately determined the drum was unscrewed from the barrel, put into a vise and bored for the cap nipple (sometimes called the tube). This nipple was as a rule set at about a 45-degree angle to conform to an alignment with the hammer. The cap nipple, a hollow steel tube about one-eighth of an inch in diameter by one-half inch long, had a base of about twice its upper diameter. This base was threaded and screwed into the drum to complete a contact with the channel that must commence with the powder charge in the breech of the gun. The nipple properly fitted, the drum was screwed back to its place. The smith, then placing the muzzle to his mouth, would force air through the barrel. If a clear channel was indicated, some loose powder was poured down the barrel, a cap placed on the nipple, the gun pointed in a safe direction, the trigger pulled, and if the ignition was proper the job was declared done. The cost for such an operation ran from $2.00 to $3.00. About 80% of all flintlock rifles and shotguns were changed to this percussion principle and were mostly done from the year 1835 to 1855.

The changes which came with the percussion lock, however, were largely confined to the system of ignition, the general stock contour of the older days persisting. Even target and hunting rifles of original percussion design and made as late as 1840–1850 are unmistakably great-grandsons of the rifle of the Dark and Bloody Ground, as were the contract Indian rifles made by the later gunsmiths of the Lancaster neighborhood.

The passing of the flint-lock presaged by comparatively few years the passing of muzzle-loading arms.

From the earliest settlement of this country to the present day, Americans have been the greatest users of firearms of any people in the world, our Canadian neighbors sharing equally the distinction. At first smooth-bore firearms, of a conglomerate character representative of everything that had been produced in Europe and the British Isles, greatly outnumbered the crude rifles of those days, and it was not until about 1750 that rifles were greatly in evidence. It is probable that, by the year 1725, the American hunting rifle had reached its full development, but for years thereafter the output of this splendid type of arm was comparatively limited. The facilities for production were restricted and the cost was much greater than that of the smooth-bore guns of the period. Again the rifle of Central Europe still held its popularity with some hunters and it took time to demonstrate the advantages of the new gun. But the small-bore, long-barrel rifle had come to stay and was destined to be the standard arm of the American hunter.

By the year 1740, from all indications, it was recognized as vastly superior and far more economical than any other firearm procurable. The vast majority of men had outfitted themselves with rifles, each to his own liking, and there was a rivalry over shooting keener than that which exists in any sport today.

Rifle matches became the first American pastime and so general was shooting that it became the national sport. Roadhouses and taverns were the favorite spots for these matches, which were held frequently, and if no such rendezvous was handy it was customary for the riflemen to get together in groups in the smaller villages and even on a neighbor's farm. For more than a century this form of amusement overshadowed all others and its inception was doubtless due to the introduction of the hunting, or Kentucky, rifle.

This was the era of the muzzle-loader. Every man took pride in his marksmanship. We were a nation of expert riflemen. Slow fire and accurate aim filled the larder, kept the Indians at a distance, and won the much-prized trophies of the match.

That a degree of skill commensurate with the high standards displayed during the early and mid-nineteenth century is seldom met with today except among a class of shooters numerically small in comparison with the population of the nation causes speculation as to the reasons underlying this circumstance.

Students of rifle shooting history know only too well that the heyday of marksmanship did not continue; that after 1850 shooting as a nation-wide sport began to lose popular favor until—and for a considerable time—this heritage of the American people was regarded as of minor importance. Generally this lack of interest is attributed to the disappearance of big game, the prevalence of which was an incentive for the younger generation to learn to shoot and to keep in practice at the various local matches; and to other and similar causes, such as the upgrowth of thickly populated communities wherein the social life provided recreations other than shooting.

All of this, to a certain extent, was undoubtedly true. But what these students in most instances have failed to recognize is that the passing of the muzzle-loader and the decline of marksmanship were more than a distantly related coincidence. In fact they were more nearly a direct cause and effect. Also, that between 1850, when the percussion muzzle-loader reached the practical stage of its development, and 1865, which marked the close of the war between the States, many other forces were at work which presaged the inevitable retirement of these fine old weapons and the temporary eclipse of the sport of marksmanship in which they figured so splendidly.

In connection with any review of the passing of the muzzle-loader, it is significant that while the flintlock Kentucky endured as a maker of rifle history from the early seventeen hundreds to about 1840—a period greater than a century—with nearly another century of use behind it in snaphaunce form both in Europe and in the Colonies, the percussion principle was discovered, reached the zenith of its development and became obsolete well within fifty years.

There was a good and sufficient reason for this, since the basic principle of the percussion lock, the use of fulminate instead of powder for ignition, was responsible for the brief existence of the percussion muzzle-loading system. Although many attempts at breech-loading were invented during the flintlock era none were found practical until Forsyth's discovery of the use of fulminate, which swept away most of the obstacles and bridged most of the gaps encountered by the experimenters of flintlock days.

And so the way was opened for change, awaiting only the occasion, which was not long in coming with the ever-growing demand for weapons which could be loaded faster and more easily than the muzzle-loader. This need was emphasized during the war between the States wherein, especially by Northern troops, many of the elementary forms of breech-loading were used. Then, and immediately following the close of hostilities, all manner of breech-loading systems were devised and tried out, first those which worked in conjunction with the use of fulminate caps and later many which were based upon the primed metallic cartridge. All of this, of course, hastened the end of the muzzle-loading era, especially when there were perfected the first multi-fire weapons which combined rapid or breech-loading with rapidity of fire. At that time, more than half a century ago, there was no organization of marksmen to keep the sport alive nor had the Government undertaken to encourage marksmanship as a factor in national defence. Therefore when a decline of interest in marksmanship came coincidentally with the passing of the muzzle-loader, there was little done to combat it. Fortunately for the future of a nation whose perpetuity was later to depend upon the skill of American soldiers with the rifle on the battlefields of the World War, marksmanship did not become entirely a lost art, but lay dormant for a generation, kept barely alive by the activities of a few scattered enthusiasts, until there came the revival which now promises to restore to America her proudest title—a nation of marksmen.

But to return to the period of decline—American marksmen of the transition period from percussion to breech-loaders soon discovered that the superb accuracy which had characterized the old cap and ball weapons was lacking to a greater or less degree in the new breech-loaders. The inventors of these new style weapons centered their attention upon the mechanics of breech and lock rather than upon perfection of barrel. That was to come later. Yet all but a few riflemen—those who were perhaps to become the nucleus of the Schuetzen Shots who flourished in the eighties—

were won away from their old favorites and adopted the new rifles largely because they were easier to load and more rapidly fired.

The lack of target accuracy in the first of the new rifles naturally hastened the decline in a sport which was predicated upon ultra accuracy, and many of the rifle shooters turned to the shotgun, which about that time began to be used in matches both at the dead mark and at the trap.

This latter form of sport with its greater thrill of shooting at a moving target became very popular and no doubt was a serious obstacle in the path of a continued popularity for rifle shooting, especially when the live bird matches were at their height. Those among the rifle shots who were also hunters found that the new rifles were sufficiently accurate for game shooting and they too abandoned the old rifle, since the new one, when properly held, would hit a mark the size of a deer at a very considerable distance even though it was not a tack-driver.

Pride in accurate aim had yielded before the desire for rapid action even at the cost of uncertain results. The rural rifle matches were but dim memories. Later on came the invasion of the small bore and by 1885 this toy—as the older riflemen called it—had reached a point of very high accuracy, as had the heavier calibered rifles, in which line development had continued in spite of obstacles, such super accurate weapons as the Sharps, Remington, Maynard and Ballard single loaders having appeared and being in use among those who still played the long-range shooting game.

After the invasion of this new rifle, few muzzle-loaders were made. One by one the old riflemakers closed their shops. The change, which began soon after the Civil War, was not rapid, but certain and slow, and was so much in evidence that by the year 1876, the Centennial of our Independence, the breech-loading rifle was recognized as a standard arm, and ten years later the muzzle-loading rifle was seldom seen on the few remaining big-game ranges.

We have today rifles, guns and pistols which measure so close to perfection that attempts to improve them seem a waste of time. Our revolvers and pistols will do remarkable work at more than 200 yards; our hunting rifles, with their superb accuracy, high velocity and corresponding flat trajectory, plus a tremendous shocking power, are perfect. Our service rifle, compact, neat and strong, a weapon with a muzzle velocity of 2700 feet, holds a record for long-range accuracy never equaled in the whole wide world. But the man on the street is no longer interested, and marksmanship has failed miserably to keep pace with ballistic improvements.

Yet the day of the painstaking, methodical rifleman, whose motto was "one hit is worth more than a thousand misses," is gone: it went with the passing of the muzzle-loader.

Reference Index

REFERENCE INDEX—Continued

REFERENCE INDEX—Continued

This special edition of

THE KENTUCKY RIFLE

by Captain John G. W. Dillin

has been privately printed for members of The Firearms Classics Library. Film was prepared from an original 1924 edition. The book was printed and bound by Quebecor Printing. The text paper was specially made for this edition by P. H. Glatfelter Company. The binding is of genuine pigskin, furnished by the Cromwell Leather Company. Endleaves are 300-denier silk moiré. Edges are gilded and spines are brass-die stamped in 22-karat gold. Cover stampings and design of the edition by Selma Ordewer.